WRITING EFFECTIVELY

HELPING CHILDREN MASTER
THE CONVENTIONS OF WRITING

LEIF FEARN AND **NANCY FARNAN**

San Diego State University

ALLYN AND BACON

Boston • London • Toronto • Sydney • Tokyo • Singapore

To our literate children: Kevin, Bridget, Michael, Jennifer, and Eric

Senior Editor: Virginia Lanigan
Editorial Assistant: Kris Lamarre
Marketing Manager: Kathy Hunter
Editorial Production Service: Chestnut Hill Enterprises
Manufacturing Buyer: Suzanne Lareau
Cover Administrator: Suzanne Harbison

Copyright © 1998 by Allyn & Bacon
A Viacom Company
Needham Heights, MA 02194

Internet: www.abacon.com
America Online: keyword: College Online

Library of Congress Cataloging-in-Publication Data

Fearn, Leif.
    Writing effectively : helping children master the conventions of writing in the elementary and middle school / Leif Fearn and Nancy Farnan.
      p. cm.
    Includes bibliographical references and index.
    ISBN 0-205-26764-5
    1. English language—Composition and exercises—Study and teaching (Elementary)—United States. 2. English language—Composition and exercises—Study and teaching (Middle school)—United States.
I. Farnan, Nancy. II. Title.
LB1576.F393 1997
372.62'3—dc21   97-11949
                                              CIP

Printed in the United States of America

10 9 8 7 6 5 4 3 2 1   02 01 00 99 98 97

CONTENTS

In editor Lisa Shaw's collection of his quotes, *In His Own Words: Colin Power*, General Colin Powell (Retired) had this to say about writing his autobiography: *My American Journey*: "I am going to write a book because I have some things I want to say, some thoughts I want to pass on. . . ."

As a writer, I am convinced that General Powell would not have been able to write his book, would not have been able to say some things, and would not have been able to pass some of his thoughts on without having mastered what the authors of this book, Leif Fearn and Nancy Farnan, call the "conventions" and what my St. Martin's editor called "the mechanicals." Without the conventions of punctuation and capitalization, nothing he wrote would have been understandable.

Without understanding, there is no communication. Without communication, there is no understanding.

Authors and editors can and do go to war over the placing of a comma. Hyphens can never substitute for ellipses. Serious changes in tone, intent, or meaning are involved. Clarity of meaning is everything in communication. Being able to say, in writing, exactly what one does mean is crucial to being understood. That's not going to get done without the conventions being properly used.

The authors of this book are correct in asserting that the earlier conventions are learned and properly used, the better. No matter what their age or condition, human beings desperately desire to be understood and insist on communicating with each other. Those who acquire the ability to communicate well, who are able, as General Powell was, "to say some things" and "pass on some thoughts," will lead a much more satisfying life than those who are not capable of doing so.

Once General Powell finished his book, he had this to say about the actual writing of it: "You're never done. I hate this profession. I am an amateur, and I am leaving the profession."

It's true. In writing professionally, one is never done, really. One simply decides that it is time to quit or the work will never be read. And more than one writer has said they hate writing—it's very hard to write well—but love having written. General Powell, having written, and written well, is no longer an amateur. He is, however, free to leave the profession. He can do so with great satisfaction, having achieved his stated goals—goals he would not have achieved unless he knew the conventions, a crucial part of the art and craft of writing.

A truism: Nobody can make a writer write. In writing this book, Leif Fearn and Nancy Farnan have given its readers, and all those future writers, a truly valuable gift.

Betty Abell Jurus

Betty Jurus is a prime mover in San Diego's burgeoning writers' community. She is the originator of the annual Southern California Writers' Conference at San Diego and the Writer's Haven Writers. She twice served as president of the San Diego Writers and Editors Guild, and she holds membership in the New York Authors Guild. Her latest book is *Men in Green Faces*, with Gene Wentz.

FROM THE AUTHORS TO THE READERS

Between us, the authors of this text have taught writing to children and youth for several decades. We have read the papers of thousands of youngsters from primary through high school grades, to say nothing of thousands of university undergraduate and graduate students. We have conducted staff development for hundreds of teachers, in scores of districts, with whom we have had many conversations on the topic of writing instruction. We have come away from those experiences with the conclusion that far too many students are unable to use fundamental conventions of writing effectively. Teachers often voice this as their most common frustration associated with writing instruction, and their concerns are well documented by the 1990 National Assessment of Educational Progress' *Writing Report Card*. The report states that students have increased the **quantity** of their writing; that is, writing instruction is conducted in such a way that young writers are becoming increasingly fluent. At the same time, however, the **quality** of their writing has not improved significantly. This evidence supports what we have observed and what we have heard from countless teachers.

We have prepared this book for the purpose of helping teachers teach their students to craft disciplined text. By disciplined text we mean writing that is cohesive and that leads to a clear message. **Cohesion and clarity are served by (although not exclusively the result of) a writer's ability to apply knowledge of the mechanics of writing—to use the conventions of writing effectively.**

The philosophy that guides all of the activities in this book has its foundations in a program called Developmental Writing, which is grounded in well-accepted practice from the fields of creativity and educational psychology. The instructional processes and activities in this text are, as well, grounded in solid research in writing and, more broadly, literacy. The following description attempts to clarify a foundation for the instructional ideas in this book.

ROOTS IN CREATIVITY

In the early 1970s we were working on ways to enhance the creative abilities of children in school. As a result, we designed creative curricular interventions, or activities, to be used directly with students in regular classrooms through the grades. These activities were designed around formal curricular content (mathematics, language, social science, and so forth) because that's what teachers and students were, and are, responsible for. Therefore, it made sense to assume that the formal curriculum was, and is, the context in which classroom creativity would occur, if it were to occur at all.

Some of the demonstration activities and lessons focused on writing. During the teaching, it became clear very quickly that if the instruction associated with writing were to be creative in any rigorous and defensible way, what passed as "creative" writing would have to be set aside. It was obvious that any attempt to implement lessons designed around what was known about creativity was largely, if not fully, thwarted through traditional "creative" writing exercises in which children just wrote a while, waiting for something dramatic to happen. Equally nonproductive was the division of genres into "creative" ones (fiction, poetry, and drama) and "noncreative" ones (essays, journalism, and reports of information).

In fact, when one **begins** with the nature of creativity, it is plain that all writing is, by classical definition, creative. What we're talking about here is the organization and reorganization of knowns. That's what every creative genius, and lots of not-so-genius (albeit creative) folks, have done since the beginning of time. Certainly, no one organizes **un**knowns, for if the data are not known, there is nothing to organize. People don't think, creatively or otherwise, in a vacuum; we think **about** things. What we think about is what we know, or are beginning to know. It would be ridiculous to suggest that we think about what we don't know.

To behave creatively in writing, then, there have to be knowns. It's all arrangement and rearrangement of knowns. And what is it that the writer has to know? Winston Churchill suggested one of them. He is reported to have complimented his early schooling by claiming that he didn't learn very much, but he did learn the constructive properties of the English sentence. Think about it a moment. English works in sentences. If one can think in and write a sentence, one can write in English; if one cannot think in and write a sentence, one cannot write in English. Of course, there are myriad other things a writer must know, but the sentence is first. Everything comes from the sentence.

That's where the focus on creativity with respect to writing led. After years of failed explanations of sentences as subjects and predicates, and later the unsubstantiated notion that if youngsters would just write a lot, sentences would eventually emerge, it appeared that even very young children were quickly developing a sense of sentence writing because they had an opportunity to **think creatively** about it.

In addition, the demonstration lessons revealed that writing is as much oral as it is psychomotor or scribal. Children understood what became something of a mantra, that writing is something you do in your head; then you either push it out of your mouth or you push it out of your pencil, but it goes on in your head.

As demonstration lessons in creativity continued, they became more and more about writing, which made it necessary to build more and more instructional "frames" (that is, clusters of activities) around creative thinking skills and writing; and then it became necessary to organize (there's that word again) the instructional "frames" that had been developed.

After several months of organizing and reorganizing, there emerged three areas of focus for what was to become Developmental Writing (L. Fearn. 1983. *Developmental Writing in the Elementary and Middle School*, Kabyn Books, San Diego).

Focus Areas in Developmental Writing

- **Content:** Sentences, relationships between and among sentences, paragraphs, genres, mechanical control, and assessment and editing. (Notice that this book is about **one** portion [mechanical control] of **one** focus area.)
- **Processes:** Creative thinking skills and interactive writing processes that are specific to the individual, the situation, and the genre.
- **Time:** The most valued commodity in school is time. Commitment of regular and consistent time reflects the value that the teacher places on writing skill, and it communicates to young writers the extent to which they should value learning to write, as well. The recommended time necessary to do it

right is 10 percent of the instructional week, or 20 to 30 minutes every day.

The basic Developmental Writing elements of content, processes, and time evolved naturally into the concept of balance applied to teaching and learning in a comprehensive writing program. What evolved was the Balanced Writing Program, where instructional planning centers on the curricular strands of **processes**, **craft**, and **genres** (for a discussion see Farnan, N. and Fearn, L. [November 1993]. The big picture: The writing program in action. *Writing Teacher*, pp. 32–34; more specifically, Farnan, N. and Fearn, L. [May 1996]. The big picture: The writing program in action. *Writing Teacher*, pp. 16–19). In a Balanced Writing Program, children and youth think rigorously, which is to say **creatively,** about the things that matter in writing (i.e., processes, craft, and genres). Craft includes, but is not limited to, conventions (mechanical control). The instructional processes and activities that we describe in this book, in the narrow area of mechanical control, focus specifically on what's creative about learning to use the conventions of writing effectively.

THE WAY THIS BOOK IS ORGANIZED

This book is divided into six chapters. Chapter 1 is "About this Book." This chapter contains critical information about the book, its activities, and its instructional processes. It provides information that is critical to the use of the text. Chapter 2 is a discussion of writing processes and the roles of creativity in writing. Chapters 3 and 4 explore 30 conventions in punctuation and capitalization that are fundamental to mechanical control in youngsters' writing. Chapter 5 defines and discusses grammatical terminology that is necessary for conversations between teachers and students about writing, capitalization and punctuation conventions, and the management of language. This chapter also includes activity ideas that are designed to help youngsters understand not only definitions of the terms, but also to have functional command of their use. Finally, Chapter 6, titled "The Teacher as Researcher in the Classroom," includes practical materials for assessment, record keeping, and communication with parents.

CHAPTER 1

ABOUT THIS BOOK

The first discipline in writing is knowing that writing is a discipline.
—Paraphrased from Archibald MacLeish in Murray, 1990, *Shoptalk*, Portsmouth, NH: Heinemann

Writers construct meaning that is displayed in some form of print or text, and readers are able to use what has been written as a foundation for their own meaning only if print adheres to predictable patterns with which the reader is familiar. Part of the familiarity and the patterning rests on the use of conventional markers—the mechanics of writing.

The conventional markers help support communication between writers and readers. This communication is critical when we think of reading as a transaction between a reader and a text. Louise Rosenblatt writes extensively about the transaction. In her book, *The Reader, the Text, the Poem* (1978), she describes text as a blueprint for readers to follow as they make meaning while reading. A blueprint is a set of directions for building, in this case for building meaning. It contains large pictures and the smallest details, both of which contribute to the whole. Although the conventional markers for writing are sometimes mistakenly seen as minor details, they are neither minor nor details; in fact they are the *markers* that readers use in the meaning-making process.

THE ROLE OF CONVENTIONS IN MEANING-MAKING

Readers use words and sentences and paragraphs to construct images and ideas. In the creation of written language, a writer uses each of these elements in a way that contributes to a reader's developing understanding. The *word* is critical in meaning-making. If a sentence contains the word *bird*, and the context is feathers and nests, the meaning that readers make will have something to do with winged creatures that fly, build nests, and lay eggs.

The *context* is revealed in the language string, the syntax, which refers to the structure of the combinations of words in phrases, sentences, and paragraphs. Readers know the "bird" in the text is a flying creature

that builds nests and lays eggs because the written language around the word *bird* describes such a creature.

However, if the "bird" in the text is written with a capital "B," and the context is a bouncing ball on a hardwood floor in a large arena, the "bird" is not a winged creature that lays eggs and flies. Rather, the "Bird" is a blond man who shoots the bouncing ball into a small hoop and makes a lot of people howl with delight. Context, a reader might say, is everything. (For readers unfamiliar with *that* context, Larry Bird was one of the greatest shooting forwards in the history of the National Basketball Association.)

But writers, while honoring context thoroughly, would argue that the marker, in the case of "bird," is at least very important. If the critical sentence were to read: "It was evening when the bird flew toward the nest," the creature in the sentence is feathered and lives in a tree. If the critical sentence read: "It was evening when Bird began to soar," the creature becomes a basketball player. The marker, a capital letter, along with the cultural literacy fundamental to all reading, serves to make the meaning.

There are all kinds of markers that carry meaning. That is, they provide details that allow readers to make meaning. Let's remain with the winged creature, or, if you like, the basketball player. What happens to the meaning if the critical sentence, the context, contains the word *birds*? Of course, the meaning changes to accommodate more than one winged creature. But if the word were written *bird's*, then we're back to one winged creature again. And if the word were written *birds'*, we've changed to more than one. It isn't merely the spelling; it's the apostrophe, and, more than that, it's the placement of the apostrophe. Furthermore, the spelling, the apostrophe, and the placement all matter, every time.

Even with very young writers, when we encourage temporary (i.e., invented) spellings to support their developing understandings of the way written language works, most teachers would not tell children **not** to think about the words they use, for then the instructional message would be that words aren't important for making meaning in print. Experimenting with language through use of temporary spellings is useful for young writers. However, the value in their experimentation lies in their ability to write increasingly effective approximations of language in its standard, accepted forms. While we may tell youngsters to write (and spell) to the best of their ability at any given moment, the message is **not** that spelling isn't important. That would be a strange message because we know it is not true, and so do they. We are not saying that youngsters can make any random scratches and scribbles on the page and that scribble-making is what writing is all about. (Even when the writings look like scribbles to adult readers, make no mistake that to the young writer they are absolutely meaningful. All we have to do is ask.) To extend this reasoning, if we tell them not to pay attention to punctuation, aren't we telling them that punctuation isn't important in meaning-making?

"Of course not," some might insist. "It isn't that punctuation isn't important; it's that punctuation isn't important at the drafting 'stage' of the writing process." For the moment we will set aside a discussion of the fact that there are no "stages" in writing processes, and the fact that hundreds of writers' self-reports, writers who are both novices and experts, and who write both fiction and nonfiction, reveal that writing is an application of process elements that are idiosyncratic to who they are, to the day and time, and to the type of writing they are doing (more on writing processes a little later).

The issue here, the one that leads to our argument, is that if young writers write without attending to punctuation (or capitalization, usage, spelling, and so forth), they are practicing writing that is free of the discipline that serves meaning. The implications here are significant. If young writers practice a certain kind of writing, they are likely to get good at it. Practice promotes expertise. Writing that is free of mechanical discipline is a form of poor writing. It is not appropriate for young writers to become expert at writing poorly.

Parenthetically, is it possible to engage in **any** complex human behavior without attending to its discipline, its details? What is riding a bicycle without attending to the pedals? (It's falling down and scraping your knees.) What is basic arithmetic without attending to the relationships between numbers and signs? (It's a bunch of unpatterned marks on paper, or ideas in the head.) What is drawing if the young artist doesn't pay attention to perspective and light source? (It's an unsatisfying lollipop that the young artist wishes looked more like a tree.) What is music without the scales, the rhythms, the instructional notes about relative loudness? (It's noise.) The noise may have

merit, but it isn't music. The lollipop isn't a tree, the marks aren't arithmetic, and the falling down isn't riding.

We purposefully use the word *conventions* to refer to the markers. One of the reasons for the use of *conventions,* rather than *rules,* is that while all markers are there to carry meaning, their use is often dictated by context. For example, in spelling, the word *color* in Liverpool, England looks as though it's spelled wrong. The British spelling is *colour.* There are numerous spelling examples. "Liquefy" is also correctly spelled *liquify.* What's the rule? A better question is, on what do we agree? The British agree that *colour* is spelled with a "u." Americans agree that it is not. We've also agreed to put a comma before the coordinating conjunction in a compound sentence; however, we've agreed that if the independent clauses are especially short or clear, we can leave the comma out. The rule says put it in; the convention says use your judgment.

Let's return to our argument about the importance of conventions in writing. In print-rich classrooms, children are writing more than ever. They are surrounded by language in books and newspapers, on the walls, and in their portfolios. They are writing more and becoming more fluent. And, just as in reading, fluency in writing is important. If writers, novice or expert, don't get their ideas on paper, then they aren't writers because they aren't writing.

Fluency, then, is necessary, but it is not sufficient. The 1990 National Assessment of Educational Progress's (NAEP) *Writing Report Card* (Applebee, A. N.; Langer, J. A.; Mullins, I. V. S.; & Jenkins, L. B. Princeton, NJ: ETS) makes that clear. NAEP reported that youngsters in Grades 4, 8, and 11 were writing more, but not better. Effective writing is achieved in the larger discipline of writing, one element of which is the control of meaning markers called capital letters and punctuation marks.

"You're missing the point of writing process," some might say. "Young writers who have mastered the process will go back during the revision and editing stage and 'fix' the piece for mechanical control." Let's again set aside the fact that revision and editing are not "stages" in real writers' writing processes. Consider the logical absurdity of the argument about *going back* to make mechanical corrections. If a young writer knows enough about using apostrophes in singular possessives to make necessary corrective changes when editing, wouldn't (s)he use the apostrophes properly when drafting? It isn't as though making a tailed dot takes so much time that a young writer's train of thought is compromised in making one or two of them. Using an apostrophe wouldn't interrupt the flow of ideas. If a writer knows about using apostrophes in possessives, the draft will show them, perhaps not in every instance and perhaps not accurately every time, but they will be there because the writer uses them as routine meaning markers just as (s)he uses words, sentences, and phrases as meaning makers.

But there's an assumption in much of what passes for writing instruction that young writers do not know about meaning markers when they are drafting, so we tell them not to worry about the markers because it's more important that they get the ideas on their paper (ideas, incidentally, that work partly *because* of the meaning markers). Then we tell them to go back and put in the meaning markers, based on the logically absurd assumption that they have suddenly and miraculously learned what they didn't know five minutes ago.

Perhaps instead of telling young writers not to worry about conventions, the message should be to write as well as they can, all the time, while at the same time teaching them directly to write increasingly well. The disciplined part of writing well is what this book is about.

THE ROLE OF CONVENTIONS IN A BALANCED WRITING PROGRAM

There are two purposes for teaching conventions for young writers. One is to cause young writers (that is, help them learn) to write conventionally accurate language. The second is to give young writers knowledge they can use to edit their work. The focus of the instructional strategies in this book is on *writing*. This means youngsters must write, using the conventions, and they must be taught directly and systematically to do so.

We realize that the existence of this book isolates capitalization and punctuation from the larger writing experience. However, the authors in no way mean to suggest that capitalization and punctuation can be learned in isolation. Therefore, all experiences with the meaning markers treated in this book are part of children's oral and written production in classrooms.

- Every activity emphasizes the sounds of conventionally structured language.
- Every activity causes young writers to apply meaning markers as they, the writers, construct meaning in whole pieces of language—sentences.

The emphasis here is on the writing. Always the writing. Always the writer's writing.

It is important, actually critical, to realize that this book addresses instruction in only one facet of a comprehensive writing program, or what your authors refer to as a Balanced Writing Program. A balanced course of study in writing includes all of writing: syntactic structures, organizational techniques, and messages, as

well as mechanical control. If any of them is missing, the larger course of study is compromised. Teaching young writers exclusively about the mechanical discipline (i.e., capitalization, punctuation, spelling, syntax, organizational techniques) misses the message-making point of writing altogether. However, to teach only message-making misses the point that the messages work because of a writer's control over the discipline. For instance, sentences only work in writing because they adhere to the conventions on which language users have agreed.

However, writing is more than effective use of conventions. It is a complex literacy act that requires a comprehensive view of instruction. A Balanced Writing Program includes attention to three major elements: (1) processes and procedures in writing, (2) genres and their characteristics, and (3) craft. Processes and procedures involve writers' growing sense of how they approach and perform writing. For example, writers' workshops (N. Farnan & L. Fearn. March 1993. *Writers' Workshops: Middle School Writers and Readers Collaborating, Middle School Journal*, 61–65) focus on reflection through feedback to writers that is direct and functional.

Study of genres involves their characteristics (i.e., their rhetorical elements or what makes each unique) and procedures that help writers create patterns of thinking and writing that are appropriate to each particular genre. For example, autobiographical writing involves patterns of thinking that are different from persuasive writing.

A third major element of a Balanced Writing Program is attention to craft. This involves learning how to write effective sentences and paragraphs and how to write in ways that use conventions that best convey a writer's message.

This book is about only one of those elements, craft, and, as such, does not pretend to offer, by itself, a balanced approach to writing. What it does offer is one element that is integral to a Balanced Writing Program.

TEACHING CONVENTIONS TO NATIVE AND NON-NATIVE SPEAKERS OF ENGLISH

Earlier, we talked about an emphasis on the sounds of properly constructed language. The sound of language has always been fundamental to language learning, including learning to write. Today, however, the sound of formally constructed language is especially important, probably even critically important, because anywhere from 10% to 100% of the boys and girls in many elementary and middle school classrooms in the United States speak a native language other than English and face the task of learning English as a second language.

Language learning is fundamentally auditory. Written language learning is also fundamentally auditory, which is not to say that writing is talk written down. All young writers, and especially youngsters writing in a second language, need instructional practices based upon the *sound* of well-constructed language. For that reason, every activity in this book has both oral and written output associated with it.

One of the benefits of the oral emphasis that we have noticed over the years is that it provides an opportunity to deliver **direct** and **useful feedback** to youngsters immediately. It can take as much time as two minutes for young writers to construct a single sentence, then as much as two more for several youngsters to share aloud and receive feedback from the teacher. Of course, teachers know best about the capabilities of their own students and must make their own decisions regarding the time allotted for any given instructional strategy. However, your authors' experience in classrooms, both their own and other teachers', has shown that children across grade and ability levels are capable of working much more quickly and efficiently than is often assumed. For example, we know that:

- fast-paced work often serves to focus children's attention (as it does ours);
- children will take as much time as we give them to complete a task (as will we), even if much time is wasted in the process; and
- a small amount of heightened anxiety associated with intense concentration and focus tends to support learning rather than compromise it.

Therefore, we would reiterate that two minutes is fully sufficient time for children and adolescents to complete the writing activities involved in the strategic teaching of mechanical control we describe in this book. In fact, there are times when one or one-and-one-half minutes will be more appropriate.

We believe that the timing and pacing associated with an instructional strategy are critical. Equally important is the element of feedback. In any learning situation, it is direct and useful feedback that helps move learners toward increasingly accurate approximations, thus the learning objective.

Regarding the teaching of mechanical control, feedback might sound something like this:

TEACHER TO CLASS: Write a sentence that contains three kinds of animals that make good pets. [Students write.]

TEACHER: O.K., someone please share what you wrote.

JOSE READS: I think the best pets are dogs, cats, and fish.

TEACHER: Jose, read your sentence again, and every time you come to a comma, call it out loud.

JOSE READS: I think the best pets are dogs comma cats comma and fish. [In the Lesson 3, Commas in Items in a Series, we discuss the issue of whether there is a comma between the last two items in a series of three or more. Everything in this literal transcription of a classroom scenario rests upon that discussion.]

TEACHER: Terrific! How many pets are in your sentence, Jose?

JOSE: Three.

TEACHER: Correct! And you separated each one with a comma.

JOSE: Yes, I did.

TEACHER: Great! You did it right. Read your sentence again while the rest of us listen carefully to the sound. [Jose reads again. The teacher tells him again that he has written the sentence correctly and calls on someone else to read.]

PATRICIA READS: I think the best pets are llamas, horses, and emus.

TEACHER: Read again. This time call out the commas when you get to them.

PATRICIA READS: I think the best pets are llamas comma horses and emus.

TEACHER: Patricia, how many pets are in your sentence?

PATRICIA: Three.

TEACHER: When we listened to Jose's sentence, there were three pets, and he separated each one from the other with a comma. Do you think you should separate each of your pets with a comma just as Jose did?

PATRICIA: My other teacher said I didn't have to.

TEACHER: Your other teacher was not wrong, but this year we're going to use commas to separate each item in a series. Patricia, if you follow last year's teacher's convention and readers understand your sentence, that's fine. If your readers do not understand, you will have to add the last comma.

We have a dilemma here. Patricia was told one thing last year and another now. Is it appropriate to second-guess last year's teacher? Suppose last year's teacher told Patricia that mountain ranges separate the country into time zones or that all adverbs end in *-ly?* Well, mountain ranges do not separate the country into time zones, all adverbs do not end in *-ly,* and if the last two items in a series are discrete, the comma is used to make that clear. Patricia has a right to know what's right, no matter what last year's teacher said.

The activity above can also be done orally, without putting anything on paper. That would sound something like this:

TEACHER: Boys and girls, think of a sentence that contains three animals you think make good pets. Write your sentence in your head. [Hands go up immediately.] Jose, read to me. [Jose reads the sentence he has written in his head, and the scenario goes on as above.]

The value of the totally oral scenario is time efficiency, for it takes youngsters five seconds to do what it might take a minute or two to do with a pencil in their hand. (Again, because individual teachers know their students best, teachers must make their own decisions regarding how much time to allow students to do the work, depending on students' developmental and performance levels.) Oral writing requires mental discipline, as children must both remember and report simultaneously. Parenthetically, real writers write orally much of the time; it's what they call planning or prewriting.

Teachers might find they want to adjust the examples we've provided to accommodate the language, performance, and developmental levels of their students. Throughout this book, your authors make suggestions about grade- and age-level appropriateness regarding the conventions. (See the "Scope and Sequence" section in this chapter.) One of our considerations is that conventions need to be taught in response to the kinds of writing that children produce. For example, if children are not routinely writing compound sentences, it makes no sense to teach commas that separate independent clauses. On the other hand, somewhere around late second to middle third grade for most children, it does make sense to teach compound sentence writing because children need them to express their increasingly complex ideas and because such sentences are showing up in what they read and write.

The key to the consideration of development is to focus on what young writers are writing and what young writers can learn to write and will find useful to express themselves. The authors have found that only a few students through the elementary grades, for example, write well enough to need or benefit from semicolons. However, at the upper elementary and middle levels, young writers begin to notice semicolons in their reading and may find them useful in their writing. For that reason, we have included the teaching of semicolons in our book.

ABOUT THE CONVENTIONS

The conventions in this book were chosen because they reflect the kinds of needs youngsters have in the elementary and middle school. For example, youngsters tend to write sentences that need a variety of comma conventions. They tend to write lengthy strings of language connected by *and* and *then*. A solution to writing such sentences (and writing too many of these sentences does present a problem in writing) is to understand and master alternative punctuation conventions, two such alternatives being the use of commas to create compound sentences and the use of end punctuation, thereby creating separate sentences.

The usefulness of the conventions we discuss depends on students' needs, and grade/age recommendations are a part of every lesson. Youngsters tend increasingly, as they get older, to write compound and complex sentences, and even compound-complex sentences. As children get older, they express their ideas with more complexity, and that shows up in their writing. On the other hand, not all youngsters will need semicolons. Therefore, we recommend that teachers teach markers such as semicolons and the difference between restrictive and nonrestrictive clauses as they see the need arise in individual student's writings. The distinction here is not between conventions that are simple as opposed to those that are difficult or complex. The distinction is between what youngsters need and use and what teachers discern that their students are not yet ready to use. The conventions we teach should be those that students use but may find confusing, conventions they may need but have not yet mastered. These should be our first priority as we decide **what** conventions to teach—and **when.**

The intent of this book is to provide conventions that are useful in writing. The student audience is primarily elementary and middle school. This is not to ignore high school and college students. It's just that the ideal instructional focus should occur before that. The professional audience is preservice and inservice teachers who intend to work with or who are working with elementary and middle-school students.

The book is **not** a dictionary of all-purpose rules and exceptions, of which there are more than 200; it is not a comprehensive editing manual. For this we would recommend a comprehensive secretary's manual or writer's handbook, both of which should be part of a classroom reference library.

HOW LESSONS ARE DESIGNED

In this book the examples are written to focus on writers and writing and on reading and literature. The examples offer a frame of reference for teaching mechanical control. We encourage teachers who use this book to add their own ideas and examples.

Each lesson is divided into seven parts. The first presents the convention with a brief definition, followed by a second part illustrating young writers' unedited writing samples that contain the target convention. The third part is an explanation of the convention, followed by a fourth part that contains examples written in the context of contemporary children's literature. The fifth part explains the convention instructionally and poses multiple ideas for teaching it. This part includes narrative, as well as examples of teacher–student dialogue that offer illustrations of possible classroom interactions. There is no implication that these illustrations represent a script for teachers. They are merely examples of classroom interactions based on many actual lessons. The sixth part is made up of multiple instructional cues or prompts that can be used as black-line masters for overhead projection or independent practice by students. These are comprised of writing, not editing, cues. This is a book about writing. Finally, each lesson includes *Tips for Teachers* that highlight instructional ideas and strategies.

The lessons also make recommendations regarding grade-level appropriateness of the activities. However, because learning is developmental and not necessarily age-bound, and certainly not grade-bound, we emphasize that our recommendations may apply, at best, only generally, and not for every student, nor for every classroom. We are aware that teachers must make their own judgments about appropriateness.

A REVIEW OF ASSUMPTIONS THAT SHAPED THIS BOOK

An assumption provides a basis on which something rests. This book rests on certain assumptions about language, writing, teaching, and learning. They provide a foundation for teaching mechanical control in a Balanced Writing Program.

- *The first discipline in writing is knowing that writing is a discipline.* Young writers must learn the conventions on which literate users of a language generally agree.
- *The discipline in writing is a collection of literacy conventions, not rules.* Conventions imply practical use and dynamic agreements over time.
- *Anything that is taught about writing needs to be taught in and through writing whole pieces of language, beginning with the smallest whole unit of meaningful print, the single sentence.* Context dictates what is learned. If something **about writing** is taught outside the context of **whole pieces of writing,** there is little or no predictable application **to writing.**

- *The complex world of mechanical control can be reduced to high frequency, high utility conventions that reflect the agreed-on transactions between readers and writers.* Mechanical control of American English need not be so complex that it cannot be mastered and applied by even young writers.
- *Youngsters, and everyone else, tend to learn what they practice, not necessarily what they are taught.* Young learners tend to learn what they write; therefore, if young writers write undisciplined prose, that's what they learn. Many young writers practice writing badly, and get good at it.
- *Learning to write is both oral and scribal.* Because language is learned in the ear, formal oral language is fundamental to a successful writing program. Writing, therefore, can occur at the end of a pencil, at a keyboard, and orally.
- *Teaching mechanical control is but one of the several enormously important parts of a Balanced Writing Program.* Mechanical control itself does not make a writer, but without it no one becomes a writer. Steinbeck could capitalize, and so can Rudolfo Anaya.

A REVIEW OF MAJOR FEATURES OF THE BOOK

- This book presents 30 mechanical conventions in American English. They were originally culled from a comprehensive secretary's manual and subsequently tested against children's writing samples in grades K–12.
- Throughout Chapters 3 and 4, discussion of each convention appears in the context of ideas from children's literature and the authentic productions of young writers.
- This is a book in which youngsters **write** to master the conventions, not merely study and memorize them and evaluate their use in prewritten sentences. The purpose of this text is not to hone youngsters' editing skills, but to cultivate and sharpen their writing skills.
- There are clearly described instructional procedures for teaching each convention.
- There are specific implications for independent practice included with each instructional procedure.
- All instruction occurs in the context of whole pieces of language (sentences) that contain authentic images and ideas generated by young writers.
- This book does not pretend to be something it is not. It is about mechanical control. It enhances the larger Balanced Writing Program.

SCOPE AND SEQUENCE—GRADE LEVEL
TIMELINES FROM AWARENESS TO MASTERY

Throughout Chapters 3 and 4, in which the 30 punctuation and capitalization conventions are defined, described, demystified, detoxified, and delivered, there are regular references to grade levels at which this or that convention can be taught. Those references come from two sources. One is the hours and hours in all sorts of classrooms in which we have tried every one of the 30 conventions at various times of the year, sometimes drastically overshooting the children, sometimes insulting their basic intelligence, but usually connecting the children with the convention. The other source is the corpus of writing samples, literally in the thousands, that we have read and scored over the years and that have provided evidence of the mechanical conventions young writers need and use, with varying degrees of effectiveness, when they write. (This is largely irrespective, incidentally, of the native language they bring to school.)

So we put together what we learned from those two sources of information and came to the conclusion that initial capital letters and terminal marks should be an awareness focus in kindergarten and early first grade. They become a direct instruction focus in the first grade and a guided and independent practice focus in the late first grade and throughout the second grade. It is legitimate to expect mastery of those two conventions by most of the children by the end of the second grade.

By mastery we mean that the third grade teacher, after reminding and reinforcing throughout the first month, need not read past the first missing initial capital letter and terminal mark on anyone's paper. When you come to the first, the very first, of either of those errors, you merely give the paper back to the young writer and say, "I don't read past the first of that sort of error. When the paper is on your side of the desk, you may do as you wish, but when it crosses your desk, it must be right. Fix it and bring it back for me to read."

Now understand, we've allowed three whole years during which children learn to use periods and capital letters before we hold them responsible for doing it right. If that feels too severe, make it fourth grade when the responsibility kicks in, or the fifth, maybe even the sixth. Incidentally, there are seventh graders who don't use terminal marks routinely in their writing. Is it too severe to hold seventh graders responsible for periods? Ninth graders? University juniors? We suggest the end of the second grade works for most children. That allows them to focus their attention on more mature matters in writing. It also lets them know that their teacher thinks they're smart and worthy of responsibility.

Of course, in any educational venture there are exceptional cases and special needs, but we're not talking about exceptions here. By and large, we've found that the sequences and three-year time frames work for most of the young writers under most circumstances, all other things being equal. If a student arrives at the school for the first time and walks into the fourth grade, there is some significant catching up to do, so the fourth grade mastery expectations won't work until the catch-up has been accomplished. The children in the third grade aren't all alike, so there are different expectations and demands. We're talking here about *most* of the students *most* of the time under *most* circumstances. We also know that classroom teachers know the young writers who don't fall into the category of *most* and know how to vary their instruction and expectations. Such teachers will, of course, provide direct instruction in periods and apostrophes to the eighth grader who arrives at the school never having had any punctuation instruction, and also will provide some portion of the eighth-grade year for the eighth grader to master the material.

All of the 30 punctuation and capitalization conventions are arranged in three-year instructional sequences below. Within each three-year sequence there is *awareness time* when teachers call young writers' attention to the conventional markers in the print they are reading, on the signs and charts around the room, and in the larger environment in which they live. There is *direct instruction* time when teachers formally teach the conventions, perhaps as recommended in this book. Then there is *practice time*, both guided and independent practice, when young writers write with the convention every day in sentences and in larger writing contexts. Finally, there is *mastery time* after which young writers are expected, after three years of awareness, instruction, and practice, to use the convention habitually.

There is, of course, one element in this instructional program that is critically important, so important, in fact, that without it the expectation of mastery becomes fragile. That three-year timeline means that all of the teachers on a school site must agree to make it happen. Everyone must get together for fifteen minutes before the new school year begins and agree that it is not necessary to have legions of fourth graders who "forget" to capitalize the names of their friends, who "forget" to put question marks at the end of question sentences, who "forget" where sentences are supposed to end and merely string them together with *and*. Everyone will have to agree there are second-grade content and skills

Instructional Timeline: Awareness to Mastery

	K	1	2	3	4	5	6	7	8
End Punctuation (1)	*************								
Commas in Dates (2)	*************								
Commas in Series (3)	*******************								
Commas in Addresses (4)	*******************								
Apostrophes in Contractions (5)			*******************						
Periods in Abbreviations (6)			*******************						
Commas in Compound Sentences (7)				*************					
Punctuation in Dialogue (8)				**********************					
Apostrophes in Possessives (9)				**********************					
Commas in Complex Sentences (10)					*************				
Quotation Marks and Underlining in Published Titles (11)					*************				
Commas in Series of Adjectives (12)					*************				
Commas to Set Off Appositives (13)					*******************				
Commas after Introductory Words (14)					*******************				
Commas after Introductory Phrases (15)					*******************				
Commas in Compound-Complex Sentences (16)						*******************			
Commas to Set off Parenthetical Expressions (17)						*************			
Dashes and Parentheses to Set Off Parenthetical Expressions (18)						*******************			
Colons in Sentences (19)						*******************			
Semicolons in Sentences (20)						*******************			
Capital Letters to Begin Sentences (21)	*************								
Capital Letters in Names (22)	*************								
Capitalizing I (23)	*************								
Capital Letters in Days and Months (24)	*******************								
Capital Letters in Place Names (25)	*******************								
Capital Letters in Person's Title (26)			******************						
Capital Letters in Published Titles (27)					******************				
Capital Letters to Show Nationality, Ethnicity, and Language (28)						******************			
Capital Letters in Trade Names, Commercial Products, and Company Names (29)					******************				
Capital Letters in Names of Institutions, Associations and Events (30)					******************				

that fifth-grade teachers ought not have to teach. If there is no agreement, then upper-grade teachers will just have to forgo teaching upper-grade material, as many do, because they must continue teaching lower-grade material, as they have.

COMMON QUESTIONS ABOUT CONVENTIONS AND MECHANICAL CONTROL

1. **Doesn't attention to mechanics interrupt children's fluency?** No. Attention to the discipline of writing is *part of* the flow. Children who have no conscious control of the discipline of language are precisely the ones whose fluency is most seriously compromised. As children gain control over the mechanics of writing, they are better able to attend to the flow of their language rather than to whether or not their language is right. They realize their writing communicates better, and they know that is the goal. Remember, of course, that nothing in this book suggests that the *discipline of writing* should be taught separately from real writing. Context. Context is everything.

2. **Won't too much attention to conventions paralyze young writers?** Too much attention to anything has a negative effect on everything else. There is nothing in this book that advocates attention to the discipline of writing to the detriment of the real purpose for writing, which is, of course, to make messages. The quality of messages, that is whether or not they work, is dependent to some extent on the writer's control of the discipline. For this rea-

son, we like Regie Routman's quote: "It's not enough that students are writing a lot . . . if their writing is not improving. We need to have high expectations for having not just the quality of the writing, but the standards, the conventions. . . . Writing has to be readable" (February 1994, *The Council Chronicle*, NCTE, p. 7).

It has been our experience over many years in classrooms that teaching the conventions of writing, as recommended in this book, in no way compromises students' motivations, attitudes, or inclinations to write.

3. **Don't writers pay attention to mechanical control only during revision and editing?** Of course not! Virtually all writers' self-reports of how they write reveal that they write as well as they can all the time. Writers don't write poorly on purpose. Writers mobilize everything they know whenever they write. The message to youngsters is not that their first drafts must be perfect, but neither should the message be that young writers can ignore all conventions while they are thinking through and writing their first drafts. Rather, the message is that youngsters should always do the *best* they can at any particular moment, knowing there will be time for more careful revision and editing at a later time. (See our discussion on writing processes in Chapter 2.)

4. **Are you saying that children can become automatic in their use of written conventions?** Certainly! People, and children are people, become good at and eventually automatic with what they practice. Put another way, it isn't practice that makes perfect; it's "perfect practice that makes perfect." (Thank you, Suzanne Jackson.)* Therefore, if young writers practice the conventions that enhance the quality of their real writing, they will become automatic with those conventions; and they can spend the rest of their time thinking about **what** they want to write rather than **how** to write it.

5. **How do I know what conventions to teach?** One way is to read your students' writing and notice the characteristic mechanical errors. Experienced teachers know that there are error patterns in every classroom. Teach to eliminate the error patterns. We also know that some youngsters make errors

that no one else in their class makes, or that only a few children make. In this case, the answer is to individualize instruction through work in small groups based on youngsters' needs. The second way to know what conventions to teach is to take a writing sample early in the year (see Chapter 6, "The Teacher as Researcher in the Classroom") in the middle of the year, and at the end of the year. Record the error patterns from the first writing sample, and establish an instructional objective to eliminate half of the error rate by the second writing sample. Halve that rate again by the end of the year. If a teacher is successful with that schedule, the average number of mechanical errors in the classroom will be decreased by 75% in one year. If next year's teacher does the same thing, it's only a matter of time before the average child in a school has become automatic with the discipline of writing.

6. **How do I know when my students have become automatic with capitalization and punctuation conventions?** One way to judge this is according to when children at an average level of performance in your room produce largely error-free writing most of the time and can correct most of their own errors given sufficient time. Another way to judge students' automatic use of conventions is to set your own criterion for performance. For example, you might conclude that your students can be judged as using capitalization and punctuation conventions automatically when the class has reduced its error rate by an average of 80%.

7. **When do I find the time to teach the conventions this way?** If children are going to learn to write well, writing instruction will consume approximately (and minimally) 10% of an instructional week. In the elementary school that's 20–30 minutes every day. In a middle-school schedule of 90-minute blocks, it would be approximately 10 minutes a day. We know that time on task is directly associated with learning. We recommend allotting time that ensures on-task behavior. The 20–30 minute number tends to be the amount of time it takes very young writers to explore even the simplest idea in writing. We know that teachers spend time on what they value, which communicates importance to youngsters. If we expect children to learn to write, we will commit the time. However, a Balanced Writing Program must encompass more than just attention to mechanical control. Students must be gaining procedural knowledge about writing, must be writing in a variety of genres and content areas, and, in addition,

---

*Suzanne Jackson is a dear friend, elementary and middle-school teacher in Round Rock, Texas, and one of many teachers who teach writing in the spirit that we describe in this book. She is on the faculty of the Writing Institute for Teachers and consults widely in writing instruction.

must be working on the craft of writing, which includes attention to mechanical control.

8. **Where do I find the time to read all the writing suggested in this book?** The most common problem in teaching writing at any level is the teacher's reading load. Here's the basic dilemma: If students are writing as much as they must in order to learn to write well, you can't possibly read it all; if, on the other hand, you are able to read all your students' writing, they can't possibly be writing enough to learn to write well. Given the dilemma, teachers have, over the years, suggested ways to deal with it.

    *   Consider that all practice need not be monitored. For example, parents do not monitor all of their infant's early experiments with oral language, and the children learn to speak anyway. Teachers do not monitor all of children's reading, nor would it be possible to do so. Similarly, it is not necessary to monitor all writing practice.

    *   Collect all students' writings so they'll know that what they write is important.

    *   Not every piece of writing needs to be graded, although it is necessary to record work having been done. It is sufficient to give students credit for having written simply by entering a check in the record book. Students get credit, you do not have to read all of the papers, and, in addition, students get writing practice.

    *   Read randomly, at the rate of approximately five papers a day, ensuring that every student has had a paper read by the end of the week.

    *   Small groups of students read each other's papers, form Writers' Workshops, and give each other feedback.

CHAPTER 2

ABOUT WRITING PROCESSES AND CREATIVITY IN WRITING

Writing is, by virtue of its cognitive and disciplinary demands, enormously complex and difficult. Our conceptions of writing and its process functions influence how we design writing instruction. Writing **is** process, and while writing processes are not the focus of this book, it seems to your authors that knowledge of processes is critical for all aspects of a writing program: Every time writers write, they are engaging in processes. As youngsters write to cues in this book, they are mobilizing all of the aspects of writing processes. And because writers mobilize these aspects interactively and idiosyncratically, youngsters will respond variously to the cues. A child may sit and think for a moment, forming the kernel of a sentence in his head before he begins writing. Another may begin writing immediately, stopping in mid-sentence to plan and reflect, crossing out false starts and then moving ahead. Yet another may write furiously, her hand barely able to move fast enough to capture the ideas tumbling out, stopping to reflect only after the sentence is written.

Writing is also a fundamentally creative process. Creativity is not an abstract or mystical phenomenon or construct. Creativity has an operational definition and a variety of skills or behaviors observable in creative geniuses, as well as in the rest of us. Those creative thinking skills are basic to the writing we describe in this book.

As background for the activities in this book, this chapter discusses an interactive view of writing process and the connection between writing and creativity.

UNDERSTANDING WRITING PROCESSES

Nancie Atwell, in her acclaimed book *In the Middle: Reading and Learning with Adolescents* (1987, Heinemann), makes the following comment about writing process:

> I'm careful never to talk about the *writing process because that article implies there's just one process through which every writer goes. I know I can talk only in general ways about what writers do, or in specific ways about what I or other writers do on specific occasions* (p. 126).

Atwell acknowledges that students might find it helpful to discuss elements of process, and she uses such

terms as *rehearsing, drafting, conferring, deciding when content is set.* However, she is careful to present these process elements as guidelines only. She discusses them with her students and then moves on. That is because, as she remarks, "Once kids have a general idea of procedures, and some of the language of the (writing) workshop, I want them to make their own decisions about what to do next as writers by looking at and thinking about pieces of their writing" (p. 127). She believes that if students remain tied to a writing process poster that shows writing to be a linear, step-by-step set of procedures, then "they're not deciding" (p. 127).

Atwell is not alone in her concern that stage-bound conceptions of writing process can be counterproductive for young writers. In the early 1980s, in his book *Essays into Literacy* (1983, Heineman), Frank Smith argued that writing is not a simple transference of thoughts from mind to paper. In other words, asking students first to prewrite their ideas, with the objective of simply transferring those ideas to written text, misrepresents writing process. Smith explains his point.

> *Writing can create ideas and experiences on paper which could never exist in the mind. . . . Thoughts are created in the act of writing, which changes the writer just as it changes the paper on which the text is produced. Many authors have said that their books know more than they do, that they cannot recount in detail what their books contain before, while, or after they write them. Writing is not a matter of taking dictation from yourself; it is more like a conversation with a highly responsive and reflective other person (p. 82).*

Reflect for a moment on your own experiences as a writer. Have you ever reread something you have written and been surprised at the way you expressed yourself, perhaps even surprised at the ideas that you captured in your writing? E. M. Forster is quoted in Murray's book, *Shoptalk* (1990, Boynton/Cook Publishers, Portsmouth, NH, p. 101), asking, "How do I think until I see what I say?" It's an experience many writers talk about and one which the writers of this book experience routinely. There seems to be a dynamic relationship between cognitive and linguistic functions when writers write.

The implication here is that, left to their own devices, planning and drafting occur almost symbiotically, an interaction discounted by a stage-bound approach to writing, even when we add recursive qualifications. Unlike what is implied in traditional notions of writing process, much of the planning that occurs in composition takes place **during** the writing, not before it. Throughout a writing, writers draw information from memory—planning, generating ideas, evaluating, and revising. That is not to say writers never plan in advance. It merely punctuates the fact that planning **in-event** is a routine occurrence, as earlier plans are revised and elaborated on in response to what a writer discovers in the course of writing.

Likewise, revision is a complex set of activities that routinely occur during the drafting of text. Revision can occur after a composition is written, but formulaic classroom instructional models of writing process would have us think that revision only occurs after a writing, something that simply isn't accurate.

Researchers seeking more adequate conceptualizations of process have explored the idea that writing process is recursive. They have done this in an attempt to avoid the linearity of stage-bound models of writing process and to make a statement regarding the complexity of it. While process elements may occur recursively, that is, a writer may cycle back to planning after drafting and may cycle back to planning during revision, the idea of recursiveness is inadequate as an explanation of process. It merely runs linearity in two directions. It does not fundamentally change linear process ideas. It seems more appropriate to describe writing process as a continuous generation of ideas that are transformed into text, text that is built upon a preceding generation of ideas and their transformations into text.

Given this, it appears that planning, drafting, and reflection (revision/editing) probably occur in most people's writing processes, but not as prescriptive states. Rather, they are functions that occur in the creation of text. Planning, for instance, is not an initial stage in writing, as suggested semantically by the term **prewriting.** Instead, it is a function that pervades writing, an artifact of mental engagement in the production of print. Early on in the writing of any given piece, planning may be explicit, meaning "observable" in the form of outlines, notes on scraps of paper, mental designs, and ideas "massaged" over time; but the preponderance of planning occurs **during** writing. Every decision a writer makes is indicative of planning, and every decision creates new problems, whose solutions demand planning. What must be understood about planning in writing process is that it occurs primarily because a writer is mentally engaged in producing text (writing).

Reflection is no more a **stage** in writing process than is planning. Writers reflect on their early plans, just as they reflect on the product of their writing and its future, in fact. But most critical are writers' reflections on every decision they make as they work their way through a writing. Reflection is mental work in-event. We see this process element at work in crossed-out words, arrows, carets, circled words and phrases, and marginal notes that remind a writer to return to the place later. It is mental consideration of ideas as they crop up **during** a writing.

Reflection is more clearly observable if it occurs toward the end of a writing. Then, it looks like what we traditionally think of as revision. Later still, it looks like editing, and still later, polishing. Any notion, however, that reflection is fundamentally, or even primarily, associated with a **postwriting stage** ignores the self-reports of experienced writers (see Dorothy Parker, William Styron, and Frank O'Conner as quoted in Cowley's *Writers at Work: The Paris Review Interviews, First Series,* 1958, Penguin Books), as well as the appearance of novice writers' rough drafts.

Drafting is the key to understanding writers' processes. Planning occurs primarily because of the draft. The draft triggers planning; it illuminates planning and plans, and only because of the draft is there material on which to reflect. If there is a unifying principle in writing process on which everything else rests, it is the draft, as it is generated in the mind and in the process of being formulated into text.

Drafting is evidence of construction of the mind that is eventually displayed on paper. It is impossible, in a neurological sense, to have text in the absence of mental constructions. Print can not be created in a vacuum. Writing can happen only to the extent that a writer has a text-in-process to produce, and the text-in-process exists in a mind that is itself in the process of construction.

Writing instruction has lived through its process childhood. (For a retrospective on writing process, see: Farnan and Fearn. May 1996."The Big Picture: The Writing Program in Action," *Writing Teacher.*) As when all things grow up, leaving childhood behind means accumulating useful experience, but it also means accruing an increasing collection of knowledge while moving into and through adolescence and adulthood. While there appear to be generic functions in writing processes, they are not stages, and they are not linear, as instruction often tends to imply. Writing functions occur, for the most part, as interactions of process elements of drafting, planning, and reflecting. Almost two decades ago Donald Murray, in an article in the National Council of Teachers of English journal, *Language Arts,* urged "researchers and teachers to read what published writers say about the writing process, since accomplished writers and inexperienced students often agree on the writing process and disagree with what is taught in writing texts and composition classes" (1980, p. 491). He recommended *Writers at Work: The Paris Review Interviews* as a starting point to learn from practicing writers.

For that reason, we look at Annie Dillard's comments as she descibes writing in her book *The Writing Life* (Harper and Row, 1989):

> *When you write, you lay out a line of words. The line of words is a miner's pick, a woodcarver's gouge, a surgeon's probe. You wield it, and it digs a path you follow. Soon you find yourself deep in new territory. Is it a dead end, or have you located the real subject? You will know tomorrow, or this time next year.*
>
> *You make the path boldly and follow it fearfully. You go where the path leads (p. 3).*

In her book, Dillard recounts feelings of joyful abandon when her writing moves forward and frustration when that momentum has been lost, albeit temporarily. She describes writing as a journey into new territory—uncertain, seeming sometimes absurd, fraught with twisting trails and forks in the road, yet always compelling. Conspicuously absent from her narrative is any mention of writing as a series of stages of steps; she implies, instead, the forward movement sustained by a planning–drafting interaction.

No matter how students engage their writing processes as they respond to instruction in this book, it is important to recognize that every time youngsters write, they are using interactive writing processes to get from left to right. As they respond to instruction in this book, they are mobilizing explicit creative thinking, as well.

WRITING AND CREATIVITY: A STRONG CONNECTION

When we engage youngsters in writing tasks (as we do in this book), some teachers often associate creativity with some writings, but not others; and the different association causes many folks to approach the writing differently. When we teach what we consider to be "creative writing," our voices tend to rise with a lilt of lightness. Our faces brighten and our voices suggest that we can all now relax and let our inner selves take over to create wonderful writings. We usually associate fiction and poetry with such writing. On the other hand, when we speak of writings that we would not label as "creative," we lower our voices; we get serious, and we insist that students adhere to complex rules and procedures in order to write effective prose.

We usually place expository (explanatory) writing in this category, writing that would include persuasive essays, as well as compare–contrast and analytic writing.

The problem is that both perspectives send erroneous messages. Young writers often get the message that if they are smart enough or clever enough or have the right inborn capabilities, their creativity will flow and somehow take the form of eloquent prose (or poetry). That's quite a tall order. On the other hand, when the writing gets serious and brows are furrowed, another set of intimidating expectations associated with difficulty and rigor is implied.

This problem is exacerbated by the language we use. When creativity is associated with writing, it is used as a modifier, as in "creative writing." The use of the modifier suggests that there must be another kind of writing. While most of us would not overtly label any writing as "noncreative," that is what the modifier implies. That is how our language works. If there is such a thing as "creative writing," then there must be such a thing as "noncreative writing."

Fiction writing does, in fact, involve creativity. Think about fiction. If it's character driven, the writer builds a story around the character. Faulkner suggested that to write a story is to invent a character and follow him (or her) around for a couple of days. The character will engage in events, talk, and move around in environments. The writer observes, listens, and records. Character-driven fiction involves elaboration on a character. **Elaboration** is a creative thinking skill.

If fiction is plot driven, the writer builds a story around a plot core (an annual ritual, for example). The plot core lives in characters (farmers) who give it texture through their behavior. The writer brings character (farmers) and environment (small Kansas town) to bear on the plot core (annual ritual: read Shirley Jackson's "The Lottery") and fashions a story. Plot-driven fiction is elaboration on a plot core.

Elaboration is a fundamental creative thinking skill and is integral to writing fiction, no matter what the writer's beginning point. Fiction is creative because it demands at least one creative thinking skill, or creative behavior. (Fiction demands others, as well, but any one establishes the creativity in the writing.)

Now what about a letter to the editor of a local newspaper? The letter puts forth an opinion (agree or disagree) about a piece of news or opinion recently published (postponing construction of a new housing development until there is a second environmental impact study). A citizen reads the news article and experiences an immediate reaction. As she reads, the reaction becomes stronger, and she is motivated to reply. She composes a short letter that contains a statement of the issue, her position on the issue, her reasons for the position, a brief acknowledgment of why someone might see the issue another way, and her conclusion.

In writing this piece, the writer began with a reaction to the news article and then in her letter, which was an opinion essay, she elaborated on the initial reaction. There is more than elaboration, however, in what she did to write her response. In her letter (as in a piece of fiction), she displayed *fluency* and *organization*, both creative thinking skills. If mobilization of one or more creative thinking skills established fiction as a creative writing process, it would seem to follow that mobilization of the same creative thinking patterns would establish an opinion essay, as well, as an act of creative writing.

And, of course, it does. A way of thinking or behaving is creative because it demands creativity. If a human behavior, in writing or otherwise, can be accomplished without creativity, then that skill or behavior is not creative. If, however, a human behavior or way of thinking does mobilize patterns associated with creativity, then that one is explicitly creative. Creativity occurs whenever it is required to do something, as in writing a piece of fiction, an opinion or persuasive essay, or an analytic essay.

Elaboration, fluency, and organization of chaos are well established in the literature of creativity and creative thinking. Another well established creative skill includes the ability to observe, to be aware, to be attentive in ways that allow individuals to take in and organize information around them in order to create a storehouse of knowledge. **Awareness** is critical for creativity, and creative individuals have stores of knowledge to access.

There's more. The fiction and the opinion letter both required **perseverance** in crafting ideas and language, and both required **courage** to put oneself on the line, vulnerable to public scrutiny. Perseverance (self-discipline) and the courage to take risks are attributes consistently associated with creative skill and behavior.

In addition, fiction writers invariably wonder about "what would happen if." That sort of wondering or speculative thinking is called **curiosity,** which is a creative thinking skill or behavior. And for those readers who have written opinion letters to the editor of a local newspaper, the origin of such letters may have been, "Gee, what's the logical conclusion of that line of reasoning?" If that were the case, the creativity associated with that sort of opinion letter is the same curiosity that fired the fiction.

Do opinion letters ever arise from the need to "see" or consider an issue from a different perspective? If so, that's **flexibility,** or flexible thinking. It's the kind of thinking that causes us to slap our foreheads and cry,

"Why didn't I think of that?" Fiction writers also tend to view the ordinary from more than one perspective, and sometimes their perspective is different from anything we've ever seen before. Maybe their perspective ends up being different from anything the writer has ever seen before. Maybe it evolved as the writer wrote; when the writer came out on the other side of the story, there it was. If the perspective is unique for the writer, the term in the language of creativity is **originality.**

It would not be the first time in the history of opinion writing, as well, for an essay or letter to display a unique thought. People routinely cut and save, or post on the refrigerator, opinion essays they find especially interesting. That level of interest is often the result of the original thinking in the writing.

There's a pattern working here, a pattern of creative possibilities associated with two seemingly disparate genres, one we easily refer to as creative (fiction) and the other that we tend not to see in that way. Creativity reaches beyond fiction and poetry right into an opinion letter to the editor of a local newspaper. It reaches into report writing, also, because a report requires the writer to have an awareness of and knowledge about a particular topic. It requires that the writer organize a collection of ideas and information in his/her own way (**originality**). It also requires that a writer begin with a kernel of inquiry or speculation and **curiosity** about a subject to be researched.

Now that we've explored some of the qualities shared by fiction, opinion, and research writing as creative writing, what writing is not? A teacher writes an exercise on the chalkboard in English class. The exercise contains the words *men* and *man* where the subject is supposed to be and the word *were* in the verb slot. Circling the word *men* as the appropriate subject for the sentence probably makes little or no creative demand on students, so the exercise is probably not creative. But such exercises aren't writing, either. We'll have to look elsewhere for "noncreative writing."

What about formulaic paragraph writing? What if a teacher were to assign a "hamburger" paragraph that requires five sentences, the middle three of which are the "meat" of the main idea? Unlike the sentence above (*men* and *were*), students will actually write something, so it qualifies as writing. But is it creative writing? To satisfy the writing task, students must generate an idea that will serve as the main one, and several more to elaborate on the idea. The task requires at least a minor degree of **fluent** thinking. Also, the teacher required a specific organizational structure. When "organizing chaos" is associated with creative people, it is the organizational behavior that is creative, not following someone else's invention (in this case the teacher's) of an organizational system. Therefore, writing a hamburger paragraph makes at least one, and perhaps two or more, creative demands on a writer. That particular writing is then, according to definitions of creativity, a creative writing task.

Notice that writing does not have to be very good to be considered creative. Notice, as well, that the assignment or prompt for writing does not have to be especially good or intelligent to be creative. Some pretty inane, and at the same time creative, things have occurred in the world. Your authors view hamburger paragraphs as rather inane because they have so little to do with real paragraph thinking and writing, or anything else for that matter. And if students write enough hamburger paragraphs, their prospects for ever writing well may, in fact, be compromised. But none of that means the writing demand is not creative.

The point in all of this is that writing, unless the writer is taking dictation, is fundamentally a creative activity. Writing is a creative process. There certainly are some nonwriting tasks in school that are not creative; but when anyone begins writing, whether with a pen in hand or keyboard underhand, and composes text, the composing is, according to well established definitions of creativity, a creative behavior.

It is certainly not wrong to use "creative" as a modifier for writing; it is simply redundant, and it implies that writing that we do not overtly label as creative must be noncreative, which is a virtual impossibility. The worst part of qualifying writing as creative or, by implication, noncreative, is that it leads to a valuing of some writing over other writing. There may even be a perception that "real" writers write fiction, that nearly anyone can write everything else. Bobby Knight, Indiana University basketball coach, chided sports journalists several years ago with a comment to the effect that everyone learns to write in the second grade and then some move on to bigger and better things. It is difficult to know precisely what Coach Knight meant by that;

he may have simply spoken in a moment of anger at sports writers. However, one conclusion is that what sports journalists do (which is write) can be learned by a seven-year-old. No one ever says that about Welty, Hemingway, or E. B. White.

In the context of this book and the cues that we use to prompt youngsters to write, definitions of creativity are instructive. For example, consider a cue that asks them to write a sentence that contains the name of a friend and to use the words "my friend" after the name. The cue requires the writer to use both fluency and elaboration, both creative thinking skills. Consider another cue, which asks the writer to write a sentence that has the idea of a favorite breakfast as the main idea, and in which *today* is the introductory word. Again, the task requires writers to mobilize both fluency and elaboration. Yet a different cue gives writers a model sentence ("Below, there are six birds flying carefully between the rock ledges.") and asks them to write a new sentence with *above* as the indtroductory word. That cue requires writers to mobilize flexibility as they reconsider and rewrite the model sentence from a different perspective. Of course, all of the above cues require the creative thinking skills of awareness and perseverance.

Other creative thinking skills, such as curiosity and organizing chaos, might more often be mobilized in larger pieces of writing. However, the cues in this book explicitly bring creative thinking patterns into the classroom, patterns of thinking that youngsters will mobilize whether they are writing sentences or larger pieces of text.

The point is, even though this book focuses on what might be viewed by some as a specifically noncreative task—that is, practicing and learning the discipline associated with writing and language use—the cues in this book engage young writers in writing activities that are explicitly creative.

CHAPTER 3

PUNCTUATION

This chapter contains 20 punctuation conventions. The lessons are sequenced according to a developmental perspective. In other words, we've started with the conventions that are of highest utility for primary grade children. They are the conventions which will appear very early in children's writings and, as such, should be addressed early in the school writing curriculum. Lessons toward the middle of the section become increasingly relevant to upper elementary grade children. By the time we get to Lesson 20 on semicolons, we recommend that teachers respond only to youngsters' needs in the upper elementary and middle school grades and not expect mastery from most until late middle school or beyond. (For suggestions regarding a grade-level timeline for teaching the punctuation conventions, see Chapter 1.)

It is our intention that each lesson be user (teacher) friendly, that each lesson represent direct and systematic application of the convention in youngsters' writings, and that youngsters engage in the lessons by constructing their own meanings and participating together as a community of learners.

TIPS FOR UNDERSTANDING AND USING THE LESSONS

- The teaching procedures in these lessons are recommendations and reflections on experience; they are not prescriptions or scripts. There is no assumption that teachers will adopt the recommended dialogue verbatim in their classrooms.
- References to time (e.g., "On the first day of kindergarten. . .") are not prescriptions; good teachers know on which day to begin.
- The "Explanation" section of each lesson is about the convention; the "Teaching Young Writers. . ." section is about direct instruction.
- Cues that call for specific sentence length (e.g., "Write a six-word sentence. . .") cause young writers to think consciously about sentence writing by having to count deliberately and think through a sentence; deliberate attention promotes learning.
- Often in these lessons, we refer to a "word wall," a wall space or bulletin board dedicated to displays of words that students have learned, are learning, and use over and over.

LESSON 1: END PUNCTUATION IN SENTENCES

The Convention

Use a period at the end of a declarative (telling) sentence, a question mark at the end of an interrogative (question) sentence, and an exclamation mark at the end of an exclamatory sentence.

Student Writing Samples (not edited for spelling)

1. My favorite plac is Sea Word. [First Grader]
2. I want to be in a plac wher ther is not violens or bad people. [Second Grader]
3. I like to climb almosat to the tip top of the tree and listen to the birds and the wind. [Second Grader]
4. The hunters are closing in on a herd of musk oxen. [Third Grader]
5. I want to feel the warmth of the sand and sun touch my skin. [Fifth Grader]

Explanation

We use end marks to signal the reader that a sentence is finished. Each kind of sentence has its own marker. The most frequent kind of sentence used by young writers is declarative, a telling sentence, one that makes a statement. The end of those sentences is marked with a period. Probably the second most frequent sentence that young writers write is an interrogative, a sentence that asks a question. Its end is signaled by a question mark. The least frequent kind of sentence used by young writers, or any writer for that matter, is the exclamatory sentence, a sentence that shows a sense of excitement. The exclamatory sentence is ended with an exclamation mark. (Always use your own judgment regarding technical terms such as "declarative." Young writers are able to write the sentence without knowing the term.)

End marks occur when young writers begin to write. Even in the earliest scribble-writing stages of writing development, young writers are working in the language they speak, a basic attribute of which is syntactic structures. In English, for our purposes, those structures occur in sentences, so when the two-year-old is scribble-writing on the wall of her bedroom, she is thinking in and representing sentence strings. Each of the sentences merits a terminal mark.

Of course, at two, no one is going to insist that she end each of her lines with a dot; for she has no frame of reference on the basis of which to understand and implement the convention. The point here is that terminal marks are part of the young writer's need as soon as the young writer begins to make writing-like marks. Put another way, it is perfectly legitimate to begin talking with young writers about terminal marks on the first day of writing in the kindergarten.

To talk about terminal marks *should not be confused with teaching their use, demanding their use, or punishing their absence.* During story reading, point out the dot right there and feign speculation about what it is and why it's there. Someone in the room will know and say it's a period and it shows the end of the sentence. Don't ask how a child on the afternoon of the first day of kindergarten knows about a period. (S)he just does. There might be someone who knows it's 95 miles from Waco to Dallas, or that pork comes from pigs. Children just know a lot of stuff, and someone will know about periods.

Make something of an issue out of it on that first kindergarten or first-grade day.

- Write a sentence on the board.
- Call it a sentence.
- Show how it ends with a period. Make the period prominent.
- Tell them that whenever they write a sentence that tells something, they use a period.
- Tell them that they'll do a lot of that this year, a lot of sentence writing that requires a lot of periods.
- Tell them it's the way real writers write; so as they use periods at the end of their sentences, they will be working just like real writers.

The key here is to be realistic with young writers. At the earliest stages of their writing development in school, they can incorporate the mechanical attributes of what they write naturally. Call attention early on because early on is when they need these first punctuation marks.

Examples of End Punctuation in Sentences

Periods in Declarative Sentences
In *Woodsong,* Gary Paulsen writes about the Iditarod, the dogsled race across Alaska.
The farmer in *Ox Cart Man* took his ox to town.
The house in *The Little House* got to move back to the country.

Question Marks in Interrogative Sentences
Have you read *The Red Pony?*
Where do you think the boy in Gary Soto's poem, "Oranges," lived?
Wasn't the first chapter of *Hatchet* exciting?

Exclamation Marks in Exclamatory Sentences
The thoughts of the party-goers were unanimous. Elbert, don't use that bad word!
I was very sad when I read the ending of *Stone Fox*!
Maniac Magee is a funny kid!

Teaching Young Writers about End Punctuation

Suggestions for teaching about end punctuation cannot be directed explicitly at a grade level, as every teacher knows, for there are sixth graders **and** second graders who need the instruction. In addition, the instruction designed for kindergarten and first-grade learning is different from sixth- and eighth-grade instruction designed for reminding and reinforcing.

At the earliest stages of instruction, young writers should **notice**, then **practice** what they notice. Young writers notice what their teacher calls attention to. So when that period occurs in the read-aloud book with children sitting sufficiently close to see, call it to their attention. Show it on the board in sentence context and involve the children in the process. "Marva, think of a sentence that ends with a period." When Marva shares the sentence she wrote in her mind, ask that she share it again and call the period when she gets to it. If she doesn't understand immediately, model her sentence and your direction. "This is what I mean. Marva's sentence was about her dad. When she shares and calls the period, it will sound like this: My dad works in the yard period. There, Marva, it's your turn. Marva shares: 'My dad works in the yard period.' " Tell the class that you are often going to ask them to call punctuation marks this year when they share their sentences aloud.

In a third grade, your authors asked the children to write a sentence that contained the idea of **old man.** During the one-minute writing time, we meandered around the room and read over children's shoulders.

We noticed several sentences without end marks. When it was time to share, we asked a clarifying question. "This **is** the third grade, isn't it?" The class did one of those two-syllable *yes's* in unison. "That's what we thought," we said. "That means we won't see even one sentence in the whole room without an end punctuation mark, probably a period. Isn't that right?"

Every time we have done that, all the children in the room reread their work, and those who didn't have the requisite end mark immediately put it in. If a teacher made a similar reminder with every writing demand all year (it only takes five seconds), the sheer weight of the reminders would increase the amount of pupil attention to end marks. The key is attention. As they pay attention, they do it correctly. It isn't that they don't know; it's that they don't pay attention. Teachers promote attention.

It's much later in the school career of the students. An eighth-grade teacher collects homework written in multiple paragraphs that feature transitions, and several students hand in work with haphazard use of end marks. As soon as the teacher notices this, he hands the papers back to those students and calls attention to one of the offending sentences. "Do you know what is troubling me here, Randall?" He'll invariably say something like, "Oh yeah, sometimes I forget to use periods." The teacher asks that he make the corrections and hand it in at the end of the period if he wants credit on his homework. The teacher also suggests that he get someone to read his writing before he hands it in the next time if he thinks he might forget again because, the teacher says, he will not read past the first such error. He assures the student that he writes well (if he does) and assures him also that the quality of his writing is compromised when his audience doesn't know exactly where the sentences end. It's *his* problem, not the teacher's.

For basic instruction, as opposed to the reminding and requesting that might be necessary for older students, the very best strategy, indeed, the *only* strategy if we're trying to make writers, is for young writers to *write* in the convention. The following are examples of instructional cues that cause young writers to write single sentences that contain a variety of end marks. Remember to incorporate oral sharing and feedback so that all students have an opportunity to **hear** the sounds of the language.

Writing with End Punctuation: Periods

Write a declarative (telling) sentence about the weather.

_____

_____

_____

Write a declarative sentence in which the main idea is about your favorite book.

_____

_____

_____

Write a sentence that needs a period at the end.

_____

_____

_____

Writing with End Punctuation: Question Mark

Write an interrogative (question) sentence about your best friend.

_____

_____

_____

Write an interrogative sentence in which the main idea is a beautiful spring day.

_____

_____

_____

Write a sentence that needs a question mark at the end.

_____

_____

_____

Writing End Punctuation: Exclamation Mark

Write an exclamatory sentence about a time you were frightened.

_____

_____

_____

Write an exclamatory sentence in which the main idea is joy.

_____

_____

_____

Write a sentence that needs an exclamation mark at the end.

_____

_____

_____

Tips for Teachers

1. It is important that young writers share their writing aloud. Always promote some sharing, even if only for one or two students each session. Sharing aloud allows you to make quick suggestions and/or to comment on especially effective writing. Sharing aloud also serves to fill the room with the sounds of sentences. Good writers have the sounds of good sentences embedded in their heads. The class will begin to function like a true learning community, where youngsters learn from and with each other.

2. Assume young writers *can* and *should* learn to write conventionally, even at the earliest stages.

3. Establish with youngsters that using end marks properly helps to make them good writers.

4. Assume young writers *want* to learn to write well.

5. Emphasize end marks *every* time they write.

6. Draw attention to end marks in books and stories youngsters read.

7. Acknowledge to the children that people sometimes forget all kinds of things, even periods and question marks.

8. Acknowledge to yourself that there are individual differences, and it is not necessary, therefore, to treat everyone in the room exactly alike.

LESSON 2: COMMAS IN DATES

The Convention

Use commas to separate the day of the week (Monday) from the name of the month (January), then the name of the month (January) and day of the month (22) from the year (1996): Monday, January 22, 1996. In a sentence that contains only the name of the month (January) and the year (1996), a comma between them is optional, but no comma is preferable. If the day of the month comes first (22), followed by the name of the month (January), then the year (1996), there are no commas necessary: 22 January 1996.

Student Writing Samples (not edited for spelling)

1. I was born on December 7, 1989. [Second Grader]
2. I found out that my mother was born on Thursday, June 5, 1960. [Third Grader]
3. My sister's birthday is next Monday, October 10, 1994. [Fourth Grader]
4. W. E. B. DuBois was born on February 23, 1868 in Great Barrington, Massachusetts. [Sixth Grader]
5. My best birthday party was last week on Wednesday, October 24, 1995. [Sixth Grader]

Explanation

It's curious that a convention seemingly so simple takes so long to write, but it turns out that a complete date can be written in two different ways, and a partial date can be written in two other ways. One of the dates (Monday, January 22, 1996) contains two commas. Another date (January 22, 1996) contains one comma.

Still another date (January 1996) has no comma at all. And (22 January 1996) also contains no comma. Young children are likely to write sentences that contain one of the first three possibilities, so they will need either two, one, or no commas. The fourth date (22 January 1996) is not a likely option for young children.

This is a convention that can be used in the first grade, certainly the second. It is a good opportunity to start the youngest writers using commas because the format is so clear, so unambiguous, so rational.

Young writers need the rationality. The comma helps readers know where the boundaries are when we write. Commas help readers avoid being confused. The comma between the day of the month (22) and the year (1996) keeps the numbers from running together visually (22 1996; 22, 1996). The comma between the day of the week (Monday) and the month (January) helps readers hear the transition from the day to the month.

Of course, when the general date is written as January 1996, there is nothing to run together, so there is no comma. If it's written 22 January 1996, there's still nothing to run together. Commas in dates are unambiguous and reliable.

Examples of Commas in Dates

I read the book, *Indian in the Cupboard,* for the first time in May 1995.

I gave my brother Gary Soto's book, *Baseball in April,* for his tenth birthday on March 10, 1985.

Nobody knows for sure when Maniac Magee arrived in town, but Amanda saw him for the first time on October 11, 1976.

Teaching Young Writers about Commas in Dates

In those earliest grades one of the first activities during sharing time is affixing the date to the calendar on the bulletin board. On the first day of kindergarten when the date activity begins, little Archie gets to pin the yellow leaf on the 6 of the September calendar. The teacher should

- write the date on the board;
- explain how it is written;
- explain what's in it;
- explain that the little marks called commas help us keep the pieces apart so we don't get confused.

That isn't all that different from what kindergarten teachers do every day. The only possible difference is calling attention to the commas and the reasons why they are there.

Sometime during the kindergarten year it will be useful to use the date as a motive to write and read sentences every day. That's when, instead of merely writing the date on the board when Maggie pins the 16 onto the December calendar, the teacher writes a sentence: **Today is Tuesday, December 16, 1996.** "Look at that," boys and girls, "the date looks the same when it is in a sentence as it does when it is not in a sentence. We're going to write sentences with the date every day for the rest of the year."

The next day is the seventeenth. The sentence could be: **The sun came out on Wednesday, December 17, 1996.** For a week or so, write the daily date in a sentence every day, but vary the sentence designs. Then solicit a sentence for the date from the class. "Today, you get to think of the sentence. Everyone, think of a sentence that contains today's date from the calendar." Call on someone who is likely to have it right. Jessie reads his sentence from his mind: **It is Thursday, January 6, 1996.** "Jessie," the teacher says with clear eye contact, "you're so smart. That's a fine sentence. I'm going to write your sentence on the board and leave it there all day. Then tomorrow we'll have a new sentence with the date in it."

The next day, introduce children to the first rule for young writers. Tell them that writing is something that goes on in their heads, then they push it out of their mouth or they push it out of their pencils, but it goes on in their heads. "So, today we're going to write a sentence that contains the date. Listen now as Jose tells us what the date is. Then I want everyone to write the date in a sentence. When you have a sentence written in your head, raise your hand, and I'll call on some-one so I can write the sentence on the board." Continue the process as part of sharing time throughout the year.

The only variation on the theme above is that there are children in the kindergarten room who will begin to write scribally during the year. When Marco gives the sentence, **It's March 11, 1997,** say, "Marco, would you like to write your sentence on the board?" Help him as necessary.

Now it's the third grade and, unfortunately, there isn't any more sharing time first thing in the morning. But there is the "Ticket to Recess" box right inside the door. In it this morning are 37 3 × 5 cards, each printed with one of several kinds of tasks or cues that direct single-sentence writing.

Write a sentence that contains your birthdate.

"Folks, the Ticket to Recess box has some new material in it this morning. Let's practice for a moment so you know what to do." Ask someone the date today. Write it on the board: **Tuesday, October 5, 1997.** "Good Amanda. Thank you. Everyone, look at the date as I have written it on the board." Point out the elements in the date and the commas. "Now, let's make this interesting. I want you to think of a sentence that contains today's date." The hands go up almost immediately. Tell them to write the sentence on their scratch paper. Give them one minute. If one minute isn't enough for nearly everyone in a third grade room to write a simple sentence that contains the date, there is need for some writing fluency practice. One minute for a six-word sentence (The date today is Tuesday, March 10, 1998) is one word every ten seconds. In ten seconds, the average third grader is perfectly able to write as many as three or four words. That means, at full speed, the average third grader could write as many as fifteen to twenty words.

After a minute, solicit some readings aloud. Ask readers to call the commas when they get to them (Today is Tuesday comma March 21 comma 1997). Listen to several. Make sure what they write is a sentence as opposed to a nonsentence. (Go ahead, if you must, and call them "complete" sentences and "incomplete" sentences. The fact is, however, that a sentence is, by definition, complete, so neither modifier is necessary.) Make sure the commas are placed properly. Then tell the class that as they enter the room after lunch today, they are to pull a card from the Ticket to Recess box and write what it dictates. The sentence is your ticket out the door for afternoon recess (and as they head on out and give you the sentence, they drop the card in the box). They write another sentence as a ticket to morning recess the next day, another for afternoon recess, and one for homework. Do that for a week. The practice will establish the comma convention.

Writing with Commas in Dates

Write a sentence that contains your birthdate.

_____

_____

Find out the birthdate of one of your friends. Write a sentence that contains your friend's birthdate.

_____

_____

Write a sentence that begins with today's date. Remember to place the commas in the date so your readers won't be confused.

_____

_____

Think of what the date will be tomorrow. Write a sentence in which tomorrow's date appears at the end.

_____

_____

Write a sentence in which yesterday's date appears somewhere in the middle.

_____

_____

Write a sentence in which the date begins with Saturday.

_____

_____

Find out the date on which Christmas will occur this year. Write a sentence that contains the Christmas date.

_____

_____

Tips for Teachers

1. One of the things so critical in the early and middle elementary grades is daily sentence practice. Use this lesson as the catalyst for some of the daily sentence cues you need all year long.

2. Don't hesitate about the "Ticket to Recess" plan. It promotes independent practice, and people learn to write largely when the practice to instruction ratio is about 8 to 1.

3. Take the sentence practice into social studies. There are almanacs and social studies books in the room. There are also encyclopedias and other reference books. Use a different cue in the Ticket to Recess box: **Write a sentence that contains the date on which George Washington was born.**

LESSON 3: COMMAS IN ITEMS IN A SERIES

The Convention

Use commas to separate three or more items in a series.

Student Writing Samples (not edited for spelling)

1. I like to go to my ant house to go swimming, play saga, and be wiht the bebe. [First Grader]
2. My favorite place to be is in a castle with a brick wall, a butler, and lots of horses. [Second Grader]
3. I wish I cud by a kasol full of candy, lots of toys, and dansin gosts. [Second Grader]
4. They both are funny, they help me when I need help, they are nice to me, and they don't treat me bad. [Third Grader]
5. I would like to see animals, water falls, birds singing in a tree, and all the other things in paradise. [Fourth Grader]
6. My dad works, my sister is at school, and my mom is at the house cleaning. [Eighth Grader]

Explanation

We use commas between items in a series to signal a reader that the items are separate. For example, read the following sentence and decide how many things Juan had for lunch: *Juan had fish tacos fried rice and milk for lunch.* Juan could have had fish tacos plus milk and fried rice, which would be three things. On the other hand, he could have had tacos and milk plus some fish and rice, which would be four things. Only the comma markers clarify for the reader how many things Juan had for lunch. The commas carry meaning.

There are a couple of ways to look at the question of whether to place a comma between the last two items in a series (that is, before *and*). One way is that if the last two items in a series are discrete (different from each other), the writer uses the comma. If they are not discrete, the *and* will suffice. For example, the items in the following sentence are discrete: *For breakfast this morning I had bacon, eggs, toast, and juice.* There are four things for breakfast in that sentence. On the other hand, consider this sentence, which contains three breakfast foods: *For breakfast this morning I had bacon, eggs, toast and jam.*

Another way to look at this convention is in the context of a language in flux. Recall our earlier conversation about conventions in Chapter 1 of this book (p. 1). We said that markers are sometimes used more according to context rather than rule. This is especially true of items in a series. It is usually obvious when the last two items in a series are different or discrete, so most writers leave the comma out.

Here, teachers should be cautious. Children begin using items in series around the second grade. What happens when a seven-year-old, while trying to figure out writing, is at the same time told, "Sometimes you use the comma and sometimes you don't. You figure it out." We're trying to teach confidence, not confusion. Therefore, we suggest that confidence is best served by telling youngsters to use the comma between the last two items in a series. As children mature, they become increasingly able to handle ambiguity, but probably not in the second grade.

Examples of Commas in Items in Series

I liked the books *The Little House, Chicka Chicka Boom Boom*, and *Knots on a Counting Rope*.

It was early in the morning when Little Willie got out of bed, put on his boots and trousers, walked into the cold snowy morning, and hitched Searchlight to the sled.

In *The Very Quiet Cricket* Eric Carle writes about a spittlebug, a cicada, and a bumblebee.

Teaching Young Writers about Commas in Series

There are several kinds of items in series to which this punctuation convention applies. There is the sentence that lists three or more names of friends, makes of automobiles, breakfast foods, and kinds of living room furniture. Those kinds of sentences begin to occur in the sentences of very young writers in the first and second grades. We need to help children understand that they want their readers to understand that they are writing about three or more things, and the commas are the signal to the reader. As always in writing instruction, the responsibility for clarity falls on the writer. The writer who wants the audience to read **three** things, then, will use commas as the meaning marker, the signal, to the audience. If the writer fails to signal the audience and the audience fails to understand that there are three or more things in the sentence, it is the writer's fault. We don't use commas to make the teacher feel good; we use commas to help the readers understand what we have written.

That message of responsibility permeates all instruction about conventions, and everything else in writing, for that matter. It becomes increasingly important as the series becomes increasingly complex. Eggs, bacon, and toast are clearly three kinds of breakfast foods, and the commas aren't so critical to anyone who already knows that. However, what if there are prepositional phrases, and it is important for the audience to know that three things happened. The young writer's sentence is about looking for a lost toy, and the message is that the writer looked long and hard. The sentence reads: *I looked under the table, in the closet, and between the sheets on the bed.* Without the first comma, the table can easily be in the closet, which would limit the search to two places and change the writer's meaning.

It would be helpful if you wrote several example sentences on the board to make the point. For example,

After the party in the hallway with our friends, we talked about our plans for tomorrow.

"Read the sentence and tell us what you think is going on here." Play with the possibilities until there are several. There could be a party in the hallway. The hallway could be where the after-party conversation is taking place. The conversation about plans may or may not have taken place with our friends. Then put one comma in and notice how meaning is clarified. Put the other one in and notice how meaning is clarified again. "That's why we use commas in series, my friends. We want to make sure readers know what we are writing about."

It is even more critical when the series contains larger pieces of sentences. Consider the example of a story character who sits at the table with her family, eats a fine meal of potatoes and fish, remembers that it's Tuesday and she has to feed her fish. She asks to be excused so she can find the fish food that might have fallen off the table in the earthquake. The story character did lots of things; if there are no commas to separate the pieces in the sentence, it reads as a long-winded sentence, maybe even a run-on that must be rewritten. But it is not a run-on merely because it is long. If it is punctuated properly, it doesn't even seem all that long.

Of course, the instructional issue with primary children tends to be the single words and then prepositional phrases. In the middle grades, youngsters still write single words and phrases in series, but the larger sentence elements begin to creep in. Young writers need to have the convention pointed out in their reading, and they need to practice the convention in their writing lessons. Then, as you call attention to commas in series in their reading, and you engage them in practice with the convention in writing lessons, you also need to call attention to the convention in their own writing and hold them responsible for making the transition from lessons to larger pieces of writing.

The following are examples of cues that instruct young writers to write single sentences with items in series. Remember to incorporate oral sharing and feedback so that all students have an opportunity to hear the sounds of the language.

Writing Sentences with Items in a Series

Write a sentence with the names of three of your friends, one name right after the other.

_____

_____

_____

Write a sentence that contains four animals that could be pets.

_____

_____

_____

Use the following phrases in a sentence: *in the house, under the bed, after dark.*

_____

_____

_____

Write a sentence that contains three commas that separate items in a series.

_____

_____

_____

Write a sentence in which the main idea is weather, and use at least three items in a series.

_____

_____

_____

Tips for Teachers

1. The purpose for this convention, as with the others in this book, is to signal readers in a way that ensures clarity in a reading. Without commas placed appropriately between items in a series, readers can be confused about how many items there are, or even what they are. It is important for youngsters to understand that the commas are critical.

2. Over time, because language use is always in flux, there has been a trend for this convention to change somewhat. The convention used to be that when there were items in a series, a writer should place a comma between each item, as well as before the *and* that preceded the last item. More recently, it has become conventionally accepted to omit the comma before *and* as long as a sentence's meaning is not compromised. We, however, recommend that, in order not to confuse young writers, teachers direct them to use the comma before *and* at all times. This way, they will never be wrong.

LESSON 4: COMMAS IN ADDRESSES

The Convention

Use commas to separate parts of an address, whether the address appears in a sentence or on the front of an envelope.

Student Writing Samples (not edited for spelling)

1. I live at 1097 North Tempe Drive, Tempe, Arizona. [Third Grader]
2. My house is at 36665 Mission Circle, The Woodlands, Houston, Texas. [Fourth Grader]
3. I don't rember exakly what it is, but it's like 103 Apple Way, Cedar Falls, Iowa 50613. [Fifth Grader]
4. It's my father's house where I go on weekends: 4153 York Avenue, Absecan, NJ. [Sixth Grader]
5. My house is on 153 Tyler Street, Vista, California 92084. [Sixth Grader]

Explanation

Use of this information begins when the children are very small. It is a survival skill, in fact. We want them to know their telephone number and the location of their house. Then we want them to know their address. For many children, one of their first writing tasks is their name and address, and that is when they are introduced for the first time to commas in addresses. It's pretty haphazard when they are three or four, but we show the model and direct them to copy. Often, that modeling begins with parents.

When children get to school, they write letters home and practice the address. We put a model on the board and insist on the commas. Most youngsters get pretty good at it, and it makes a nice, early writing activity.

On the front of an envelope, there is the name of the person to whom the letter is directed. If it's Aaron H. Sledge, it's written just that way. But if Mr. Sledge is the mayor, his name is followed by a comma, then the title: Aaron H. Sledge, Mayor.

This might be old hat for us, but it isn't for a first or second grader, so we'll go through it line-by-line just to be sure. Mayor Sledge lives on River Road, and there is a number on his house: 118 River Road. But there are two River Roads in the city, and the mayor's is West River Road: 118 West River Road. That's just the way they do it in Grundy Center, which is the name of the town where Mr. Sledge serves as mayor. The town is in Iowa: Grundy Center, Iowa, and there is a Zip Code, 50601. The address then reads as follows on the envelope:

> Aaron H. Sledge, Mayor
> 118 West River Road
> Grundy Center, Iowa 50601

There's nothing very complicated about that, but young writers have to do it several times to get the hang of it. Maybe they should prepare mock envelopes for about twenty friends and relatives. Twenty might be enough practice for the first several weeks.

Then they have to learn how to write the mayor's name and address in a sentence. There are more commas because everything has to be separated from everything else.

Mayor Sledge's address is Aaron H. Sledge, Mayor, 118 West River Road, Grundy Center, Iowa 50601.

The key to the usage is clarity. Each element in the address, when written in a sentence, must be clearly separated from every other element in order to avoid confusion. So we added a comma after the word *Mayor* because that must be separated from the street address. We also added a comma after the street address in order to separate it from the town. Young writers need to write twenty more sentences over a period of a week or two as practice with the new comma skill.

Examples of Commas in Addresses

Ramona Quimby lives at 1234 Klickatat Lane, Portland, Oregon.

If Brian in *Hatchet* had an address, it might be 3493 Lakeshore Drive, Somewhere, Canada.

The Very Quiet Cricket was published at 200 Madison Avenue, New York, New York 10016.

Teaching Young Writers about Commas in Addresses

For older children in the fourth grade and higher, the initial writing direction can be to write what their home address looks like on the front of an envelope. It is important to begin there because the envelope is a real-world example. Make sure everyone has it right. Use the example of the envelope address to show how the comma is used in that format: to separate the city from the state. It may be useful for young writers in these upper grades to write as many as a half-dozen envelope addresses, one for someone in the room, one for the school, another for the President of the United States, and so forth. There are hundreds of addresses in an up-to-date almanac, an invaluable resource for every classroom.

It is important to remind the older elementary children that there are two different places where addresses can be written. They have written several addresses for envelopes. Now they are going to write some of those addresses in sentences. Provide a cue: Write a sentence that contains the full mailing address of the President of the United States. They will need a minute or so for the sentence. Then ask them if they have named the president in the sentence. "My friends, don't we always include the name of the person when we write an address?" This will be an item by item revision process. First they have to write in the name of the president. Then, they have to use the title and separate the title from the name with a comma.

Go through the entire process: comma after the title, after the street, and the city. Share several of the sentences aloud, each time having the reader read it once, then again calling the commas aloud: Abraham Lincoln comma President of the United States comma 1600 Pennsylvania Avenue comma Washington comma D.C. 20500. Follow that activity with perhaps two sentences that contain addresses each day for two weeks. That seems like a whole lot of sentences, but think of it this way: The sentence writing is practice. Students will be writing every day anyway. This is just one of the things they will write. It doesn't take very long, and they are practicing thinking and writing sentences, as well as using commas in those sentences.

For younger children, the second and third graders, the process takes longer. They can practice fewer sentences at a time but over a longer period of time. One sentence session begins with a mock envelope address on the board. Help as they copy it on their paper. Then generalize the process to their own home address, leading them line by line through the name, the street, the city, state, and Zip Code. Over a week or two, each child in the room should write an envelope address for as many as a dozen of the other children in the room, working in pairs on the task. They can also write envelope addresses for their school, city hall, and the local college or university. Don't be concerned about writing envelope addresses without mailing anything. This is about addresses, and it has the added advantage of informing children that there are addresses for all individuals as well as the agencies they hear about all the time.

The next stage is to write some of the envelope addresses in sentences. Write one sentence on the board, then lead the children through one of their own. Practice the sentences on a schedule of one per day for several weeks or until it is clear that they know how to write such sentences and use the punctuation properly in the process.

In the earlier grades, when practice is so crucial, it may be useful to conduct a series of lessons and practice sessions during the fall and again in the spring. Of course, youngsters are writing all sorts of other things at the same time, so there is a lot of writing in the classroom. The teacher can review much of what the children write, with a careful reading being limited to two pieces each week, perhaps one of the teacher's choice and one of each student's choice. If young writers are writing as much as the teacher can read, they aren't writing enough to learn to write well. If they're writing enough to learn to write well, the teacher can't possibly read it all.

Writing with Commas in Addresses

1. Write a sentence that contains your home address.

    _____

    _____

2. Write a sentence that contains the address of your best friend.

    _____

    _____

3. Write a sentence in which the address of your school is included. Make the address begin with the name and title of the principal.

    _____

    _____

4. Look in the almanac or check your local newspaper for the address of your representative in the United States House of Representatives. Write a sentence that contains the name of the representative and his or her address in Washington.

    _____

    _____

5. Write a sentence that contains the address of your post office, your bank, or your grocery store.

    _____

    _____

6. Write a sentence in which an address appears toward the beginning.

    _____

    _____

7. Write a sentence so that the address of one of your friends appears toward the end.

    _____

    _____

Tips for Teachers

1. Make sure to provide young writers with a model of what an envelope address is supposed to look like.
2. Show them the difference between an envelope address and an address in a sentence.
3. Make sure they practice enough times to solidify the routine use of commas in a sentence that includes an address.
4. This punctuation convention won't be used all of the time, but it does require use of the comma, which youngsters should learn.

LESSON 5: APOSTROPHES IN CONTRACTIONS

The Convention

Use an apostrophe where one or more letters are omitted in contractions of words or numbers. Place the apostrophe where the one or more letters or numbers are omitted.

Student Writing Samples (not edited for spelling)

1. It's my favorite place beckus it is fun. [Second Grader]
2. Mi favorite place is Sea World becaus there's sharks and fish. [Second Grader]
3. I would like to be in Hodywood because it's fun ther. [Third Grader]
4. That's why it's my best room in the house. [Third Grader]
5. I'm in my room, and I lik it ther. [Fourth Grader]
6. I like the rides alot because they're fun and fast, and they have alot of edventure. [Fourth Grader]

Explanation

To contract means to shorten. A contraction is something shortened. In writing, contractions are associated with shortened forms of words or phrases. In this lesson, a contraction is a shortened form of a word, in fact, two words, or a shortened form of a number. More specifically, a contraction in this lesson occurs in the following instances.

- When one or more letters are omitted from a word, that's a contraction ('n as a contraction of in when writing a breakfast food, bread 'n jam).
- When one or more numbers are omitted from a larger number, there's a contraction of a larger date ('61 as a contraction of 1961).
- When one or more letters are omitted and two words are contracted, that's a contraction, as well

(it's as a contraction of it is when writing it's painful).

While there are three kinds of contractions on the list, the most characteristic kind of contraction in writing instruction for young writers is the third, the contraction associated with contracting two words to make one and replacing the omitted letter or letters with an apostrophe. That is (or that's) the focus of this lesson.

Typically, there are certain contractions that are taught in the spelling program. In this book, however, the issue is not memorized spelling words; it's (or it is) how the language works, and because young writers understand the language, they will spell contractions properly.

The basic principle is important here. Contractions of words are formed when two words are put together and, in the combining, one or more letters are left out. To show the removal, an apostrophe is put in where the letter has been omitted. In the contraction that's, therefore, we have that and is, but the i in is has been removed. In its place, there is an apostrophe.

That last sentence is an especially interesting one because it contains the most routinely misused grouping of letters in this discussion of contractions. The word its can be a simple word in some sentences and a contraction in others. It's (it is) a contraction when it signifies the combination of two words, as it does in this sentence. However, when its placement in a sentence does not signify the combination of two words, as in this sentence, it is not a contraction. A word that is a contraction contains an apostrophe where a letter was omitted. A word that is not a contraction has no letters omitted, so there is no apostrophe.

Sometimes, as in the paragraph above, its is a possessive pronoun (The dog had **its** toenails clipped). In that sentence, the word its is about toenails that belong to or are possessed by the dog. The word is not a combination of it is. Check it. Read the sentence about the dog's toenails, and when you get to the word printed in bold, say *it is* or *it has*. If those two word pairs do not (or *don't*) fit or make sense, the word is not a contraction. Of course, the dog did not have "it is toenails" clipped. That is ridiculous, or *that's* ridiculous, whichever you like, but the ridiculousness remains in either case.

When the word is a contraction, it is because **it's** a combination of the two words *it is*. Check it here, as well. Read the opening sentence in this paragraph, and when you get to the word printed in bold, say *it is* instead of the contraction. If *it is* fits, then the contraction is right.

Contractions are used in all sorts of word combinations, and in every case *there's* (*there is*; the apostrophe replaces the vowel in *is*) the same pattern. *That's* (*that is*; the apostrophe replaces the vowel in *is*) why it makes sense for young writers to **understand** contractions rather than merely memorize their spelling patterns. Contractions represent a mechanical device in writing that young writers can understand and on which they can rely.

Examples of Contractions in Sentences

I guess I'll just have to land this plane myself, thought Brian.

No matter how hard he tried, the tiny cricket couldn't hear his chirp.

Alexander thought he'd be happier in Australia.

Teaching Young Writers about Apostrophes in Contractions

The first part of the instructional process needs to be awareness. Young writers need the sound of contractions in their ears and the appearance of contractions behind their eyes. Therefore, it is important, beginning in the first grade, and certainly no later than the second, to begin formally **noticing** contractions in what children read and what teachers read to children. And the **noticing** needs to be both visual and auditory.

While reading aloud to children in small groups, call attention to contractions, occasionally writing one on the board and explaining how it works, reading the sentence both with and without the contraction. "Listen to how it sounds, boys and girls. Part of how we learn about language is to listen very carefully and get the sound of the language in our ears and minds."

In the second grade, or once they can read a piece that has been read to them, give them awareness pieces filled with contractions.

The cow **didn't** know she **couldn't** give milk to the farmer who **didn't** have a bucket. So she met with the other cows and asked **who'll** help her. "**Don't** you know," they asked, "that there **aren't** any ways to give milk if there **isn't** a bucket?"

"**I'm** sure **we'll** be able to find a way," she said. "Maybe **it's** not a big problem. Maybe it **doesn't** mean that we **can't** get him the milk."

When such language is read aloud, the sounds of contractions fill the air. After reading once, direct the children to listen for the contractions and count them when they hear them. The point is the **listening,** not the right answer. That they are attuned to the sound of contractions is the important instructional focus.

Someone in the class will write with a contraction or two, even in the first grade. After all, children use contractions in their oral language long before they come to school. It is inevitable that *they'll* pop up in children's writing. When the first one surfaces, call attention to it directly. "Boys and girls, listen to Juanita's sentence."

I didn't know the cookies were in the bag.

Call attention to the second word. Ask Juanita what that second word is. When she calls *didn't* aloud, ask if she knows what *didn't* means. If she appears to be forming the response, wait a few counts, but if the question seems strange to her, jump in. "Listen to the sentence again." Read it as she wrote it. "Now listen to it this time, and see if you can hear something different. *I did not know the cookies were in the bag.*" Read the two sentences several times if necessary and emphasize the contraction. She'll hear it eventually, and others in the room will have their hands waving wildly if she doesn't get it as quickly as they do. When Juanita shares what she heard, write the two forms on the board and talk about the apostrophe. Call it by name, show it alone and in the contraction. Call the word by its right name. Don't necessarily teach a lesson; just call attention to the form in Juanita's writing.

Other instances will follow naturally, but now that you have called attention to the form, there will be even more. Make an issue out of them as they appear. On The Word Wall, begin pinning 3×5 cards, each with a contraction written in bold print that comes from their writing. In small print underneath each contraction, write the two words from which the contraction comes.

The words on The Word Wall are a reference point for young writers in the primary grades. They are always free to visit The Word Wall and find a word they need, in this case a contraction. The teacher's direction to the children is, "If you want to use a contraction in your writing, go to The Word Wall and make sure you have it right before you bring your writing to me or any other audience." This is one of many reminders in the elementary school writing program that it *doesn't* matter what their papers look like as long as they are on the writer's side of the desk, but when the paper crosses the desk (goes to an audience other than the writer), it has to be right. The Word Wall is a reference that helps them make it right, at least with respect to contractions.

Here's a word about worksheets used for independent practice. If there is a specific **independent practice** objective, and a worksheet can satisfy the objective, use it. There are several differences between good and poor worksheets; one good worksheet characteristic is that it satisfies a worthy **independent practice** objective. A characteristic of a poor worksheet is that its purpose is **seatwork.** A worthy independent practice worksheet regarding contractions is one on which young writers are confronted with a contraction that they make into two words, or two words that they make into a contraction; and they write a directed sentence that uses the form.

(did not) *(contraction)* **Write a sentence in which your word is in the third position.**
The girls didn't stay out late.

Young writers who work on those kinds of activities have to make the contraction, spell and punctuate it properly, and write with the contraction. They also have to plan in their writing because the position of the contraction is dictated. Unlike in many worksheets, in this case young writers *don't* have the luxury of beginning with a big letter and hoping something happens before they get to the period. Here, they have to write according to a plan at the sentence level. They have to be purposeful in their thinking and writing (and writing is the objective) as they focus on their understandings to construct meanings.

Writing with Apostrophes in Contractions

1. Think of a contraction for the words *did not*. Write the contraction in the space. _____ Now write a sentence that contains your contraction.

_____

_____

2. Think of a contraction for the words *is not*. Write the contraction in the space. _____ Now write a sentence that contains at least six words, and make your contraction one of the words.*

_____

_____

3. Think of a contraction for the words *that is*. Write the contraction in the space. _____ Now write a sentence that contains at least six words, and make your contraction the third word. The spaces are for a six-word sentence.

   _____   _____   **_____**   _____   _____   _____

4. Choose a contraction from the three in the brackets. *[can't—don't—aren't]* Write the words that make the contraction you selected.

_____

Write a sentence of at least seven words that contains the two words, not the contraction.

_____

_____

5. **could not** Write the contraction. _____ Write a sentence of at least seven words in which your contraction is in the fourth position.

_____

_____

6. **they are** _____ Write the contraction. Write a sentence in which the main idea is a girl and her sister getting ready for a party and include your contraction.

_____

_____

*The *Given Word Sentence* is used with the permission of the publisher, Kabyn Books, San Diego, California.

Tips for Teachers

1. Call everything by its right name: contraction, apostrophe, and so forth.
2. When young writers write a sentence, put a time limit on their writing. Our experience tells us that everyone in the room will become accustomed to low-level pressure. Once the pattern is set, the teacher won't have to be waiting for the last few to finish because they've procrastinated for several minutes before getting started.

3. Once there has been considerable awareness, sufficient instruction, and plenty of practice, hold young writers responsible for using the convention correctly. It is understandable that first and second graders might forget occasionally, but by the third grade, and certainly the fourth, it is no longer necessary to accept, or correct, for that matter, writing that includes first- and second-grade miscues.

LESSON 6: PERIODS IN ABBREVIATIONS

The Convention

A period is used when writing abbreviations such as personal titles (Junior and Doctor), organizations and agencies (Federal Bureau of Investigation and the National Football League), Latin terms (*anno Domini* and *versus*), and scientific terms (inch and cubic centimeters). The period appears after the abbreviation in some instances (Doctor) and within the abbreviation in other instances (*anno Domini*).

Student Writing Samples (not edited for spelling)

1. I'm in a special class called H.O.T.S. [Third Grader]
2. You get there on S.W. Airlines, that's Southwest Airlines. [Fourth Grader]
3. I lay down right there and watch my favorite T.V. programs as much as I like. [Fifth Grader]
4. If I'm happy, I turn on my radio or C.D. [Fifth Grader]
5. The P.E. building is a closed gym where we have fun playing games. [Sixth Grader]

Explanation

There is some ambiguity in this convention, but the general rule of thumb for punctuation applies here, as elsewhere. Because the purpose in writing is to convey messages as clearly as possible, punctuation is used to serve the purpose. Thus, we use a punctuation mark to clarify or to avoid confusion.

This convention is about words that are abbreviated routinely, not those that occur in order to economize randomly. The convention, therefore, does not apply to the following message pinned to the refrigerator door.

I'm at Geo clss. Wl be back for din.

That's shorthand reserved for refrigerator messages, or perhaps grocery lists. It isn't the sort of writing this book, or this lesson, is about.

There are categories of conventional abbreviations, and there are categories of abbreviations that have become conventional. In the first case, the period is expected by those who read and write English. In the second case, the period is often optional. In both cases, **using the period** is not wrong, but **not using the period** is often wrong. We prefer that young writers err on the side of using the period. That promotes a sense of predictability for the young writer. Later, when (s)he is better able to handle the ambiguity, it makes more sense to introduce the sense of exceptions, which most practiced writers take for granted.

In the first case, then, there are abbreviations that require the period. Those include professional titles for medical doctors (M.D.), dentists (D.D.S.), and Catholic sisters (Sr.). There are also academic titles for holders of the doctorate in philosophy (Ph.D.), master's degrees (M.A.), and the doctorate in law (J.D.). And there are personal titles for the first holder of the name (Sr.) and then his son (Jr.). Periods in those kinds of titles are conventional. They're expected.

Also in the first case (that is, the periods are expected) are Latin terms in common usage. Those include, but are not limited to, the following: *exempli gratia* (e.g.), *et cetera* (etc.), *ante meridiem* (A.M.), and *post meridiem* (P.M.). Finally, there are certain scientific terms, characteristically associated with measurement, such as *inch* (in.) and *foot* (ft.). It is important to note that many measurement abbreviations do not take a period because their spelling patterns are not like any other word (Btu, cm, and rpm, for example).

In the second case, there are abbreviations that *may* use the punctuation, the period, but the abbreviation is in such common use without the period, it has come to look odd with it. Take, for example, the Federal Bureau of Investigation, which is routinely referred to, both orally and in print, with three letters. Think, now, when you see the three letters in print, are there periods after each letter, after the third letter only, or are there no periods at all? Do you most often see it with periods but occasionally with no periods? Is it wrong to write the three letters as FBI? Is F.B.I. more right than wrong? In fact, that is one of the many abbreviations for which the period is optional but most often absent. Using periods in such abbreviations, however, is not wrong. Look at the following abbreviations and see if they "feel" better with or without the periods.

FBI   CIA   N.C.A.I.   GM   NASA   A.C.L.U.
GOP   HUD   N.C.A.A.   UN   A.M.A.   M.G.M.

A key to understanding this punctuation convention is what young writers need. There are some abbreviations (Mr., Mrs., Ms., Dr., Sr., Jr., in., A.M., and P.M.) that are very likely to occur in the writing of anyone who writes even a fair amount. There are other abbreviations far less likely to occur (Btu, cm, and NCAI). Young writers need to become familiar with the meaning, spelling, and proper punctuation of the higher frequency abbreviations. Much of the rest of the possible abbreviations will be handled as instances come up along the way.

Examples of Abbreviations in Sentences

Mr. Grayson was the caretaker at the ball park.
The gardener was able to treat Elbert's problem even better than James Shultz, M.D.
The bell in *The Polar Express* was 10 cm. in circumference.

Teaching Young Writers about Periods in High Frequency Abbreviations

On a given day in about the second grade, or as soon as the first abbreviation occurs in someone's writing in the room, pose a question. "If it's three o'clock, is it when you are sleeping or is it in the afternoon when you are playing? In what part of the day is three o'clock?" The conversation needs to turn, eventually, to the fact that there isn't any way to know when three o'clock is unless it is written as morning or afternoon. So how do we say it is three o'clock in the afternoon without using the word *afternoon*? Someone will know. Someone always does. Someone will say that you can tell because it is P.M. in the afternoon and A.M. in the morning. "So what does P.M. mean, Justin?" He'll almost certainly say it means afternoon and night. If he

says it means *post meridiem* and that the Latin means "after noon," call his mother and ask what he eats for breakfast.

"Yes, Justin, it does mean that it's afternoon or night. So you're saying that if we write 3:00 P.M., we mean that it's three in the afternoon?" Justin will say that's exactly what he means.

Explain that what Justin is talking about is called an *abbreviation*, something we write that's shorter than the whole word. Ask what we do when we are writing about a doctor, whose name is Doctor Gladys Cooper, and we don't want to write out the whole word *doctor*. It will be Juanita, or maybe Janine, who knows. Call on Juanita. "It's Dr." she says. Tell her to come on up and write that on the board.

Pretend she writes the correct letters and doesn't use a period in the abbreviation. "Right here, Juanita, we put a period. Boys and girls, we have to tell the reader that we've written an abbreviation. We do that by putting a period at the end. If we don't put the period in, it just looks like we made a mistake. We will learn about lots of abbreviations this year. The one for *doctor* is one of them. The one for the afternoon is another. Oh, and what's the abbreviation for afternoon or night? Carlos?"

On another day, use P.M. as the lead-in to A.M., and teach those two as a pattern. Write sentences that contain the time of day, and make sure to direct them to use the abbreviation. **Write a sentence that tells about something that happened at 2:30 in the afternoon. Use an abbreviation to show what time it is.** Put the abbreviations on the word wall.

On another day, introduce some personal abbreviations: Jr., Sr., Mrs., Ms., and Mr. Direct the young writers to write the words and the abbreviations, calling attention to the punctuation. Direct them to write sentences, as well. Put some personal abbreviations on the word wall.

In this age, it is important to know abbreviations for metric terms. Introduce those abbreviations with which they are familiar from science class: in., cm., mm., and so forth. Write the words and the abbreviations. Write sentences that contain the abbreviations. Put the abbreviations on The Word Wall.

Most second graders won't need the Latin abbreviations **e.g., i.e.,** and **vs.,** so those can wait for several years. In fact, the abbreviation for *versus* might not be important until they are in law school, and then the legal abbreviation is merely **v.** They will probably need B.C. and A.D., so include those in the instructional plan along the way.

It will be helpful to make the abbreviations part of the spelling lists as the year wears on—a couple here, a couple there. The focus, of course, is the abbreviation and the punctuation; but in the larger sense, the focus is writing, using every part of the language to make writing work. Abbreviations are part of the language.

What do we do about the National Football League and the National Council of American Indians? The local newspaper has abbreviated the former as NFL, just that way, without any punctuation between the letters or at the end, for so long that the unpunctuated abbreviation has become the accepted convention. On the other hand, it is not wrong to maintain a punctuation pattern, so the children could abbreviate it as the N.F.L. Collect abbreviations and write them on a special section of the word wall.

Writing with Abbreviations

1. Write a sentence that contains an abbreviation for the word *mister.*

    _____

    _____

2. Write the abbreviation for the word *doctor.* _____ Write a sentence that contains the abbreviation for the word *doctor.*

    _____

    _____

3. Write a sentence that contains an abbreviation for the word *inch.*

    _____

    _____

4. Use the abbreviation **A.M.** in a sentence about what you had for breakfast.

    _____

    _____

5. Write a sentence that contains the name of a doctor and an abbreviation, but don't use the abbreviation **Dr.** Use the abbreviation that comes *after* the doctor's name, not before the doctor's name.

    _____

    _____

6. Write a question sentence in which there is an abbreviation of your choice.

    _____

    _____

7. Write a sentence that contains an abbreviation for a woman who is married.

    _____

    _____

Tips for Teachers

1. Don't overwhelm the children with abbreviations. There aren't very many high frequency and high utility abbreviations.

2. Introduce abbreviations a couple at a time over the year, and insist they write with them. Also direct children to include in their larger writings the abbreviations they have learned.

LESSON 7: COMMAS IN COMPOUND SENTENCES

The Convention

Use a comma before *and* (or any other coordinating conjunction: *but, or, for, so, yet, nor*) to separate two independent clauses in a compound sentence.

Student Writing Samples (not edited for spelling)

1. You can make your own food, and it tastes real good. [Second Grader]
2. It has a lot of rides, and it is fun. [Second Grader]
3. I went to the redwoods, and I got GI Joe for my birthday. [Third Grader]
4. They have told me all about the great rides they have there, so I am trying to save up money to go and have a good time. [Third Grader]
5. I like natur, and I like to sing the soogs about natur. [Third Grader]
6. Some guys or girls my age ask me to teach them, and I feel good about myself when I have the chance to help someone. [Sixth Grader]

Explanation

In compound sentences, the comma marks the division between two (or more) independent clauses (or simple sentences). In the following sentence, the word *and* separates two ideas in one **simple** sentence.

I went to the ball game and had a terrific time.

The two ideas (**went** to the ball game and **had** a good time) occur in one sentence, one clause, one sentence sound. As it is written, there is no more than one sentence, or one independent clause, if you will.

In the next sentence, on the other hand, the comma clearly separates **two** independent clauses (two complete and separate but closely related ideas):

I went to the ball game, and I had a terrific time.

Now, there are two clauses, two sentences or sentence sounds. We could, for instance, put an end mark after having gone *to the ball game.* If we capitalized *and,* we could make a second sentence out of the part about having had a good time, or we could just drop the *and* and have a second sentence. Incidentally, while primitive, perhaps, there is nothing ungrammatical about beginning the second sentence with *and,* just as there is nothing ungrammatical about beginning sentences with *because,* as we shall see along the way in this book.

The two example sentences are quite different, and that's what young writers need to notice. In the first sentence, the *and* does not separate two independent clauses (sentence-like constructions). It separates two pieces of action (two verbs: *went* and *had*). Therefore, no comma is needed. In the second sentence, *and* does separate two independent clauses, so the comma is needed. That's called a compound sentence, and that's what the convention is about.

Now, primary teachers know the age of onset for compound sentences to be during the first grade months for some children, the second grade for most, eventually the third for the rest. Children who have had opportunities to explore language and thinking through writing are writing compound sentences by the end of the third grade because they are thinking in main ideas that cannot be accommodated by simple sentences. Orally, and in writing, one way they make language express their thoughts is by stringing pieces of sentences together with *and.* They don't have to be taught the syntactic labels for what they're doing; they only need to learn to handle it properly. We recommend that in the primary grades teachers don't try to teach youngsters about independent clauses and coordinating and correlative conjunctions. Just teach them how to control what's running out of the end of their pencils.

Early on, control means learning to punctuate, in this case compound sentences, properly. Later on, it can mean mastering terminology and using the mastered terminology to cue more writing (Write a sentence that contains two independent clauses joined by the conjunction *so*).

Elementary grade teachers often face seemingly endless strings of simple sentences connected by *and*. Then we make rules intended to eliminate the problem. We admonish: Don't use *and* more than four times in this piece. You can't begin a new sentence with *and*. When you use *and* more than twice, you will write a run-on sentence. We conduct lessons on reverse sentence combining, in which young writers reconstruct the writing of someone else to eliminate constructions connected with *and*.

Some teachers don't make an issue of students' overuse of *and*, thinking that if children are getting their ideas down, and if they write enough and receive the right minilessons, they'll eventually come to understand how to do it right.

However, they don't all eventually come to understand how to do it right. Many youngsters practice doing it improperly and eventually habituate it. The reverse sentence combining doesn't change their writing behavior because it is practiced with writing they didn't construct. The psychological dynamic associated with youngsters constructing their own ideas in purposefully designed syntactic structures is quite different from arranging someone else's ideas and structures.

If we focus their attention on their own writing with the convention, they will practice doing it properly through their own thinking and writing behaviors. Remember that practice doesn't necessarily make perfect, but perfect practice does. If we want young writers to master compound sentences, they have to write them properly, they have to punctuate them properly, and they have to do those often enough (through direct instruction and in the context of their larger writings) that over time they become automatic. The goal is always automaticity.

Examples of Commas in Compound Sentences

The two bad ants climbed into the coffee cup, and they swirled around in the black liquid.

Winnie liked the Tuck family, but she found them rather strange.

The chocolate bar cost a dime, yet the saleslady allowed the boy to pay with a nickel and an orange.

Teaching Young Writers About Commas in Compound Sentences

In order to write compound sentences, children do not need to know the meanings of terminology, such as independent clause and coordinating conjunction. They do not learn to write compound sentences, nor to punctuate them, by learning the terminology. (They also do not learn them by punctuating someone else's writing.) However, as youngsters move into the upper elementary and middle school grades, there is nothing wrong with using the terminology to identify what they already know.

In the meantime, direct third graders to think of a sentence in which they do two things. You might say: "If I were going to think of that sentence, I think I might come up with something such as *I like to swim and I like to dance*. What might your sentence sound like?" Of course the first volunteer will model: "*I like to play jump rope and I like to play baseball*." The objective here is to use their sentence as an object lesson. That the first volunteer models from the teacher's example is fine.

Write the student's sentence on the board and lead a conversation about there being **two** things she likes to do. Help youngsters notice that the **two** things can be made into **two** sentences without adding new wording. Show them that the word *and* separates the **two** whole sentence ideas. Then add the comma, indicating that when there are **two** sentence ideas as there are in the child's sentence, the **two** sentence ideas are separated with a comma. "Read your sentence again, and this time call the comma when you get to it." The volunteer reads, and when she gets to the comma, she says "comma." There are two points of information for youngsters in the lesson: a rational explanation of the convention based on a child's sentence and the sound of the sentence. Used together, frequently and over time, and with work from the young writers in the room, those informational cues increase the probability that the convention will eventually become habituated.

Solicit a second compound sentence from the class. Write it on the board. Show its characteristics again. Put in the comma. Direct the writer to read it with the comma. Put the third sentence on the board, but this time ask the writer to read the first idea, then the second. Ask the writer where the comma should go. Direct the students to read the sentence with the comma. Go through variations on the theme as many as five or six times in the lesson. Tell them that they performed terrifically, that they'll do this again tomorrow, and drop it. No homework. No directions to write five more just like those they did. It's just the first lesson. Tomorrow or next week is soon enough for them to prove that they have learned the lesson.

Conduct a similar lesson the following day and the day after that. On the third day it may be time to direct them to write one or two compound sentences before recess. Check their work. If there are two groups (most will do it right, a few may not), take the few aside the following day and reteach. The rest get the twice weekly reinforcing practice that takes as little as a few minutes.

Elementary and middle school students speak in and write compound sentences naturally. In virtually every writing activity in the primary and middle grades, a youngster will write a sentence and begin the next sentence with *and (My mother bought me a present. And I had a really good time.).* The other common construction is stringing together independent clauses with *and* and no punctuation *(My mother bought me a present and I had a very good time and we played great games and I can't wait until my birthday next year.).* Every teacher sees those kinds of constructions a hundred times a week. What to do?

A teacher can work individually with students and with the whole class. Looking over a child's shoulder, a teacher might say, "Luis, read your first sentence." (Luis reads, "My mother bought me a present.") "Terrific! Read your second sentence." (Luis reads, "And I had a very good time.")

The teacher stands over Luis and says, "Luis, look what I'm doing. I'm switching your period with a comma, and I'm going to make your capital 'A' a small 'a'. Now read the sentence the way I revised it, Luis." (Luis reads, "My mother bought me a present, and I had a very good time.") The teacher continues, "Luis, listen to your sentence. Read it again." (Luis reads.) The teacher now asks, "Luis, how many sentences do you hear?" Luis responds, "One." The teacher says, "That's right, Luis, because we just revised your two sentences into one." Then, to the rest of the class, having written Luis's sentence on the board, "Boys and girls, look at the way Luis's sentence is written." Point to the first independent clause ("My mother bought me a present. . .") and say, "Here's one sentence sound (independent clause), and there's another (pointing to "I

had a very good time"). They are separated by a comma and connected by the word *and.* You remember how we wrote those before. Everyone, write a sentence like that about what you like to have for dinner."

While it may not be grammatically incorrect for students to string a page full of independent clauses together with coordinating conjunctions, or to begin every sentence with *and,* it is stylistically unacceptable. Students' writing becomes more effective when they develop a sense of how to write well-crafted compound sentences.

After students write several compound sentences in isolated lessons for practice over several days, direct them specifically to write compound sentences in their larger writing through the grades. Initially, the practice sounds like this: "Write a compound sentence in which the two parts are separated with *and.* Luis, remind us what I mean when I ask for a compound sentence." Over time, direct similar sentences in two- or three-minute sessions using other conjunctions. "Write a compound sentence, and separate the two parts with *but (or, for, yet,* and so forth)." There is a list of conjunctions in every language arts book. This is the time to use the list, not to memorize it, but to write with it.

Once young writers appear to be able to deliver compound sentences on command, it is time to draw their attention to using them in larger writing tasks. In a Balanced Writing Program, everyone is working out of a portfolio filled with writings in various stages of completion. "Today as you work on a piece from your portfolio, I want you to find a good place to use a compound sentence. It might be in the piece that you turn in for the **Best Effort Board.** That way I'll have a chance not only to see your work, but also to see how you are using compound sentences." (The Best Effort Board is a small bulletin board on which students post their best writing on any given day.)

Writing Compound Sentences

Write a simple sentence that includes your name.

_____

_____

Write a simple sentence that tells how old you are.

_____

_____

Now, write a compound sentence that includes the ideas in both of your sentences above.

_____

_____

Write a compound sentence that joins two ideas with the word _but_.

_____

_____

Write a compound sentence in which the main idea is your favorite holiday.

_____

_____

Write a compound sentence in which the joining word (coordinating conjunction) is the sixth word in the sentence. (Use the word _conjunction_ only after you have used it **in writing** during several lessons.)

_____

_____

_____

Write a compound sentence of at least nine words, and use _or_ as the joining word.

_____

_____

_____

Tips for Teachers

1. Remember that young writers write compound sentences with no information whatsoever about independent clauses or coordinating conjunctions. That means that teaching them about clauses and conjunctions will not necessarily help them write better ones. It's the writing, not the analysis.

2. It's not necessary that youngsters have all of the technical terminology as they are learning to write effective compound sentences. The terminology (independent clauses and coordinating conjunctions) can be daunting for young children. However, we can help them develop a sense of sentence, and that sense of sentence will stand them in good stead as they "listen for" a sentence on both sides of the joining word (*and, but, or, nor, for, so, yet*).

3. A language user's sense of sentence comes through the ear, not through learning about complete thoughts or subjects and predicates. The more systematic and direct oral work that surrounds sentencing in your classroom, the more quickly youngsters will begin to internalize the sense (the sound) of a sentence.

LESSON 8: PUNCTUATION IN DIALOGUE

The Conventions

Mario had prepared for his expert's presentation to the class: "Use quotation marks to show someone's talk is beginning and has ended." Mario looked directly at the class, his audience, and said, "Use a comma to separate the name of the person doing the talking from what the talker said." Then Mario eyed his very best friend, Benchley, and with a steely eye, warned, "If you end a sentence with what someone said, put the period inside of the quotation mark." Everyone in the class clapped as Mario finished. Mario cleared his throat. "That isn't all," he said. "Commas also go inside of quotation marks. But if there is a colon or semicolon in the sentence, those go outside of the quotation marks. Remember," he said, "commas and periods inside, colons and semicolons outside. Also, if the speaker asks a question, the question mark goes inside the quotation marks."

"That was very well done," the teacher said. "And who can tell us the final part of the conventions for writing dialogue? Kim?"

"It's that every time a new person starts to talk, you have to indent so readers know the talker has changed."

"Why is that important, Kim?"

"We do that because if we do change paragraphs every time there is a change in the talker, we don't have to write *he said* and *she said* every time."

Student Writing Samples (not edited for spelling)

1. My dad said, "Don't forget to fed the dog." [Third Grader]

2. "Where did you come from?" the monster said. [Third Grader]

3. I think the girl should have said, "If that's where we are going to go, I'm going home." [Fifth Grader]

4. "But I guess he will have to wait a couple of more years for that dream to come true," Gaby said. [Sixth Grader]

5. When my mother got off the phone, she said to my dad that the teacher called and wanted them to go in for a conference. She said, "I think there is some kind of prize or award that he is going to get." [Sixth Grader]

Explanation

This convention is primarily about dialogue. Everything else in this lesson revolves around using quotation marks to signal readers that someone is talking and, if there are two or more people talking, when one takes over from another.

The quotation mark is the signal, and that signal encloses each piece of talk. If someone asks Ramona what she thinks about the flavor of the soup, she answers. **"I've always loved chicken soup on a rainy day."** Notice that the end mark, the period, is inside of the quotation mark.

Sometimes, the writer might try to add to Ramona's image at the moment by interrupting her talk. **"I've always loved chicken soup,"** she said as she gazed out the window, a tear welling in the corner of her eye, **"especially on a rainy day."** Notice that what Ramona said is divided into two pieces, each enclosed separately with quotation marks. Notice, as well, that the comma at the end of the first part of her talk is inside of the quotation mark, and the period at the end of the second piece of her talk is inside of the quotation mark.

Then there are times when a writer introduces a character's talk. **And that's when Ramona said directly to Park, "I'd like you to see my office when I've finished redecorating it."** The writer gave readers directions about who was doing the talking (Ramona) and to whom she is talking (Park). Notice the comma after the introduction and the period, again, inside of the final quotation mark.

Now, there's the matter of the question mark with quotation marks. We place the question mark after the question itself. **Park asked, "When will your office be ready?"** The quoted material, not the whole sentence, is the question, so the question mark goes inside of the quotation mark.

However, some sentences are not written that way. **Why did Park ask, "When will your office be ready"?** In that case, the whole sentence is the question. If the whole sentence is the question, the question mark is for the whole sentence, not just the speaker's words, and goes outside of the quotation mark. If the question relates only to what is inside of the quotation marks, the question mark goes inside, as well.

There's understandable logic to all of this, and with practice, over protracted time, the logic will be clear, and young writers will use it to understand the conventions. The key words here are **protracted time** because no single lesson, or unit, will establish these interrelated conventions. Instruction must occur in pieces that are critical to what young writers are working on at the time. The fact is that their needs focus overwhelmingly on the routine use of quotation marks, commas, and periods.

It's very unlikely that young writers will have to deal with the colon and semicolon, which are exceptions to the rule that punctuation goes inside of quotation marks. In fact, we can read novels for months and run into only a half dozen instances of this. Anyway, picture the restaurant where Ramona and Park are having their lunch. It's raining outside. They are sitting at a window table, peering occasionally across the road to the Brazos River. **"There are three things," Ramona began, "that are important in this discussion"; however, that's when the lamps on the tables began to rattle and everyone looked around in terror.** Ramona was about to say what was important to her when something interrupted. Notice that the quotation mark shows the end of her talk. Notice, as well, that the semicolon that precedes *however* is outside of the quotation

mark. Everything else in the sentence follows the conventions stated above.

The colon in dialogue occurs very infrequently. But can't we just hear Ramona, once the rattling dies down and the soup stops sloshing over the edge of her shallow bowl, thinking about some books she'd like Park to read? **"There are two good reasons," she said, looking at Park, "why you should read 'Fire and Ice'": you'd appreciate the images, and you'd see the meanings in Frost's short poem."** We grant that it's unlikely that young writers will get themselves into a situation like that, but if someone did, the teacher, who read this material, would know how to help.

Examples of Punctuation in Dialogue

Ramona said, "Hand me the hammer, Henry."
"What are you going to do with it?"
"I'm going to fix the door, silly."

Teaching Young Writers about Punctuation in Dialogue

Remember the statement above to the effect that the overwhelming need of young writers in writing dialogue is using quotation marks, commas, and periods. That's where to begin this lesson, and it is most useful to begin when someone in the class asks how to do it or does it and needs guidance to make it right.

"Claudia's presented me with a problem, folks, and I want us all to look at it together." Write Claudia's dialogue on the board.

He said don't run away. That's when she said okay I won't.

You have already spoken to Claudia and made sure it would be okay to use her writing as an example. That being the case, it's safe to turn to her and ask her to read the first sentence. "What did *he* say, Claudia?"

Because you've already had the conversation, she is secure about how she will respond. "Don't go away."

"Well now, how will the reader know what he said in that sentence?" Claudia might have figured it out already, but there will be several others in a second- or third-grade room who will know. Someone will put quotation marks into the conversation. "Where?"

"In front of what he said," Claudia answers. So you put one set of quotation marks in front of *don't*.

"Claudia, this might be a hard question, so I want you to think about it. Is what he said a sentence? Is *don't run away* a sentence?"

"Sure," she tells you.

"Well then, we need a capital letter, don't we? If *don't run away* is a sentence, the first word should have a capital letter. Is it okay for me to put it in there?" She agrees, so now the writing on the board has quotation marks in front of the talk, and the talk begins with a capital letter. "So where does his talk stop, Claudia?"

"It's at the end of the sentence, there at *don't run away*."

"So I should put quotation marks here after *away*." She agrees again. "But where? Do you think I should put the quotation marks in front of the period or after the period?" If you aren't sure that Claudia will say the quotation mark should go after the period, put the chalk there and suggest that you put the quotation mark after the period. She'll most likely agree.

This is a good time to inform the class that readers need a warning signal that someone is going to talk and that we use a comma as the warning. Put a comma in after the word *said*. Now the board shows her first sentence.

He said, "Don't run away."

Ask Claudia to read her sentence aloud from the board. Ask her to read it again and this time with every punctuation mark when she comes to it. She'll have to concentrate, but it's fun, and she'll eventually get it just right. "He said comma quotation marks don't go away period quotation marks." Tell Claudia that she's terrific.

Go on to the second sentence and make the adjustments there, soliciting help from others in the class. Show them that the two sentences in Claudia's piece make two paragraphs, so when you put them on the board, indent them both. Tell them that whenever there are two or more people talking in a story, each time one finishes and the other starts, there is a paragraph change. Show the class how that works in the story books from which they are reading. Assure them that there is a lot to remember when they write dialogue (use the term; it isn't as long as *refrigerator*, nor as abstract as *cute*, and they know both of those) and that you will help them every step of the way.

Call on Pauline to give you a dialogue sentence for the board. She thinks a moment and calls one out loud. This takes a little getting used to for them, so don't despair when Pauline says, "My mother says not to get dirty before we go to church."

Tell Pauline that you want her to rethink her sentence because she didn't let her mother talk in the sentence. Her sentence is about what Pauline said, not what her mother said. That's called an **indirect quotation;** and if you think it would be useful, go ahead and use the term with students. Give Pauline about three seconds to think about what you've said. If she seems stymied, put the sound out there for her and the rest of the class to hear. "I would rethink your sentence this way: My mother said (long pause) don't you get dirty before church." Pauline will very likely raise her hand quickly and say something like, "It has to have those things, the quotation marks." Tell her how smart she is for noticing that and write her sentence on the board.

My mother said don't get dirty before church.

Ask Pauline to come on up to the board and show how to punctuate and capitalize the sentence so readers will know exactly what's going on. Help her if she needs it, but don't let her hesitate too long. When she's finished, ask her to read it aloud, reading all the marks as she goes along.

Conduct the same scenario once more on that first day. Then tell them to go back to their own writing, and if they want to write some dialogue, make sure to do it the way they did on the board. Roam the room and give help as needed.

The next day conduct the scenario again with perhaps three more sentences. During that second lesson, use a direction similar to the following: "Think of a sentence that contains someone's talk." When Leticia gives her sentence (*I want a nice birthday party*), ask her who said that. She says, "I did." Tell her that her sentence has to tell readers not only what the character said, but who the character is, too. If she doesn't get it immediately, show it on the board: *Leticia said, "I want a nice birthday party."*

On another day, make the direction just a tad more complex: "Think of a sentence in which Marcia says something to Marie." (*Marcia told Marie, "Let me have your extra cookie."*)

We suggest that the conventions associated with colons and semicolons wait until they are needed. There is no need to teach conventions that are demanding of writing skill beyond that of the students in the class or that aren't part of their reasonable writing needs.

Writing Dialogue

Read the following sentence:

> **The men all screamed at once run for your lives because the tigers got out of their cage.**

Rewrite the boxed sentence and put in all the correct punctuation and capital letters.

_____

_____

_____

Write a sentence in which Craig talks to Kim about a lost puppy. Make sure both Craig and Kim each talk at least once.

_____

_____

_____

_____

> **Anita and Charlene are talking to one another about a test they took in school. One of them feels good about the test. The other one thinks she didn't do very well on the test. Write a conversation they might have. In what you write, make sure both Anita and Charlene talk at least two times each. Remember that your readers have to know at all times which character is talking.**

_____

_____

_____

_____

_____

Tips for Teachers

1. While there are quite a few conventions associated with writing dialogue, they are relatively consistent (for example, commas and periods inside quotation marks at the end of a speaker's word, a new paragraph with every change of speaker, and so forth). Teach the conventions as you see the need in students' writings.
2. Point out how writers punctuate dialogue in the stories your students read. Use the readings as models for how the conventions work in the writing of dialogue.
3. We are confident that youngsters can learn to write conventionally accurate dialogue. Promote awareness, give students plenty of practice, both under teacher guidance and independently, and hold them accountable for doing it right once they have learned.

LESSON 9: APOSTROPHES IN SINGULAR AND PLURAL POSSESSIVES

The Convention

Use an apostrophe in nouns and certain pronouns to show possession. The position of the apostrophe depends on whether the possessive noun is singular or plural.

Student Writing Samples (not edited for spelling)

1. I like to be in my mom's room. [Third Grader]
2. It's my dad's house because it has three beds, and it is nice to be there. [Third Grader]
3. The place I like most is Heather's house. It is a two store house, but Heather's room is kind of small, but her back yard's big. [Third Grader]
4. I like to be at Allen's cos we play Sega and Super Nintendo. [Fourth Grader]
5. We all like being at my sister's house on the holidays, but I like being in my brother's bedroom mostly. [Fourth Grader]
6. The ranch at my grandmother's house is where the animals are. [Fifth Grader]
7. At my best firend's house there is a forest in the back, and we go there to be alone. [Sixth Grader]

Explanation

There aren't many mechanical matters in writing that produce more confusion than apostrophes in possessives. They are placed incorrectly in singular or plural forms. They appear on signs all over town whenever there is a word that ends in s. And there are disagreements about how they should be used, even among professional editors. We will attempt to simplify and clarify.

Apostrophes show possession. There are three kinds of possession.

- Apostrophes show ownership: That is the **bird's** nest.
- Apostrophes show identity: Those are **Asimov's** words.
- Apostrophes show time or space: It's a **mile's** distance in an **hour's** time.

Some pronouns use an apostrophe to show possession. It was *anyone's* guess that *someone's* book would show up and relieve *everyone's* concern. (The pronouns *ours, hers, his, theirs,* and *yours* are always possessive pronouns and **never** use an apostrophe.)

Using apostrophes to show possession is, in the first place, an ambiguity for many people. They aren't sure when or how. The **when** is whenever we're writing about something that belongs to someone or something, as in the *man's* hat, the *radio's* sound, or a *friend's* house. We also use an apostrophe if we're writing about identifying something, as the *girl's* mother or the *horse's* job. And then there is an *hour's* worth of effort, a *minute's* time, and a *yard's* length of cloth. Those represent when the apostrophe is used.

The matter of **how** can be complex, but if we think about **why** we are using the apostrophe at all, how it is used becomes clearer. If the sentence reads, "The **bird's** nest fell to the ground," we know we are talking about one bird. When the noun is spelled as though there were only one of it (*bird*), then possession is accomplished by adding an apostrophe before the *s* (*bird's, house's, cake's*).

Now, if the sentence reads, "The **bird's** nests fell out of the tree," there is still one bird, but more than one nest; it is a bird with a second home. As long as we are writing about one bird, the spelling remains the same.

What if the sentence reads, "The **birds'** nest fell from the tree"? Well, there is more than one bird trying to live in one nest, and the nest has fallen out of the tree, leaving the birds homeless. Notice that the word *birds* that appears right before the word *homeless* in the last sentence does not contain an apostrophe. Why should it? It represents more than one bird, which makes it plural, but the birds do not possess anything. They certainly don't possess "homeless."

Okay, now the sentence reads, "The **birds'** nests fell out of the tree." Here we have more than one bird and more than one nest, and the nests belong to the birds. So far, so good. Change the sentence to "The **birds' nests'** eggs fell out of the tree." Now there are nests that belong to the birds, but those nests did not fall out of the tree. What fell out of the tree were the eggs from the birds' nests. The eggs are identified as connected to the nests, and the nests belong to the birds. The apostrophes make all of that clear. At least it all becomes clear if we spend enough time "playing" with it and having a conversation about what the apostrophes do to change the meaning of the sentence. That's what instruction is about. Instruction is certainly not about putting apostrophes in words someone else wrote for an exercise.

There is one more variable that has to be dealt with here. Let's say we have a boy named James, and he has a hat that a strong wind has blown off his head and down the street. What do we do with James and his hat? The sentence reads, "The wind blew suddenly and lifted **James's** hat off his head." There is only one James, so the apostrophe is placed exactly as it is when there is only one bird; the apostrophe is between the correct and full spelling of the word (*James*) and the *s* that makes the word possessive. Thus the hat belongs to James; it is **James's** hat.

However, readers will see sentences in which the possessive does not appear that way. The sample sentence can also appear as, "The wind blew suddenly and lifted **James'** hat off his head." People who write the possessive that way do so because they don't want to add another syllable to the word. That's perfectly acceptable.

Examples of Apostrophes in Singular and Plural Possessives

The Widow's Broom was written by Chris Van Allsburg.
Alexander's rotten day made him think about going to Australia.
Winnie's drink was cool and refreshing.

Teaching Young Writers about Apostrophes in Singular and Plural Possessives

Using the apostrophe to show possession begins to occur in children's writing quite early. First graders write about their **daddy's** shoes and their **dog's** tail. It is not unusual to find sentences in the early grades in which students write about the **living room's** furniture, the **cars'** tires, and their sister **Marla's** bracelet. Occasionally, there are apostrophes in the words, usually there are not. When there are apostrophes, they may or may not be placed properly. The apostrophe that is used to signify possession is a punctuation convention that can be introduced in the earliest grades, reinforced for several years, taught directly in about the fourth grade, and used properly on a consistent basis by the end of the fifth, certainly the sixth, grade. Teachers need to be prepared to work with it over time.

We posed the following sentences in a second-grade class:

Sam's pet snake got lost. It wrapped around the table's leg and wouldn't let go.

"How many snakes are in the little story?" (One.) "How do you know?" (It says there's one snake.) "No it doesn't. It doesn't say 'one snake' anywhere. How do you know?" (Right there. It says *snake,* not snakes.) "Yes. Of course. We know it's one snake because it says *snake.* So what's the boy's name?" (Sam.) "Yes. How many boys are there?" (One.) "How can you say that? You said there's one snake because there isn't any *s* at the end of the word. Well, there's an *s* at the end of the boy's name, so why not think there's more than one boy?" (Because it has that thing there, the postrfe.) "The apostrophe, boys and girls, let's hear it, the apostrophe. Everyone." (Apostrophe.) "Yes, it does have an apostrophe, but how does that tell us there's only one boy?" (You said when we were reading that if it's in the word, it's only one thing. You said.) "So I did, and it's very smart for you all to remember that. Good for you. You see, we've seen it in our reading, but this is the first time we have seen it in writing. The sentences on the board aren't mine; they're Clay's. He wrote them, and I put them on the board because that apostrophe business is important for all of us to think about.

"Just to stay with Clay's sentences, how many table legs are there for the snake to wrap himself around in Clay's sentence?" (One.) "One table leg? How do you know?" (Because it has the apostrophe.) "Good. Then let's look at it this way. Suppose Clay had written his sentences this way."

Sam's pet snake got lost. It wrapped around the tables' legs and wouldn't let go.

"How many table legs did the snake wrap himself around?" (Two.) "How do you know?" (Because it says *legs.*) Yes, it does. How many tables?" (One, just like before.) "But look at the apostrophe. Is there anything different? Is the apostrophe in a different place?" (Oh yeah. It's moved over.) "Where?" (It's after the word now.) "Yes, it's outside of the *s*. In Clay's sentence, it was inside of the *s*; now it's outside of the *s*. If it's inside of the *s*, there's only one table. If the apostrophe is outside of the *s*, there's more than one table. Look at the picture in your head. Can you see the snake wrapped around one table leg in a sentence with the apostrophe inside of the *s*? Now, put the apostrophe outside of the *s* and look at the picture of the snake wrapped around the legs of two tables. Can you see?" (They'll all say they do.) "This is what is important here, my friends. The position of the apostrophe changes your picture from one table to two tables. The apostrophe has a lot of meaning, and we're going to think about and write sentences and words that contain apostrophes all year. And we're going to find them in our reading and talk about what we find. Oh, and if you want to use them when you write, go ahead, but make sure you are using the apostrophe correctly. You may check with me, one of your friends, or anyone else who might know."

Not too many days later, the next day if possible, pose the following situations. "Boys and girls, I'm going to put some words on the board. I want you to tell me whether there is one thing, or more than one." *(bird—bird's—birds'—car—car's—cars'—Jim's—horse's—cups')* Use several words. Explain the relationship between where the apostrophe is placed and whether there is one or more than one. It's a game. Play it daily for a long time. Many of the children will get the idea eventually.

Call attention to the apostrophe in their reading. Connect what they see in print to what they know from the apostrophe game on the board.

Now in the second or third grade, "getting it" doesn't mean they will always write properly with the idea. It's also too early to give a test and expect that everyone will demonstrate their apostrophe competence. It might be useful, however, to suggest one day that they write a sentence that contains a word that has an apostrophe that means *one* thing. That isn't a test, either. But if there are several who write that kind of sentence correctly, assign more, and move them to the next level. Those who appear confused at the writing level of performance are only second and third grad-

ers. It isn't reasonable to expect that everyone will get a handle on this one at the same time, but they are moving from the level of awareness or identification to application. It's a critical move, for awareness and application are two very different cognitive processes.

But if it's late in the fourth grade or sometime during the fifth, it's time to get it settled. The instructional processes described above for second and third graders remain useful in the fifth, but at that level it's necessary to get to the writing (the application) quickly. It's also necessary for many of the students to get it right, soon. But we can expect that, because students are a year or two older, and they've been getting orientation to the apostrophe for two years, they've been trying to write with it in directed sentences for two years, as well. Now it's time to introduce the more correct vocabulary (when there's one, it's called *singular*; when it's more than one, it's called *plural*). It's time to call it all by its right term, if this hasn't been done before. These constructions are called **possessive** because it's almost as though the leg belongs to the table—the table possesses the leg, Sam possesses the snake, you possess your feelings, and so forth.

"Come to think of it, if David possesses his feelings, we would write a sentence this way."

The children were not paying attention to David's feelings.

"Whose feelings are in the sentence?" (David's.) "How many Davids?" (Just one.) "If we wrote about the **bird's** (write the word on the board as you ask the question) nests, how many birds?" (One.) "What if we wrote about the **birds'**?" (There's more than one.)

"Write a sentence that contains a singular possessive. Write a sentence that contains a plural possessive. Write a sentence in which a singular possessive is in the third position." The cognitive function here is construction; the thinking process is application. These are the processes required in writing.

Conduct such sentence writing activities daily for several weeks, maybe two minutes' worth each day. Post several of the sentences each day. Direct the students to include a possessive in whatever they happen to be writing in their portfolio.

Writing with Apostrophes in Singular and Plural Possessives

1. Write a sentence that talks about one cow that lives in a large pen. Write the sentence so that the word *cow* is spelled with an *s* and an apostrophe before the *s*.

    _____

    _____

2. The sentence you wrote for Number 1 above had one cow in it. If there is one cow, and an apostrophe before the *s*, the word is called a singular possessive. Write another sentence that contains the word *bear* as a singular possessive.

    _____

    _____

3. Write a sentence in which the main idea is bad weather. Include a singular possessive in your sentence.

    _____

    _____

4. Write a sentence that contains the word *trees*. Make sure your sentence has more than one tree in it. Use an apostrophe to show that the word *trees* is a plural possessive.

    _____

    _____

5. Write a sentence that contains a plural possessive. Make the plural possessive something that you can wear.

    _____

    _____

6. Write a sentence in which the main idea is a birthday party. Include a plural possessive in your sentence.

    _____

    _____

7. Write a sentence that contains the word *birds* as a plural possessive.

    _____

    _____

8. Write a sentence in which your name is written as a singular possessive.

    _____

    _____

Tips for Teachers

1. There are two keys in learning to write singular and plural possessives in sentences. One of the keys is a lot of awareness and conversation about words, what they look like when they are written as possessives, and what the placement of the apostrophe means in each word.

2. The second key in learning to write singular and plural possessives in sentences is to write lots of sentences that contain singular and plural possessives. That means writing one or two, maybe even several, every day. Write one as a ticket to morning recess, one as a ticket to lunch, one as a ticket to afternoon recess, one as a ticket out the door at the end of the day, and two for homework. Do that for a five-day week. That's thirty sentences in one week. Continue for as many weeks, beginning about

half-way through the fourth grade, as necessary for the students to demonstrate reliable mastery.

3. Recognition and application are two entirely different cognitive processes. Asking youngsters to place apostrophes correctly in prewritten sentences is not the same as asking young writers to construct their own writings, using singular and plural possessives in which apostrophes are placed appropriately. The latter is the cognitive ability required in writing. The former is not.

4. Once the idea of possessive has been taught and practiced, insist on its proper use in all of their writing, all of the time. Part of it is learning; the other part is a sense of responsibility for doing it right.

LESSON 10: COMMAS IN COMPLEX SENTENCES

The Convention

Use a comma to separate the introductory dependent clause from the independent clause that follows.

Student Writing Samples (not edited for spelling)

1. I would lik to be in the montins becse it would be fun. [Second Grader]
2. I like Mexico because it is where I come from. [Third Grader]
3. Becaus it is cool, I like Disnyland the best. [Third Grader]
4. If I could pick anything I want, I would have a KFC. [Third Grader]
5. When you first get there, you will see the rides and hear them. [Sixth Grader]

Explanation

Sentences appear in a variety of designs or configurations. There are **simple** sentences that feature an independent clause designed around a subject, a predicate, and an object: **The man fed the dog.**

There are **compound** sentences that feature more than one independent clause in the same sentence. Lesson 7 is about compound sentences, where independent clauses are connected with certain kinds of words (conjunctions): **The man fed the dog, and the dog wagged its tail happily.** The question about whether or not two short independent clauses such as those require a comma before the conjunction doesn't affect the

fact that the example **is** a compound sentence, comma or not. For instructional purposes, and given the age when young writers need some stability regarding conventions, we think the comma should be habituated. When young writers develop sufficient skill and conventional mastery, they will be in a position to make informed and reasonable adjustments in standard conventions.

There are also sentences with more than one clause, but one of them will not stand alone, is not independent, and is, therefore, dependent. Such sentences are called **complex,** and they look like this: **While the master craftsman sanded the wood for the box, his helper prepared the hot glue.** In that sentence there is a sense that there must be something following the opening clause about the master craftsman. The opening piece of the sentence, or dependent clause, suggests that something is going on *as* the master craftsman is working. What is going on is in the second clause, the one that will stand alone as a sentence, the independent clause. **His helper prepared the hot glue** has the design characteristics necessary to be a sentence, all by itself. That's what makes it an **independent** clause. The first clause won't work all by itself to make a sentence, so we call it **dependent.** Complex sentences combine dependent and independent clauses. When young writers prepare such sentences with an opening dependent clause, as in the example above, the two clauses are separated with a comma, as in the example above.

The complex sentence construction involves a sentence that begins with words such as *although, since, as, while, if, when,* and *because* (e.g., Although the sun was shining, it rained across town. As the rain fell, everyone scattered for cover.).

Because is a marvelous example of the necessity of teaching this convention. Some teachers routinely tell young writers not to begin sentences with *because*, precisely because when young writers do so, they often write fragments, failing to include the independent clause. To take *because* away as the first word in a sentence does not solve the problem of writing fragments; it only deprives young writers of a perfectly good word and of the information necessary to write the construction properly. The instructional alternative is to teach the complex sentence with its appropriate punctuation.

A clause is a group of words that has the sound of a sentence. Language is learned in the ear, not through labels and definitions (e.g., a sentence is a group of words with a subject and predicate). All language users develop a sense of sentence, and it begins as auditory stimulation, in the ear. This sense of language can transfer to writing if the sound of language is emphasized in the writing program. A sentence sounds like this: "It is raining today." It does not sound like this: "Raining it today." It does not sound like this: "Raining today." By emphasizing the sounds of an English sentence, youngsters (and this is especially important for children for whom English is a second language) develop a sense of sentence. An independent clause is a sentence sound. A dependent clause is a sentence sound that begins with words such as those we mentioned in the first sentence of this section.

Examples of Commas in Complex Sentences

Although Kate and Emily were friends, they didn't agree on everything.

When Kate said she thought old people were scary, Emily reminded her of Mrs. Thurstone, who was 86.

As the child followed her father through the woods, she heard the owl call eerily in the night.

Teaching Young Writers about Complex Sentences

The teacher says, "Boys and girls, think of a sentence in which the first word is *although*. (This lesson design has been used successfully about half-way through the third grade. Specify the first word in order to ensure complex-sentence thinking.) When you think of one, let's hear it."

Students think. Basically, they are writing the sentence in their heads.

The teacher calls on a student whose hand is raised. "Marcia."

Marcia reads the sentence that is in her head: "Although I wasn't supposed to eat cookies, I ate one anyway."

The teacher responds, "Terrific! Read it again!"

Marcia reads.

The teacher says, "Listen, boys and girls, to the two pieces of the sentence as Marcia reads again. Marcia, read just the first part of your sentence."

Marcia is likely to read "Although I wasn't supposed to eat cookies." The teacher asks her to read the second part. She reads, "I ate one anyway." The teacher emphasizes what Marcia has just done. "Boys and girls, there are two parts in Marcia's sentence. Make sure your sentence has two parts." Pause. "Somebody else read."

When Jorge reads his two-part sentence, the teacher asks where he would put a comma. Jorge hesitates, then responds, "Between the two parts." (If Jorge says, "After *although*," the teacher tells him that the comma goes *between the two parts*.) The teacher listens to several other students read (again, from the sentences in their heads). She asks them to say the word *comma* out loud when they come to it in their sentence. The point here is to accentuate the two parts and the punctuation needed. So far, students have not put anything on paper; they've been reading from what they've thought, prepared, written in their heads. Now, the teacher says, "Think of a sentence in which the first word is *because*. Remember the two parts. Write your sentence on your paper."

Students can usually write a sentence in a minute; ninety seconds is plenty of time. Just before the teacher is ready to call time, (s)he asks them again to listen for the two parts and not to forget the comma.

When the teacher calls time, (s)he asks for a student volunteer to read aloud. With each reading, the teacher emphasizes the two parts and the comma. (S)he asks students to differentiate the first part from the second by reading one, then the other. After several days of such five-minute lessons, the teacher points out that the first part of the sentence will not work alone; but the second part will. "The first part depends on the second part, boys and girls, just like your puppy depends on you to feed it. The second part works all by itself; so it's independent, just like your mother and dad are not dependent on you to feed them." That is sufficient terminology for students at this point. Explanations of clauses can come later; however, once the explanation of independent and dependent has occurred, the teacher can stop referring to "the first part" and "the second part." (S)he can use the appropriate terminology for the two parts because students already understand what they are.

Initially, it is important for students to learn how this language structure works and how it sounds. The oral sharing is necessary and creates a real learning community, as students practice writing complex sentences and learn from each other. In addition to the five-minute oral and written lessons on complex sentences, which should persist until the children write and punctuate them correctly and automatically, the teacher should direct young writers to include one or more complex sentences in whatever genres they are writing. Students can now be held accountable for writing and punctuating them correctly in their own writing; and they can learn the labels for what they already know how to do, that is, write complex sentences. Labels are only confusing and intimidating when the concepts they name are difficult or unclear. When learners reach clarification and understanding first, the labels are merely serviceable, that is, in service to the learner.

Writing with Complex Sentences

Write a sentence of at least eight words in which the first word is *although*.

_____

_____

_____

Write a complex sentence in which the first word is either *because* or *since*.

_____

_____

_____

Write a complex sentence in which the first word is either *while* or *as*.

_____

_____

_____

Write a sentence about multiplication in which the first word is *if*.

_____

_____

_____

Write a complex sentence in which the main idea is two books you have read.

_____

_____

The following sentence begins with *when,* but it is not a complex sentence. What kind of sentence is it?

_____

When will dinner be ready?

Write a complex sentence that begins with *when*.

_____

_____

Tips for Teachers

1. The terminology associated with complex sentences is, well, rather complex. It includes dependent, as well as independent, clauses. As we've discussed before, this terminology can be intimidating for youngsters. However, it becomes less so, and maybe not at all, if they already know how to write complex sentences, if they have the sound of a complex sentence in their ears. The systematic and direct filling of classrooms with oral sharing of complex sentence constructions will help ensure they have the sound.

2. When language pervades the air in a classroom, youngsters have the opportunity to function as a community of learners. They learn from each other as the sounds are displayed. In the case of complex sentences, the sound has two parts. Youngsters can learn, through the sounds, that commas separate the two parts when the first part **begins** with *because, since, although, if, when,* and a few others. That's the dependent clause. Again,

it's not the terminology; it's the sound. When that clause comes at the end of the sentence, the comma is not needed to separate the two parts. This is something almost every youngster can master by the end of fifth grade.

3. You, the teacher, are part of this community of learners. Your language models and your immediate feedback on their constructions are a critical part of the mix.

4. Remember, we ought not take sentence structures away from youngsters merely because they do not handle them properly (for example, sentences that start with words such as *because*). It is necessary to help them learn to handle such constructions properly.

5. As youngsters learn to handle complex sentences quickly and well, and, at that point, if you think it is important that young writers know the terminology, begin teaching it and using it in your cues.

LESSON 11: QUOTATION MARKS AND UNDERLINING IN PUBLISHED TITLES

The Conventions

Quotation marks are used to show the titles of magazine articles, short stories, chapters or sections of books, short poems, songs, television shows, and radio programs. Underlinings are used to show the titles of books, names of magazines and newspapers, full-length movies, and plays. (To make a complete list for underlining we could add names of sculptures, David; long poems, Walt Whitman's Leaves of Grass; and paintings, Mona Lisa.) Underlinings and italics can be used interchangeably. However, within any one writing, a writer should be consistent.

Student Writing Samples (not edited for spelling)

1. The oldest book I culd find in the libary is called *Think and Do.* [Third Grader]
2. My best poem is "The Snare." [Third Grader]
3. If I could read any book, it would be the one my mother has in the living room. It's name is *The American Reader.* I would want to read that book because it's about all the things that great people have said and written. [Fifth Grader]
4. I'm hearing my favorite song, "I'm Your Puppet." [Sixth Grader]
5. My parents watch "60 Minutes" every Sunday, but I don't watch it very much. [Sixth Grader]

Explanation

These conventions are statements that are generally accurate. When writing a bibliography, however, the conventions for quotation marks and underlining change depending on the form (the style manual) required. The conventions described in this lesson are those used generally in writing and are used for clarity only. They inform readers that a title of some sort is being used in the sentence. If the title is underlined, it is a book or magazine or play or one of the other items included in the underlining convention. If it isn't underlined, it's any one of several other kinds of titles.

Anything **within** a book or magazine tends to be set off with quotation marks. The name of the book or magazine, however, is set off with underlining. If it's a television show (**"60 Minutes"**), it's set off by quotation marks; if it's the magazine that lists all the television shows for the week *(TV Guide)*, it's underlined.

The poem by R. D. Allen is called **"Winter at No Name Inlet."** It appeared in the September 1989 issue of *Crazyquilt Quarterly*, published in San Diego. In the May 1986 issue of the same magazine, there appeared K. A. Burkhart's short story, **"The Final Form of the Butterfly."**

George Will, noted newspaper columnist and television commentator, wrote of **"Examining Academic Malpractice"** in the July 1995 issue of the *San Diego*

Union-Tribune. Notice the pattern throughout. The title of the publication is underlined; the title of the piece within the publication is enclosed in quotation marks.

Julie Andrews sang **"My Favorite Things"** in the movie about a woman who wanted to be a nun but married a handsome sea captain. Can you name the movie? (The title of the movie should be underlined.)

Chris Van Allsburg has written some marvelous books for young people, among them The Polar Express and The Wreck of the Zephyr; but by far my favorite books for young readers are The Winter Room by Gary Paulsen, Maniac Magee by Jerry Spinelli, and The Boat Who Wouldn't Float by Farley Mowat. The book titles are all underlined. They are not printed in bold face in this paragraph, because we didn't want readers to misunderstand. All of the titles in this lesson are either enclosed by quotation marks, or they are underlined.

Examples of Quotation Marks and Underlining in Sentences

"A Clean, Well-Lighted Place" is a great short story by Ernest Hemingway.

Merlyn's Pen is a magazine dedicated to publishing children's writings.

Big Bird is a character on the most popular children's television show of all time, Sesame Street.

Teaching Young Writers about Punctuation to Show Titles

This punctuation convention should occur relatively early in the lives of young writers because they will most certainly be writing about books and stories they are reading. Do not misunderstand what we are suggesting here. We are not suggesting that second graders should be writing book reports or reviews of the stories they read in their literature anthologies or trade book collections. We are suggesting that they are writing responses to literature as they write in personal and interactive journals, essays, letters home, and so forth. Even in the primary grades, therefore, young writers need to learn how to signal readers by punctuating titles appropriately.

It's the second grade, and we've been reading a book for the past several days. Inquire about the name of the book. "It's Elbert's Bad Word," Suzanne calls out. Ask what they have noticed in the book. They'll talk about the lawn party and the gardener. Someone will say that he thought the butler was funny. After a bit, ask about the name of the book again. Write the name

of the book on the board. "Is that it?" They'll nearly yell that it is. "Good, but how do we know it's the title of the book? I mean, it's three words. Maybe it's the first three words in a sentence about a boy's bad word. Maybe it's the title of a story in another book that has lots of stories in it. How do we know it's the title of a book?" Someone will say that we know because it is.

Write something else on the board: **Chickens Aren't the Only Ones.** "What do you think is the rest of the sentence?" There will be all kinds of speculations because it's fun to finish sentences that start in interesting ways. Write several of the speculations on the board. Then interrupt. "You know, my friends, I just remembered that isn't the beginning of a sentence at all. When I wrote it on the board, I didn't add something very important. I got confused for just a moment, but now I have it right. Here, this is the way I should have written it so I would remember.

Chickens Aren't the Only Ones

Ask what they think it is. There will be several ideas, then someone will ask in a tentative voice whether it's a book. You pull out the book (by Ruth Heller, Grosset and Dunlap, 1981) and show that it is, indeed, a book. "How might we signal that we're writing a book title?" They'll all agree that the key is to put a line under the words when they are a title of a book. Of course they'll all agree. Second graders always do when the lesson is conducted just right and the message is clear. It's the way second graders are.

Now it's time to write lots of sentences that contain titles of books. Youngsters should write one in the morning as a ticket to recess, another as a ticket to lunch, another as a ticket to afternoon recess, and one for homework, the latter containing the title of a book they have at home. That's four such sentences per day, three days each week, for a total of twelve sentences each week. Incidentally, when they do this, second graders are also writing twelve planful sentences. Every time they write a planful sentence, they get one more opportunity to practice becoming better at writing planful sentences. After students have written several thousand planful sentences, no middle-level teacher will ever complain about seventh graders who can't write sentences. And for whatever it's worth, several thousand is an attainable number; for 12 per week for 36 weeks makes 432 planful sentences. Do that through the second, third, fourth, fifth, and sixth grades; and youngsters will have written at least a couple of thousand (2160, to be precise), and that's only for book titles and doesn't include what they write in response to a cue such as the following: Write a sentence that includes the names of two state capitals west of the Mississippi River and south of Nebraska.

The scenario above works the same for the titles of poems, articles, short stories, and songs. Provide a cue: Think of a sentence that contains the title of your favorite poem. As they share their sentences orally, ask how they would write their sentence on paper so readers would know they are writing a poem title. One will say to use capital letters. "That's good, but that's what we do with book titles, too. So how would we know you're writing about a poem and not a book title?" Someone will almost certainly say to put a line under it. "That's what we do with book titles, Ruben. What might we do with the poem so readers will know it isn't a book title?"

This is not the sort of question that should remain open until Thursday. Give it a response or two, then write the following sentence on the board.

My favorite poem in <u>Where the Sidewalk Ends</u> is "Recipe for a Hippopotamus Sandwich."

"What's the name of the poem in my sentence?" They'll know immediately. You will probably have to read the poem, so have it close by. Then they'll want to hear more from the book. Limit them to several and promise more tomorrow. "What's the name of the book?" They'll know that, as well. "How can we tell the difference between the book title and the poem title?" They'll know that one, too. Tell them that the immediate future holds lots of practice writing sentences that contain the names of poems and the titles of books.

Extend the lessons over the next several days, or weeks, to include short stories, song titles, and article or chapter titles.

Writing with Punctuation in Published Titles

1. Write a sentence that contains the name of your social studies book.

   _____

   _____

2. Write a sentence that contains the name of a chapter in your social studies book.

   _____

   _____

3. Write a sentence that contains the name of a short story and the name of the book where the short story can be found.

   _____

   _____

4. Think of the best song your whole class sings together. Write a sentence that contains the name of the song.

   _____

   _____

5. Look through a book that has stories and poems in it. Find a poem or a story that you like. Write a sentence that contains the name of the story, or the poem, and the name of the book.

   _____

   _____

6. Write a sentence that contains the name of a dictionary in your room.

   _____

   _____

7. Write a sentence that contains the name of a chapter about electricity in your science book. Include the name of your science book in your sentence.

   _____

   _____

8. Write a letter to your mother or father about the best book you have read so far this year. Write the name of the book in your letter.

   _____

   _____

Tips for Teachers

1. This is an excellent opportunity to get children to look carefully at books in the classroom. Use the opportunity.
2. This is also an excellent opportunity for children to communicate with their parents and others at home about what they are reading in school. Use the opportunity.
3. Keep it simple: Book and magazine titles, movie titles,

and newspaper names are underlined; chapters, poems, songs, and articles are enclosed with quotation marks. Remember, we are talking about instruction for second and third graders, or seventh and eighth graders, perhaps. It will be thesis time in their graduate programs before they have to worry about the idiosyncrasies of a particular style manual. For now, all they have to do is communicate clearly.

LESSON 12: COMMAS IN A SERIES OF ADJECTIVES

The Convention

Use a comma between two or more adjectives when they modify the same noun and when the word *and* could be used between them without changing the meaning of the sentence.

Student Writing Samples (not edited for spelling)

1. It's a pink, pretty bedroom that I live in. [Third Grader]
2. I always like to go to the park because it has those giant, ancient trees in there. [Fourth Grader]
3. There are nice, clean restaurants there. [Fifth Grader]
4. This spot is where a big, green three is. [Fifth Grader]
5. Mr. Burns was my favorite, best teacher when I was in fourth grade. [Sixth Grader]

Explanation

When there are several short helpful adjectives in a row in a sentence, there is the possibility of misunderstanding a writer's message. In the previous sentence, for example, a reader could wonder whether there are short adjectives and helpful adjectives, or whether there are helpful adjectives that are short. But then a reader could stop to ask whether the issue is about adjectives that are short and helpful, or, on the other hand, about helpful ones that are short. The commas between adjectives in a series serve to eliminate the question. If the sentence reads, **When there are several short, helpful adjectives. . .**, there is no question about the meaning.

For our purposes as teachers, the technical term for such adjectives in a series is **coordinate adjectives,** or adjectives that modify the same noun or pronoun and

that can be reversed without changing the meaning of the sentence.

The older of the two men is a silent, shy type.

The two adjectives in the sentence (*silent* and *shy*) are called coordinate adjectives. They both modify the noun *type*, and they can be reversed (*shy* and *silent*) without changing the meaning of the sentence. In either order, the older of the two men remains both shy and silent, and the two adjectives, in either order, modify the noun *type*.

In the fourth or fifth grade, however, when the issue is likely to come up, the explanation depends on what students already know. If their sense of sentence parts is anchored in terms such as "describing words," then the explanation has to do with more than one describing word in a row. That will get the job done in a primitive manner at least, rather as a chainsaw would get the roses cut. But if fifth graders have some sense of how words affect one another in sentences, how they can be used to enhance the power of other words, and they know that the enhancement is called **modification,** we can tell them in a clear, precise manner (where both *clear* and *precise,* in either order, modify the noun *manner*) how and why to use commas in the sentence (see pages 138–139 for a discussion of adjectives).

There remains the question of order when putting adjectives in a series in a sentence. In the sentence, **The large, fluffy cloud seemed to sit on top of the hill,** there is no reason why the adjectives *large* and *fluffy* can't be reversed to read *fluffy* and *large*. In the previous explanation regarding the use of commas to separate two or more adjectives that modify the same noun, one criterion is that the order of the adjectives can be reversed without changing the meaning of the sentence. It seems, then, that the order is not relevant.

However, at times it may seem as though the order of appearance may influence meaning, as in the following examples:

The large, old man got out of the car.
The old, large man got out of the car.

The writer is in charge of deciding what (s)he prefers and intends. This lesson focuses on the punctuation for the adjectives in a series. The question of meaning and order is another issue. It is useful, if young writers ask about order and meaning, to be able to give them examples they can ponder.

Examples of Commas That Separate Adjectives in a Series

Jacob Have I Loved is a book about twins with different, perplexing, and unique personalities.

Omri's birthday present from Patrick was a sturdy, wooden cupboard that happened to have an Indian in it.

Journey is about a book with characters who have interesting, unique names: Cat and Journey.

Teaching Young Writers about Commas in a Series of Adjectives

This is another punctuation situation best left at the ready stage, waiting for students to ask or to use the construction in a sentence. The wait is worth it, for if there is a serious writing program in operation in which young writers write every day through the genres and across the curricular areas, a sentence will come up.

"Jason, share that sentence you just showed me. I want to put it on the board."

The video store had a weird funny department that had all the worst movies of the year.

Point out that Jason wrote a sentence in which two words tell about the department in the video store. "And what might those two words be?" Miriam will know. She always does. "Yes, Miriam, that's right. The words *weird* and *funny* both describe the department in the video store. What are those kinds of words?" After the whole-class response in unison, "Good. I knew you'd know. Adjectives. There are two adjectives in Jason's sentence, both describing the department in the video store. Jason, my dear friend, when you do that, when you write two adjectives beside each other that way, you need to signal your readers by putting a comma between the two adjectives. Come on up here

and do that on the board, then do it in the sentence on your paper."

In a situation like that, there is usually some interest piqued, and that's the teachable moment. Take advantage of the moment. Tell students that you know they're all thoroughly absorbed in their thoughts about their own writing, but since you're the teacher, you get to teach almost whenever you want, and you want to teach right now. They'll understand because this wouldn't be the first time you've pulled rank on them. They might roll their eyes once or twice, but that's mostly because they're fifth graders, and most fifth-grade teachers ignore the preteen affectation.

Direct them to think of a sentence that has a white dog in it. Remind them that they are to think and write in their heads. Then tell them to think of something in addition to *white* that will describe the dog. Tell them that you want them to think of a sentence that contains **two** adjectives, side by side, that describe the dog.

Miriam is likely to be first.

The nice white dog sat on the front porch.

Ask her what the adjectives (or describing words) are. Ask that she read her sentence again, this time reading the comma between the adjectives.

The nice comma white dog sat on the front porch.

Ask that she read it again, but this time reverse the order of the adjectives in the sentence. When she reads **The white nice dog sat on the front porch,** ask others in the class if the sentence still works when the adjectives are reversed. Someone will certainly indicate that the sentence sounds different when the adjectives are reversed. The conversation now can focus on how the meaning actually changes when the dog is both white and pretty no matter what the order of the adjectives in the sentence, but *nice and white* might sound or feel different from *white and nice.* Tell them it's a sense that language users have, that the difference is something that people just know as the result of using English for a long time. Let them know that they have already shown, by noticing the difference, that they have that sense, so they must be experts. And let them know, as well, that if they write sentences that contain two or more adjectives in a row, and they can't seem to sense which one should go first, it probably doesn't matter.

Solicit more sentences with specific directions for two or more adjectives that modify the same noun. Listen to them as they are volunteered. After three or four oral sentences, all read twice, the second time calling the comma, direct them to write one on paper. Given that this is the fifth grade, and your daily writing work has promoted considerable fluency, one minute of writing time will be sufficient.

Now, listen to several sentences read from their papers. Roam the room and call on volunteers who happen to sit near where you are standing. Read over the reader's shoulder as (s)he reads. Notice whether the comma is inserted between the adjectives. If not, remind everyone together to look at their sentence and make sure they have the comma between their adjectives.

In situations like this, it's fully appropriate to notice how the words are spelled. Don't make a public issue of the spelling, but there is no good reason for not leaning over and saying, "Meg, you know how to spell *horse*. Please fix your word." There is also no good reason for not whispering, "Ryan, this word is spelled this way," and writing it at the top of his paper: *pollution*. "Now fix yours." Those kinds of small, short moments remind young writers that spelling is always important. It will not immobilize them as they write, but it is something to think about as they write, and after they write. The **thinking** is important because it relates to **spelling conscience,** which, as a descriptor for **attention,** is critical to spelling well. (For more on this subject, see Grothe, B. F. [1966]. A study of spelling conscience. *Elementary English 43,* 774–775; Johnson, T. D., Langford, K. G., & Quorn, K. C. [1981]. Characteristics of an effective spelling program. *Language Arts 58,* 581–588.)

Writing with Commas in a Series of Adjectives

1. Think of a sentence in which the words in brackets are used side by side to describe an animal in the zoo. *[brown—huge]*

   _____

   _____

   _____

2. Think of two words that could be used to describe a piano player at a recital. Put the words in the brackets. [_____] Write a sentence in which the two words you wrote in the brackets are used as adjectives side by side to describe a piano player at a recital. Remember the comma that separates the adjectives.

   _____

   _____

3. The man's arms are special when you see him for the first time. He walks into the room, and everyone immediately looks at his arms. Think of a sentence about the man's arms, and use two adjectives side by side to describe those arms.

   _____

   _____

4. Think of a sentence in which the main idea is a very hot day, a day in which the sun is out and there is no breeze. Write your sentence and include two adjectives side by side to describe something in the sentence. Remember the comma between the adjectives.

   _____

   _____

5. Write a sentence in which the words *colorful* and *sweet* appear as adjectives side by side to describe a special birthday gift.

   _____

   _____

6. Imagine riding along in a car on a two-day trip somewhere. Look out the window and notice something that you could describe in a sentence that contains two adjectives side by side.

   _____

   _____

Tips for Teachers

1. For those teachers who wonder why the lesson about adjectives in series isn't folded into the lesson about other words in series, there is a reason. We're trying to make these lessons as clean as possible, as unfettered with multiple variables as we possibly can. Nouns in series aren't just like adjectives in series, so we separated them into two lessons. If you think the separation is artificial, combine them when you teach.

2. It is possible to conduct this lesson without the vocabulary (*adjective*) and the idea (modification of noun), but it is much harder. Why not use the writing lesson to teach adjectives? (See Chapter 5.) Avoid definitions and lists of words. Just ask for certain kinds of sentences that contain certain kinds of words, as described above. Then use the word *adjective* as you go along, slowly and adroitly making it part of the way you talk about writing. They learned the word *horse* that way, too.

LESSON 13: COMMAS TO SET OFF APPOSITIVES

The Convention

Use commas to set off or separate an appositive from the rest of the sentence.

Student Writing Samples (not edited for spelling)

1. Sometimes my friend, Taylor, and her sister, Cera, come over and spend the night. [Third Grader]
2. The lats tiem my fren, Butch, came we had cak and iscrem. [Third Grader]
3. I can play with my mom's pertty brown dog, Teddy, and she let's me feed her. [Fifth Grader]
4. It's Six Flags, the most fun of all the places around. [Fifth Grader]
5. It's something I feel, freedom. [Sixth Grader]

Explanation

Sometimes, a writer names someone or something that, for immediate clarity, has to be defined. Third-grade Lisa wrote a three-sentence autobiographical incident that read as follows.

> **I am in third grade. My teacher Mrs. Liddle is smart. I do a lot of things in third grade.**

Lisa just knew that her audience wouldn't necessarily know her teacher's name, so she named her teacher. Of course, she could have named the teacher in the first place, but then she would have had to slip in something that told that Mrs. Liddle was her teacher. Either way, she had to define, tell more about, and place in context something she named. If she named the person as her teacher, she had to follow it with the name of her teacher; and if she named the teacher, she would have to slip in the fact that Mrs. Liddle was the teacher. The definition, the added information, the context, those are called **appositives.** Appositives are set off from the rest of the sentence with commas.

Appositives are related to parenthetical expressions, but there is sufficient difference between the two to merit separate lessons. First, there is the matter of definitions. The word *appositive* comes from the word *appose* which means *to put side by side or opposite.* Opposite to what, or side by side with what? An appositive is a noun (see Chapter 5) or noun form that follows another noun or noun form for the purpose of defining the first noun or noun form. That would be pretty hard to understand, perhaps, if we didn't already have that third grader's autobiographical incident. She wrote her teacher's name (noun) after the noun *teacher* in order to define who "teacher" is. She didn't know the definition of what she did, perhaps, but she certainly knew she had to do it.

How is what third-grade Lisa did different from a parenthetical expression? There's a parenthetical expression in the last sentence of the paragraph right above this one. The word *perhaps* is not a noun or noun form, and it does not follow another noun or noun form, and it also does not define or clarify anything that came before.

We can define **appositive** even further. It means to place a word or phrase beside another in explanation. So for those third graders, if that's what you're thinking about, or older students, for that matter, forget the "noun and noun form" business and think only about **explanation.** If the word or phrase specifically **explains,** it's an appositive. You see, in the third sentence of this paragraph, there are two parenthetical expressions. They provide extra information about the sentence; they are not explanations.

Of course, if the young writers in your room know about nouns and pronouns and can understand that a phrase in this case means *all of the other words that go with a noun or pronoun,* then talk with them about defining and explaining with nouns and noun forms. But if they don't, you can still instruct in appositives by telling youngsters that appositives explain something that might not be known to the reader.

Oh, and begin teaching them about nouns. This is one of those examples where **noun** is part of the vocabulary of writing, and it's very hard to talk with young writers about what they are doing if there isn't a shared vocabulary (see Chapter 5).

Examples of Commas to Set Off Appositives

Winnie, the girl from Treegap, thought about what it would be like to live forever.

Alexander, a young boy of eight, wanted to go to Australia.

Winnie the Pooh carried his basket, a fair-sized basket filled with crackers.

Teaching Young Writers about Using Commas in Appositives

This is another of those instructional situations to which we should respond when the need arises. In other words, there is no reason to deal with appositives in the first several grades, perhaps up to and through the fourth or even fifth, unless someone in the room uses one. That's the instructional moment, at least for the young writer on whose paper there appears a noun or noun form that defines or places in context an immediately preceding noun or noun form in a sentence.

Slip in alongside Lisa and in one-to-one conference ask her to read her second sentence. "You're writing about Mrs. Liddle in that sentence?" you ask. She acknowledges. Tell her she did a good job of letting her audience in on the fact that it is the teacher she's talking about and that her teacher has a name. Tell her it's sometimes hard to get all the information the audience needs into one sentence, but she managed it very cleverly. Write her sentence on a paper.

My teacher Mrs. Liddle is smart.

"You remember how I said that punctuation marks and capital letters are often used to signal your readers about what you've written so they can understand better? Well, when you do what you did in that sentence, you have to signal your audience." At that moment, Lisa reaches for her pencil, repositions the paper so it

faces her correctly, and puts a comma between *teacher* and *Mrs. Liddle.* Then she hesitates a moment and puts another at the end of the appositive.

When we ask why she put commas before and after the name of her teacher, she replies, "Because," she says, "it doesn't sound like it's part of the sentence; it's kind of like something extra."

"So if you were to write something like that again, you'd remember to put commas around it, wouldn't you?" She assures us that she will. In the third grade, on that day, in that situation, that is enough.

But assume it's the middle of the fourth grade, and the language arts series has a chapter about punctuating sentences that contain appositives. Direct the fourth graders to write a sentence of at least seven words with the name of someone in their family somewhere in the middle. Remind them to be sure to use the person's name in their sentence. If the children seem not to understand, model on the board. (My sister Ellen takes piano lessons on Saturday mornings.) When you solicit sharing, Elisa's hand goes up first.

It rained on the day my mother Ramona came home from the hospital.

Conduct a scenario similar to the one with Lisa we described a couple of paragraphs ago. Remind the class that punctuation is often used in sentences to signal readers about what is happening. "If we wanted to signal readers of Elisa's sentence that she is naming her mother right in the middle of the sentence, how do you think we might use commas?" There's nearly always someone in a fourth grade who knows what to do. If there isn't, model it. But there nearly always is, so when Cameron raises his hand, gesturing, acknowledge his enthusiasm: "Yes, Cameron, what do you think we should do with Elisa's sentence to signal readers about what she has done?" When he begins to tell, stop him and ask that he come on up and do it right on the board.

Knowing Cameron, we can assume that he'll put commas on either side of the word *Ramona,* but if he doesn't, the lesson isn't out the window because everything young writers do is fodder for instruction, as they take risks and make errors on their way to new learning. Pretend that Cameron puts a comma after *mother* and begins walking back to his desk. "Why there, Cameron?" He will say something about wanting to separate the word *mother* from the **name** of the mother. Tell him that's terrific thinking, and he's half-way home. Up will go Elisa's hand. "Yes?" She rises, runs to the board, and puts another comma after *Ramona.* "And why, Elisa? Why that comma?" She may say something about the word *Ramona* feeling like it just adds something extra and that we should tell readers that it isn't a mistake.

Listen to other sentences youngsters construct. Write them on the board and make an issue of the punctuation. After several students read their sentences, tell those who follow that they are to be sure there are commas in their sentence and they are to call the commas out loud when they get to them. There will be sentences similar to this one.

My father's name is Hank comma and he is a bus driver.

Reinforce the sentence and the **correct** punctuation. Tell them that Amanda invented a different way to write a sentence with the word *father* as well as her father's **name,** and she used the punctuation properly. Reinforce Amanda for remembering the lessons about compound sentences. Then, "Amanda, I'd like to see if you can rewrite your sentence so that it is similar to the ones we have been writing in today's lesson. Think about how it might read if it started with "My father" and then gave your father's name. Every Amanda we've ever known in such a situation rewrites the sentence in her head and calls it aloud immediately.

My father comma Hank comma is a bus driver.

"That's terrific, Amanda. You rewrote your sentence in your head, didn't you?" Amanda has a broad smile on her face, one of those that says, "I did it!" Ask if she could write another sentence like that, this time with another family member in it. She'll start right off. Direct the rest of the class to write another sentence with a different family member. Tell them that this sentence will be their ticket to recess. Then stand at the door at recess time and collect the single-sentence scraps of paper as they file out. Pin those that contain appositives properly punctuated on the Best Effort Board.

The next day, call attention to the sentences on the board, direct several of the students to read theirs, and use one or two from the board as models for more writing from others in the room. They should write a sentence or two on the second day, again on the third, and again on the fourth. That will be as many as eight or ten sentences, counting the first day. Then, open the language arts book to the section about appositives. The children will have some prior knowledge on the basis of which to learn what the language arts book is teaching.

Writing with Commas that Set Off Appositives

1. Write a sentence that gives the name of one of your friends. Right after the name, the sentence will contain the words *my friend*.

    _____

    _____

2. Rewrite the sentence you wrote in the space above, and this time write *my friend* first, and then right after that write the name of your friend.

    _____

    _____

3. Read the sentence in the box.

Both of the boys, Adam and Nick, won prizes at the fair.

    Write a sentence so that it's about girls instead of boys, so that there are names for the girls, and so that they both win prizes at the fair.

    _____

    _____

    Read your sentence to make sure the commas are used correctly.

4. Think of a sentence in which the main idea is something you do with a friend. Make *we* the first word in the sentence and write the people's names right after *we*. Make sure you use commas properly.

    _____

    _____

Tips for Teachers

1. Many of the children in the fourth or fifth grade will understand the lesson about sentences that contain appositives. Some won't. They'll still be able to write well.

2. Don't give a test on this lesson. Do encourage these kinds of sentences in their daily writing.

LESSON 14: COMMAS AFTER INTRODUCTORY WORDS

The Convention

Use a comma to separate introductory elements from the rest of the sentence.

Student Writing Samples (not edited for spelling)

1. Man, I like the mall because you could buy lots of close for school. [Fourth Grader]
2. Yes, I love my room because there I can use the phone and talk to all my friends. [Fifth Grader]
3. Well, I can just see it now. [Sixth Grader]
4. Basically, by mother and father are the best parents in the world. [Sixth Grader]
5. Also, it's the place where I sit to see the stars in the sky at night. [Sixth Grader]
6. There, no one can tell me not to think and daydream the way I do. [Sixth Grader]
7. My favorite place is in my mind. There, I can say anything I want. No one can hurt me or tell me what to do. There is music in my mind. [Sixth Grader]

Explanation

There are several **introductory elements,** that is, words, phrases, and clauses, which, if not separated from the rest of the sentence, might compromise the meaning of the sentence. This lesson is about punctuation that is needed after introductory **words** only. The lesson does not include introductory clauses because those are treated separately in other lessons (Lessons 10 and 16). Also, the lesson following this one (Lesson 15) is about introductory phrases.

Go back to the first sentence in the paragraph just above. It ends with a reference to compromising the meaning of a sentence. A comma separates introductory elements from the rest of the sentence when its absence risks confusing the reader. In this lesson we assume that its absence will *always* confuse the reader, so we don't deal with exceptions and judgments. Because we assume that basic punctuation conventions are being taught to young writers during their most tender learning years, the years when they are most vulnerable to confusion, we are absolutely sure that the youngsters have a great need for security that does not come wrapped in exceptions and judgments. It comes clear and clean, a secure statement on which a young writer can depend, not so much to be *right* every time, but *never to be wrong.*

Therefore, even though some books may say there is wiggle room in using punctuation after introductory words, in this lesson there is a comma between every introductory word and the rest of the sentence, every time.

"But doesn't that confuse them, as well?" Some folks may ask that because at some point in a young writer's experience someone may say that the comma isn't necessary because its absence doesn't compromise meaning. We believe the answer is "No." When youngsters are ten years old, it's ambiguity that's confusing, not security. When they're fifteen or twenty and they find out they may slightly "over comma" their writing, they already have a sense of security about punctuation. They are better able to adjust to ambiguities in punctuation just as they are in crossing the street.

Now, what does "compromise meaning" mean? Read that sentence again. Is it possible that on first reading, one could read, "Now what—does 'compromise. . . ," then realize that it has to be read, "Now —what does. . . ?" Of course. Yes, it is the reader's responsibility to construct meaning and make the meaning adjustments necessary to make the text make sense. But it is the writer's responsibility to eliminate as many possibilities for meaning confusion as possible. Introductory words and phrases are possibilities.

An introductory word appears in the following sentence: **Sometime, we will have to go to the store.** There isn't much risk of confusing meaning here, but the first word is clearly introductory in the sentence, so we put a comma after it.

Here's another sentence with an introductory element.

Now I don't understand how she made that work.

Does the sentence mean that *at this moment* the person doesn't know how she made that work? Does the sentence mean something like *Now look here fella*, I don't know how she made that work? Without a comma, it *feels* like a moment in time; with the comma, it's more like, *Hey, I don't know how she did it*. The comma serves to clarify the meaning. If it's a moment in time, *Now* isn't introductory; it's just the first word in the sentence. If it's about *Look here*, *Now* is introductory and requires a comma to make the meaning clear.

Here's another example.

Well, let's wait and see.

The first word is set apart from the rest of the sentence because the sound of the writer's intended meaning is akin to **Well—,** followed by a pause to emphasize what comes next, which is **let's wait and see.** The comma makes that clear.

Below, the river raged along a rocky course.

Without the comma, it can just as easily read, **Below the river. . . .** Of course, the accomplished reader would then change course to the accurate meaning. Writers should not make readers do that.

The key is to teach consistency early on and allow the writers' sense of mastery to carry them through the inevitable ambiguities as their writing matures, and as their ability to deal with exceptions and ambiguities grows.

Examples of Commas That Separate Introductory Words from the Rest of the Sentence

Oh, I always cry when I read *Stone Fox*.
Well, when I read, I like to curl up on my bed.
Sometimes, characters in books feel like my friends.

Teaching Young Writers about Commas after Introductory Words

We all played in the park and had a wonderful time yesterday.

Inquire about what the students notice in the sentence on the board (or the overhead screen, the butcher paper, the computer screen). There isn't much to notice, in

fact, but they'll volunteer all sorts of things because the teacher asked. Put up another sentence on the board.

Yesterday, we all played in the park and had a wonderful time.

Inquire again about what they notice. They'll say they notice how you changed the sentence by putting the last word first. Someone will notice that there is a comma in this sentence. "Yes, that's right. There is a comma, and it's in the right place for the right reason. Why do you think I put that comma right after the first word? I don't usually put commas after the first words in sentences. Why this time?"

The teacher is searching for some auditory sense of pause after this particular first word, in which case there is reason to define the word as **introductory,** not just **first.** The distinction is subtle but real. It isn't that it's the first word; it's that the word introduces the rest of the sentence.

Erase the introductory word so the sentence reads as follows.

We all played in the park and had a wonderful time.

"See, we can have the sentence without that word. If it were the first word in the sentence, the sentence wouldn't work without it, but this one works just fine without that word." Write another sentence.

Yesterday was the first day of the month.

"See, that sentence doesn't work if you take out the first word. In that sentence, *yesterday* is the first word, not the introductory word. That's what makes the word introductory, not just first. Introductory words are special words, and they have to be separated from the rest of the sentence with a comma because they're not just the first word in the sentence."

Young writers should write several sentences in which *yesterday* is the introductory word. They should share them aloud and call their comma when they get to it in their readings. These are prototype sentence writing cues that promote *yesterday* as the introductory word.

1. Write a seven-word (or five, eight, eleven, thirteen, and so forth) sentence that is introduced with the word *yesterday*.
2. Write a sentence that contains the idea of weather (or whatever else), and make the introductory word *yesterday*.

3. Write a sentence about your favorite kind of pet, and introduce the sentence with the word *yesterday*.

4. Write a sentence in which *yesterday* is the introductory word.

Listen to and comment on the sentences. Write "yesterday" sentences for a day or two. Yes, it's artificial. So is writing itself. So are reading and arithmetic. Left to their own devices in an educationally nondirective world, most youngsters wouldn't learn the three times tables. But we teach it, not because it's natural or authentic, but because there is a greater good that the three times tables serve. The artificiality gives youngsters broader skill, and the skills broaden their options.

During other days, pose other words that can function as introductory words in sentences. Yes, there are other words that can work that way. Why, there might be as many as a dozen such words with which young writers can work. Sorry, we're not likely to make the list right here. Indeed, a list might even be counterproductive because the best way to notice introductory words is in sentences where they introduce, not on lists where they don't. Well, that should close the matter for this paragraph. So, we'll leave it for teachers and young writers to find sentences that contain introductory words. Hey, that's what learning is, isn't it? Paying attention and noticing, then practicing, are the behaviors that work.

Writing Sentences that Contain an Introductory Word

Today is the first day of November.

Read the boxed sentence and notice the first word. Now, write a sentence in which *today* is an introductory word. Remember that the sentence will work even if the introductory word is taken out.

_____

_____

_____

Write a sentence in which the main idea is your favorite breakfast and *today* is the introductory word.

_____

_____

_____

Think of a sentence in which *look* is the introductory word. Be sure to use a comma to separate the introductory *look* from the rest of the sentence.

_____

_____

_____

Below, there were six birds flying carefully between the rock ledges.

Read the sentence and notice the introductory word. Notice how the introductory word is separated from the rest of the sentence with a comma. Now, write a new sentence in which the word *above* is the introductory word.

_____

_____

_____

Tips for Teachers

1. This is not a high-frequency punctuation convention. Teach it to the whole class if you wish, but it is also appropriate to teach it only to those young writers whose writing shows the kinds of sentences that need the convention.

2. When this convention has been taught, it is very important to fold it into whole written pieces. "Use a sentence with an introductory word in your story this week."

LESSON 15: COMMAS AFTER INTRODUCTORY PHRASES

The Convention

Use a comma to separate introductory phrases from the rest of the sentence.

Student Writing Samples (not edited for spelling)

1. Just for fun, I could play Sega or lift wats. [Third Grader]
2. Thinking of it, it is small and really warm. [Fifth Grader]
3. Let's see, what is the best vacation of all? [Fifth Grader]
4. Thinking of my best idea, I would say it's a day walking in the forest. [Sixth Grader]
5. Seeing the green plants, I remembered about the dream. [Sixth Grader]
6. Looking in my bedroom, I remember all the times I was sick and had to lay down on my bed. [Sixth Grader]
7. Watching the waves, I dream away into the sky. [Sixth Grader]

Explanation

The introductory phrase is another **introductory element** similar to the introductory word in Lesson 14. In this book, the lesson on introductory phrases is separate from the lesson on introductory words in order not to burden young writers with more material to handle than necessary. Once children see and work with introductory words, they can make the transition to introductory phrases, or vice-versa if introductory phrases pop up in their writing before introductory words. Either way, one paves the way for the other. Together, they provide insights that young writers can use to construct sentences in greater variety. Sentences with introductory words and phrases open the door to variety, even within simple sentences.

Most introductory phrases are participial phrases and prepositional phrases, which often function as ad-verbs (see Chapter 5). Now, let's simplify. It is not necessary to teach sentence diagrams in order to understand and write introductory phrases. It isn't even necessary to understand what a participle, an adverb, or a preposition is. Of course, it would help youngsters to understand participles, adverbs, and prepositions, but clearly one does not have to master the labels and definitions before one can write an introductory phrase. Otherwise, these constructions would not appear in elementary students' writings, and they do. Many young writers will recognize them as early as the late third grade because many use them in their speech, and they know what the phrases sound like and what they do.

We would like to emphasize that while introductory phrases will begin to appear in some youngsters' writings in the middle and late elementary years, the concept of introductory participial and prepositional phrases is abstract and, therefore, fairly complex to understand. We recommend that teachers begin with youngsters they see using these constructions and, as we have consistently emphasized in this book, begin with the **sound** of the language. For some youngsters, direct teaching of introductory phrases won't be appropriate until middle school. Still others will not be ready until high school. This is where your professional judgment, as the teacher, is so critical. Only you know what your students need to know and are ready to learn.

Let's take a look at several kinds of introductory phrases. An introductory participial phrase begins with a participle. **Sounding like a way to introduce the main idea in a sentence,** an introductory participial phrase, in fact, does introduce a sentence. Look carefully at the previous sentence. Its main idea, what the sentence is about, is that the introductory participial phrase introduces a sentence. The bold face part of the sentence is an introductory participial phrase. Notice that it **sounds** introductory to the main idea of the sentence. Its first word is a participle, an *-ing* action word that is not the verb in the sentence. The verb in the sentence is *introduce*, helped along by the ancillary verb, *does*.

Trying to understand the introductory participial phrase, people sometimes become despondent because the idea isn't so clear as they would like at first. **Working hard on it,** some of us begin to see the pattern more clearly. **Writing in introductory participial phrases,** most of us begin to see how participial phrases feel and sound as a way to set up or introduce a sentence. **Feeling good about a sense of understanding,** we move ahead and use introductory participial phrases confidently in our writing. **Using them with confidence,** we also separate them from the rest of the sentence with a comma.

Of course, five introductory participial phrases lined up in a row in one five-sentence paragraph is an awful read. We wrote that paragraph, however, because when there are several in a row, their characteristics are so apparent that they become tedious. The very tedium makes the basic characteristics of the introductory participial phrase clear.

- The introductory participial phrase begins with an *-ing* action word that is not the verb in the sentence.
- The introductory participial phrase is the set-up, the lead-in, to the rest of the sentence.

An introductory adverbial phrase is often a prepositional phrase that behaves like an adverb. It just doesn't follow the verb, as it does in the sentence below. Notice the difference.

The moon rises like a bright orange from the east.

From the east modifies the verb *rises* because it tells **where** the moon rises: The moon rises from the east. In the next sentence the phrase also tells **where** the moon rises, only this time it introduces the rest of the sentence.

From the east, the moon rises like a bright orange.

Still, the moon rises, and it rises from the east. The phrase modifies the verb *rises*, again, by telling **where** the moon rises.

Here's another example of an introductory phrase:

After breakfast, David ran outside to play.

When an introductory phrase is short and the sentence is clear without the comma, the comma can be omitted. For example, the following sentence has an introductory prepositional phrase, but it is clear without the comma.

In 1996 I bought my first car.

Although at times the comma may not be necessary, it is never wrong to separate an introductory phrase from the rest of the sentence with a comma. As with other conventions in this book, we recommend teaching young writers to use the comma after introductory phrases. As they become more sophisticated in their language use, they will begin to notice subtle differences between when meaning is compromised and when it is not. At that time, they can decide for themselves whether to use the comma or to leave it out.

Therefore, we recommend teaching that when the phrase is introductory, it is separated from the rest of the sentence with a comma. When it opens the sentence, it starts the thought; it's introductory, and as an introductory phrase, it is followed with a comma.

Examples of Introductory Phrases in Sentences

One warm day, a little cricket was born.
During the party, Elbert shocked the guests with his bad word.
While untangling the ball of string, Maniac realized that everyone was watching.

Teaching Young Writers about Commas after Introductory Phrases

It has been apparent to teachers for decades that most young writers do not apply mechanical conventions in their writing when the conventions are taught through proofreading and editing. We know, as well, that young writers don't use a comma between an introductory adverbial phrase, for example, and the rest of the sentence merely because they know that the phrase modifies the predicate in the sentence. Nevertheless, much of the time, we provide a linguistic rationale for mechanical conventions, even for third and fourth graders. When we teach writing as though it were proofreading and editing, or as though foundational content depended on sophisticated linguistic study, there is a lot of instruction that does not directly affect daily writing. What is a teacher to do?

This lesson about introductory phrases illustrates an alternative way to teach youngsters to punctuate introductory phrases in sentences. We are likely to be teaching commas after introductory adverbial phrases, and occasionally even participial phrases, in the middle elementary grades, because that's when some young writers tend to use them in their spontaneous writing. The linguistically technical explanation is not effective because most third, fourth, and fifth graders won't understand it.

We also know from decades of experience that young writers can perform proofreading and editing exercises with a great deal of skill and still not write using the conventions properly. Proofreading and editing **are not** writing behaviors, so the ability to perform the exercise does not necessarily generalize to performing writing.

We know, then, what **won't** succeed. What **will** succeed is young writers' use of the conventions in their proper context, properly, frequently, over time, and in their own writing. There are explicit implications for instruction.

- Using the conventions means thinking and writing with them.
- The proper context is writing, not proofreading and editing, though that does not mean young writers cannot use what they know to proofread and edit their work.
- Using these conventions properly means using them correctly, every time.
- Frequently means nearly every day.
- Protracted time means long enough for an age-appropriate performance to appear.

To teach this convention, place a sentence, such as the following, on the board or overhead transparency.

They all fell to their knees after they ran the race.

Ask a student to read. Then ask, "When did they fall to their knees?" (After the race.) "Of course. They fell to their knees after they ran the race. You're a very good reader. Try something, Kendra. Think of a way to change the sentence so that what comes last now comes first." Ask Kendra because she's one of those who is likely to understand what the question is about. Perhaps even she doesn't understand what you're asking. So try it another way. "How would the sentence read if we started it with *after the race?*" Now everyone will get it. Write it on the board.

After the race, they all fell to their knees.

Ask again when they fell to their knees. Show them how it doesn't matter whether the phrase is at the beginning of the sentence or at the end, it always tells **when.** If this is a class which has learned about modifiers of verbs, or predicates (a class in which adverbs have been taught), show them that the phrase acts like an adverb, so it is called an **adverbial** phrase. If this is a class that is not sensitive to modification and thinks the definition of *adverb* is that it ends in *-ly,* don't make an issue of modification at this time. Merely tell them that the phrase tells **when** or **where** or **how,** and when it's at the beginning of the sentence, it is followed with a comma. Give them several examples on the board.

Across the road, two birds splashed in a puddle.

(See, the phrase tells **where** the birds splashed.)

After the party, the children went home.

(Here, the introductory phrase tells **when** the children went home.)

As a result of the fall, the boy broke his leg.

(The phrase tells **how** the boy broke his leg.)

During the rain, everyone huddled together in their ponchos.

(**When** did they huddle, or why?)

Now, suggest that students think of a sentence that begins with an introductory phrase (or an adverbial phrase if they know about adverbs) like the one above that begins with *across.* Listen to several, direct them to write some, listen to their readings, remind them to use the comma, direct them to call the comma aloud when they come to it in their sentence, and reinforce their good ideas. In the examples above, *across, as, of,* and *during* are all prepositions. Around the middle or late elementary years, teach youngsters about prepositions (see Chapter 5), so they will understand the word when you use it.

On another day, solicit sentences that begin with an adverbial phrase that starts with *after.* You may get some complex sentences here. If you do, now is the time to go back to the lesson on complex sentences (Lesson 10) and show youngsters the difference between an introductory phrase, which does not contain a verb, and an introductory clause, which does. This may be difficult for some of your students, but some of them will understand. For others, you may want to revisit this idea at a later date.

On another day, direct students to write a sentence that begins with *while.* Ask them to work their way through the list of examples above. Direct them to find such sentences in their readings, whether in reading and literature, or in content area books. Direct them to listen as others talk, in the classroom, at home, on television. Listen for adverbial phrases, and when they bring such sentences into the classroom, post them on the cork board in the writing center.

Writing Sentences That Contain Introductory Participial and Prepositional Phrases

1. Read the sentence in the box and think of a way to write it so the last part comes first.

We had a quick lunch before the game on Saturday.

   _____

   _____

2. Think of another sentence that has an introductory phrase that starts with the word *before*. Think first. Now, write your sentence. Remember the comma right after the introductory phrase.

   _____

   _____

3. Write a sentence with an introductory adverbial phrase that begins with the word *after*.

   _____

   _____

4. Write a sentence with an introductory adverbial phrase in which the main idea has something to do with the *weather*.

   _____

   _____

5. Read the sentence in the box and then rewrite it with proper punctuation in the blank space.

Walking quickly up the hill Marcus almost tripped over a rock on the path.

   _____

   _____

6. Think of a sentence that begins with a phrase that starts with the word *hopping*. Remember the comma at the end of the phrase.

   _____

   _____

7. Write a sentence with an introductory participial phrase that begins with the word *thinking*.

   _____

   _____

8. Write a sentence with an introductory participial phrase in which the main idea has something to do with a trip to the zoo.

   _____

   _____

Tips for Teachers

Introductory adverbial phrases are very hard to teach if the youngsters don't bring prior knowledge about adverbs and modifiers to the lessons. There are three tips to think about here.

1. Teach adverbs and the relationship between adverbs and verbs as soon as the youngsters seem ready. Yes, the evidence is clear that knowledge of such terms and relationships does not necessarily transfer to better writing. But this is not the reason for teaching adverbs and modification anyway. It is impossible to converse clearly and instructionally about writing if the students don't understand the vocabulary. We can't converse instructionally about geography without its terminology, either, but we don't avoid teaching the vocabulary and attendant relationships merely because the words and relationships don't make geographers. Vocabulary and relationships don't make writers, but students have to have them in order to talk about writing. So teach adverbs, participles, and prepositions because merely pointing to words and calling them words isn't very helpful to anyone.

2. Just because we teach introductory adverbial phrases doesn't mean that everyone in the room will begin needing them in their sentences, or will ever use them, for that matter. There are perfectly fine writers of English who might report having never written a sentence that contained an introductory adverbial or participial phrase. So why teach them in the first place? Actually, we don't recommend it unless one or more of your students were writing such sentences and not punctuating them properly. Then we would either teach a minilesson only to those who were writing the sentences, or we would teach to everyone in the room on the possibility that instruction might give others an idea they hadn't considered before.

3. Youngsters will use introductory adverbial and/or participial phrases effectively in sentences largely to the extent that they practice writing such sentences. Practice means numbers of times. The number is certainly more than one and almost as certainly less than a thousand. If it were a thousand, fourth graders would have sufficient practice if they wrote about six every day through the fourth grade. But that would be too much. Three every day in the fourth and fifth grades would do it; so would a few less than a dozen per week in the fourth, fifth, and sixth grades. Then the seventh graders would have mastered writing with introductory participial and adverbial phrases. But it doesn't require even that many because the number isn't a thousand. The point holds, however. Practice is everything.

LESSON 16: COMMAS IN COMPOUND–COMPLEX SENTENCES

The Convention

Use commas to separate the clauses in sentences that are both compound and complex at the same time. Those sentences will have two or more independent clauses joined with conjunctions (see Lesson 7, Commas in Compound Sentences) **as well as** dependent clauses that are related to the independent clauses (see Lesson 10, Commas in Complex Sentences).

A compound–complex sentence would read as follows: **Although my friends wanted me to go with them, I stayed home with my sister, but I really wanted to go.** The first part of the sentence (*Although my friends wanted me to go with them*) is a dependent clause. The second part (*I stayed home with my sister*) is an independent clause. The third part (*I really wanted to go*) is another independent clause, and the two independent clauses (the second and third parts) are connected with a conjunction (*but*). The example is a compound–complex sentence because it contains the characteristics of compound sentences and complex sentences, both in the same sentence. That young writers can write and properly punctuate compound sentences and complex sentences doesn't necessarily mean that they can properly punctuate the two kinds of constructions in the same sentence. That is why there is a separate lesson for sentences that combine the two.

Student Writing Samples (not edited for spelling)

1. My favorite place is Disneyland because I get to go on the rides, and I get to see Mickey Mouse. [Second Grader]
2. Mi favorite place is Disleylan, and I like to go ther because it lokes like fun. [Second Grader]
3. So when my little brother trys to find me and get me angry, I just go to almost the top of the tree, and I don't say a word and don't move. [Second Grader]
4. It's Disneyworld because it is fun there, and they have a hunted house. [Third Grader]
5. My room makes me want to live in it, but I can't because I have to go to school. [Third Grader]

6. My favorit place is with my mom because I love my mom very much, and I know she loves me very much. [Fourth Grader]

7. When we move, my brother is going to live with us, and finaly when I'm bored, I'll have some body to play with. [Fifth Grader]

Explanation

When there are several clauses in one sentence and readers aren't sure where one ends and another begins, there is the risk of miscommunication. The example sentence above about staying home with my sister instead of joining friends for a day of fun and games is probably clear enough without punctuation. Consider the example below, however.

There is a dark wooden bookcase in my room and although there is lots of room for all my books in the bookcase they are spread around the room where I can find them.

There are three pieces in the sentence, but this time it could require more than one reading to be sure where they are and exactly what the sentence conveys. Of course, the sentence could be better crafted for clarity, but this is the sort of sentence a fifth or sixth grader is likely to write. The young writer will be read more clearly if (s)he uses a comma between the clauses. **There is a dark wooden bookcase in my room, and although there is lots of room for all my books in the bookcase, they are spread around the room where I can find them.** The second example is easier to follow. The commas provide *road markers,* perhaps signals akin to the bread crumbs of Hansel and Gretel.

There is an implied advantage in focusing on the compound–complex sentence alone, even though each of the structural attributes of sentences has been treated before, and the advantage is apparent in the "bookcase" example above. Some young writers begin writing that way sometime around the fourth grade, and often their writing isn't so clear as that in the example. If they have spent some time in their writing instruction noticing various kinds of clause structures in the sentences, they will have some background on the basis of which to begin thoughtfully planning their own writing. They will also have some background for looking at their own writing for revision purposes.

Examples of Compound–Complex Sentences

When I read *Catherine Called Birdy,* I learned something new about the Middle Ages, and I liked what I learned.

When I read *Farewell to Manzanar,* I learned a lot about the Japanese internment camps of World War II, and it was a true story about the author's family.

I love Sustained Silent Reading time because I get to read my favorite books, and the time just flies by.

Teaching Young Writers about Commas in Compound–Complex Sentences

As with the other conventions in this book, teaching about using commas properly in compound–complex sentences must involve direct instruction through students' writing. We recommend that youngsters should first have worked with compound sentences and complex sentences, both in isolation, so they could experience explicit practice, and in context so they could experience transfer of their practice to their own real writing. As youngsters' writing gets more sophisticated, pose a variation on the theme. This variation, compound–complex sentences, may be appropriate to teach as early as fourth grade for some young writers, perhaps fifth or sixth for others. However, our experience is that many fourth graders are able to master and use this construction.

Point out that they have already seen how they can write in structures that are more than one simple sentence (Simple sentences: **The girl walked home. She ate her dinner.**) and that by connecting the simple sentences, they have a new kind of sentence (compound). Point out as well that they have already written simple constructions (**The girl walked home.**) and know that when they add a certain kind of introduction (**Although she was offered a ride**), they have another new kind of sentence (complex). "What do you think, my friends? You've combined two simple sentences to get a compound sentence. Do you think you can combine a complex sentence and a compound sentence? Can you add a compound and a complex sentence?"

We have discussed that this works best when this is conducted as a project, a puzzle, an experiment. The teacher's question is an honest one: "Can you do this?" The youngsters have to "own" the idea if it is to be useful later for their own writing, and for revision and editing purposes. If the teacher poses the question, gives three or four examples, and then shows how it's done, the whole point of "ownership" borne of discovery falls apart. The discovery (i.e., learning) occurs only when youngsters have the opportunity to construct their own meaning; therefore, if, after several tries on the third Wednesday of October in the fourth grade, no one in the room has come up with a compound–complex construction, leave it with a promise. "I want to pursue this, so think about it and make some tries on your own. I will read your tries, and we'll all give it a try together tomorrow again." Oh, and follow through with the promise.

Come back to it the following day. If someone in the class turns in a homework assignment the following morning and one of the "sentences" is an especially long construction that can be visioned again, or revised, keep it as the trump card for the coming lesson. "You remember yesterday when we tried to think of ways to put a compound and a complex sentence together, and I promised I'd read your ideas. Well, let's try it again. Mark, you had a good idea. Read what you did and I'll write it on the board."

**When the man went to the store,
and he bought some pop.**

"That's a good idea, Mark. You're saying that the man bought some pop when he went to the store. Isn't that right?" Mark agrees. "Then you just write it that way and take out the *and* so the sentence tells what you want it to tell." Mark protests because he's overgeneralized the *and*. If there's an *and*, there has to be a compound sentence, thus a comma, and he already has the introductory clause that will give him a complex sentence. Good for Mark! He's beginning to construct his understanding of the compound–complex sentence.

Take Mark a little further. "Mark, when the man went to the store, he bought some pop, right?" Mark agrees. "Let's pretend there's a friend of his at the store. After he buys the pop, what happens?" Mark suggests that the man says hello to his friend. "But he has to see his friend first." Mark agrees. "So try your sentence again, and make the man see his friend."

**When the man went to the store, he bought
some pop and saw his friend.**

"That's a perfectly fine sentence, Mark. Let's say you want to report who was his friend. What would you say?" Mark tells us that he'd say the man. "OK. How would you do that in your sentence?"

**When the man went to the store, he bought
some pop, and he saw his friend.**

Bingo! Oh, it may not be a *bingo* for every teacher on the second day, but someone in the room will figure it out eventually. That's when we capitalize on **his or her** idea as a catalyst in the classroom learning community. This is how a teacher's guidance and feedback interacts with youngsters' developing understandings to create learning, in this case for learners to notice that interesting sentences can be both compound and complex. When there is one example on the board, the rest will come in bunches. They won't come from everyone, of course. Discovery almost never comes all at once by everyone on the same terms. Remember, this is only the third Wednesday in October of the fourth grade. There's tomorrow, and the session only takes three to five minutes.

Once there is one such sentence in the room, promote more, not as homework for which a third of the class must depend on a mother or older brother for the answer, but as fluency. Students write them on 4 x 6 cards, and the teacher posts them on the Best Effort Board as fast as they come in, all spelled properly and punctuated precisely, of course. And in the observational essay they are writing this week, encourage those who can to include at least one compound–complex sentence, properly punctuated, of course.

But what about those seemingly endless strings of language that are sometimes even overlong to be called run-ons and that come in every day?

**I remember how we went to the beach in the
summer and it was really cold and we went
swimming anyway and we got so cold
our lips turned blue for over an hour.**

Write one on the board. Remind them of compound sentences, complex sentences, and compound–complex sentences. "How can we make a compound–complex sentence out of Marisa's writing?" Use students' current understandings as a foundation on which to extend their learning. Combining their ideas and the teacher's leadership, they come up with a new construction.

**Even though it was cold at the beach that day, we
went swimming anyway, and we got so cold
that our lips turned blue for over an hour.**

Writing Compound–Complex Sentences

Write a simple sentence about a pet dog.

_____

_____

_____

Write a compound sentence about a pet dog.

_____

_____

_____

Write a complex sentence about a pet dog.

_____

_____

_____

Think of a way to write a compound–complex sentence about a pet dog.

_____

_____

_____

Write a compound sentence about something that has happened to you recently that made you feel good.

_____

_____

_____

Think of an introductory clause that you could add to the compound sentence you wrote above. That would make a compound–complex sentence. Write the compound–complex sentence.

_____

_____

_____

Write a compound–complex sentence that begins with the word *although*.

_____

_____

_____

Write a compound–complex sentence that could be the first sentence in a story in which one of the characters will find a lost puppy wandering down a sidewalk.

_____

_____

_____

(Example: Because it was an hour before school started, Jana walked slowly down the sidewalk, and she was surprised to see a small black and white puppy running toward her.)

Tips for Teachers

1. Always assume that the young writers in the room **can** understand what you are asking them to do.
2. Always assume, as well, that if they don't **do** what you are directing, it's because they don't understand what you're asking (it may be that the question isn't clear), they don't know how to do it (it may be that they haven't had experience with the activity), or they don't want to. Most children don't decide that they don't want to do something unless they've found out that they don't understand what it is or that they don't know how.
3. This is an activity that can take a very long time and will move along in small pieces. If you begin early in the fourth grade, it may be the end of the fourth grade before very many of the children can write these sentences and well into the fifth before the rest can do it.
4. The eleven children in the room for whom English is a new language are not, merely because of their native language, unable to write these and other sentences.
5. Always try to make a writing lesson as auditory as possible. That means young writers must read their work aloud, and the teacher must repeat as much as possible to reinforce the sound.
6. Once a punctuation convention has been taught, hold students responsible, in an age-appropriate manner, for using it properly thereafter (see Chapter 1 for ideas about age-appropriate instruction).

LESSON 17: COMMAS TO SET OFF PARENTHETICAL EXPRESSIONS

The Convention

Use commas to set off from the rest of the sentence a word or word group added to the sentence in order to add emphasis to or clarify a main point in the larger sentence.

Student Writing Samples (not edited for spelling)

1. I love chicken, ecpesheley hot and crispy chicken. [Third Grader]
2. I could do a lot of things, like play my Sega game, except I can't go out alone. [Third Grader]
3. I think it would be a place with lots of wildlife, where I could see whatever I want to see, all there on desplay for all to see. [Sixth Grader]
4. There is another place that is very much fun to go that's called Parque de las Palomas, meaning Pigeon Park, where there are a whole bunch of pigeons. [Sixth Grader]
5. It's like my other house, but not just like it, in Mexico. [Sixth Grader]

Explanation

By definition, **parenthetical** means to amplify or to add emphasis. A parenthetical expression is a remark or passage that departs from or adds to the main point of the sentence. It is an interlude, or perhaps a digression, that clarifies or emphasizes a point. In the immediately preceding sentence, *or perhaps a digression* is a parenthetical expression because, in fact, it does add emphasis to the main idea as an embellishment on the main point. (*In fact* is also parenthetical.) Whenever there is a parenthetical expression, it is enclosed with commas, one after the word just before the word or phrase begins and one at the end.

Parenthetical expressions are extra words or phrases, where the emphasis is on the word *extra*, because were the parenthetical expression (*or perhaps a digression*) removed, there would be no violence done to the sentence. In that previous sentence, **incidentally,** the parenthetical expression, *where the emphasis is on the word extra*, adds to, clarifies, and emphasizes the point of the sentence; but its removal would do no damage to the integrity of the sentence. Read the sentence without the parenthetical expression. Read the second sentence in this paragraph without the parenthetical word *incidentally*. The second sentence in this paragraph also works just fine without the parenthetical expression (word). And notice that each parenthetical expression is separated from the rest of the sentence with commas.

So why is *incidentally* added to the sentence in the first place if it only provides emphasis, and can be removed without changing the meaning of the sentence? Well, we wanted to make the reader pause just a count before the crux of the sentence came along. The comma, of course, will make something of a pause, but we wanted the pause to be a little longer. We wanted an introduction. The parenthetical expression is a small toot on a horn as in "ta da," maybe even something like a barely audible drum roll. The parenthetical word says to the reader, "Okay, you've had a chance to take a little breath. Now here comes the point."

Is it true that if we had planned the sentence better, we wouldn't have to stick in a phrase along the way? Shouldn't the nouns, verbs, and basic modifiers offer as much emphasis and clarification as necessary? Look at the sentence above in which *where the emphasis is on the word extra* serves as a parenthetical expression. The sentence begins with a perfectly serviceable explanation to the effect that parenthetical expressions are extra words or phrases. The rest of the sentence is about what would (or would not) happen if the phrase were removed. That parenthetical expression adds emphasis or clarification, but its removal doesn't violate the integrity of the sentence. However, the parenthetical expression isn't just thrown in there as an afterthought or a cover for bad planning. That particular parenthetical expression is in there for a reason, and the reason is to make the meaning of the sentence clearer, **perhaps even more memorable,** certainly to draw the meaning closer to what readers already understand.

There are several kinds of parenthetical expressions, **each separated from the rest of the sentence with commas.** There are **linking** expressions that tie sentences together. Those are not, of course, the only kinds of parenthetical expressions. Notice that in the previous sentence *of course* serves to remind the reader of the sentence that came before. That's what *linking* means.

There are expressions that add emphasis. Everyone knows, **of course,** that emphasis can be critical in some writing. **In this case,** we are emphasizing that everyone knows how important emphasis is.

There are expressions that clarify by noting what something is not. If we were talking about the ability of students to write, **not read,** this would be a different explanation. The clarification of what we are talking about sometimes comes in the form of what we are not talking about.

There are *echo questions.* We all know, **don't we,** that good writers can all read? There are times when we place adjectives in a different order for the purpose of emphasis. We could write about the hungry and watchful wolves, or we could write about the wolves, **hungry and watchful.**

Clearly, then, there are several kinds of parenthetical expressions, each enclosed with commas, and in every case included to make a point, to emphasize a point, to clarify, or to elaborate. The sentence-writing lesson here focuses on learning how to recognize and use parenthetical expressions to make writing more mature. The punctuation lesson involves learning how to use commas to show readers where the parenthetical expression is in the sentence. Writing the sentence is important. Punctuating it is important, as well.

Finally, in many explanations of parenthetical expressions, there is included a related sort of clarifying expression also known as the **appositive.** While the appositive is also a parenthetical expression, it appears as a separate lesson in this book because its function is very specific. Teachers who want to treat the two together, however, should not hesitate, for they are sufficiently related to combine, especially for younger children. Older students, upper elementary and middle level, are in a better position to understand the difference between the two.

Examples of Commas That Set Off Parenthetical Expressions in Sentences

> Bilbo, at home in the woods, is one of the main characters in *The Hobbit.*
> The boa constrictor slithered down the trunk, not afraid of anything, toward the sleeping man.
> Piglet came a little closer, looking to see what was happening, and saw Eeyore with three sticks.

Teaching Young Writers about Parenthetical Expressions in Sentences

It is difficult to identify by grade level the punctuation lesson for writing parenthetical expressions; for some quite young children write sentences that need the punctuation lesson, while much older youth and adults, **for that matter,** never use such expressions when they write. When young writers of any age begin to write parenthetical expressions in their sentences, they should be helped to understand what they are writing and to handle it mechanically, which is to say to punctuate it when they write it. In addition, it may be useful toward the end of the intermediate grades (grades four and five) to conduct a series of whole-class lessons, not to ensure that everyone in the class produces sentences that contain parenthetical expressions by Friday, but to ensure that everyone knows what they look like, what they sound like, what parenthetical expressions will do for them as writers, and how to punctuate such a sentence properly. That way, the writing device is available to anyone who finds it useful or appealing. In fact, it is possible to write English very well without ever using a parenthetical expression, so such a device ought not be an exit competency in the writing or larger language arts program.

I would like to know the President of the United States because he is our president, and that in itself makes him important to know.

Fifth-grade Dan wrote that sentence in a short essay titled "A Person I Would Like to Know." There were two stages in a short conference with Dan. First, Dan needed to be conscious of what he did, so we asked him about that *in itself* business. We asked why he put it in the sentence. He said it just seemed right because being a president would be a good enough reason to know a person. We agreed, but, we asked, why didn't he write it the way he said it? Why did he stick in that *in itself* in the middle of the sentence? Dan was adamant. He put it in because it sounded right.

Who knows where he got the sound? There are all kinds of language sounds in the world where eleven-year-old Dan lives. He just knows about the sound, and it makes sense to him. He also understands it because he described it accurately when he was first asked about it. We told him that "the expression 'in itself' is parenthetical to the rest of the sentence, and that's why it's called a parenthetical expression." Those were the words we used in the conference, not because we wanted to scare Dan with academic terminology, but because we wanted to give him the appropriate terminology.

Then we defined the word *parenthetical* as "extra," used to **make meaning more clear** or to **emphasize** something. "What are you trying to make clearer or to emphasize, Dan?" He answered directly and with confidence when he said that he'd already told us that being president is enough reason to want to know someone. Then we told him that his parenthetical expression must be enclosed with commas. We told him in the same way we tell everyone about punctuation conventions. "It's one of the things people who read and write English have agreed on." Dan put commas around his parenthetical expression. (He also had written a compound sentence, which he punctuated properly.)

We asked him to write another sentence that contains a parenthetical expression. It was just short of five minutes when he came back and showed the result of his labor.

**The fact that owls eat mice is, by itself,
a reason to protect them.**

He had the **by itself/in itself** expression nailed down. One of his table mates was right behind him with her turn. She handed us her stab at parenthetical expressions.

**River Road is, the best street in town,
is being tarred over.**

"What is River Road?" we asked Cherista. She said that it's the best street in town. We told her she had it just about right. We suggested she scratch out that first *is*. Then we asked that she read the sentence aloud to us. We asked that she read the sentence without *the best street in town*. We showed her that the sentence worked without the phrase when she took out that first *is*, but it wouldn't work if she left it her way. She went back to her seat and furiously wrote another.

**West Fourth Street, on the West End
of town, goes to the airport.**

The following morning we told the class that Cherista and Dan had written some interesting sentences. We asked Dan to read aloud his sentence that contained a parenthetical expression and to read the commas when he got to them. We asked Cherista to read hers the same way. We wrote the sentences on the board as Dan and Cherista read. We explained that the phrases in between the commas were called **parenthetical expressions**, that they help to make the sentence clearer, and that they are set off with commas. Then we risked a prompt and asked the class to write: "Write a sentence that begins with *My room* and is followed with a parenthetical expression." The first three sentences volunteered, in order, were as follows:

**My room, down the hall from my parents'
room, is the best room in my house.
My room, is big and has a great bedspread.
My room has red carpet, even in the
closet, that feels good on my feet.**

We wrote all three sentences on the board. We inquired whether the first sentence contained a parenthetical expression. We asked the young writer who said there is one to read the sentence without the parenthetical expression. We asked if the sentence worked without the parenthetical expression. The class agreed that it did. We went to the third sentence and went through the same scenario. Then we went to the second sentence. The absence of a parenthetical expression was obvious, partly because there was no way to find a discrete phrase such as those in the other two sentences and partly because there was no way to read the sentence while leaving a phrase out.

Fifth-grade Ruben raised his hand. He said he knew how to make the phrase. We invited him to write it on the board.

**My room has a bed, and a great bedspread,
in the corner near the closet.**

We asked Ruben how he did that. He said he looked at the other sentences and saw how the middle part just kind of told the reader something more, so he put in something that did that. "And you put commas around it?" we asked. "Read your sentence without the parenthetical expression," we directed. He did; we asked if the sentence still worked, and he said it did. So we asked what the parenthetical expression did for the sentence if it works without the phrase. "It tells more about the bed," Ruben said. We asked Carla what the parenthetical expression did in her sentence about the best room in the house. She knew immediately: it tells where the room is.

For a week in that fifth grade we "played around" with parenthetical expressions, always calling attention to the fact that when there is one, it has to have a comma at both ends. We suggested that when they were writing and found a situation in which a parenthetical expression might make a sentence work better, they should use one and remember to use the commas properly. The immediate result was that there were lots of parenthetical expressions in their writing for several weeks. Then they dropped off to a periodic trickle that lasted, the teacher informed us, all year. There were, then, two results of the week of informal instruction.

1. All of the fifth graders in that room were introduced to the parenthetical expression—what it looks like, what it sounds like, how it works, and how it's punctuated.
2. Several fifth graders in that room were ready to master the form and use it when they wrote.

In the case of a construction without which writers can write quite well forever, this lesson offers one effective way to handle instruction. Terminal marks, on the other hand, are always necessary, as are apostrophes in singular and plural possessives. Both terminal marks and apostrophes occur so frequently in everyday writing that everyone needs to learn and use them. Commas in parenthetical expressions are also necessary, but the frequency of parenthetical expressions is such that making youngsters aware of the construction and providing reminders along the way are sufficient for instruction.

Writing Sentences with Parenthetical Expressions

1. Read the sentence in the box and think how it could be rewritten to include a parenthetical expression.

> **The birds flew overhead on their way south.**

_____

_____

2. Using *pet* as the main idea, think of a way to write a sentence that contains a parenthetical expression.

_____

_____

3. Marcy and Clifford skipped down the street. They came on a lost kitten. Think of a sentence that describes, with a parenthetical expression, the lost kitten. Remember the commas on each side of the parenthetical expression.

_____

4. Write a sentence in which the main idea is an old man walking on a rainy day. Include a parenthetical expression in your sentence.

_____

5. Think of a way to complete the following sentence with the parenthetical expression already written.

_____, even with the lights out, _____.

6. Think of a way to complete the following sentence by writing a parenthetical expression in the space.

Down at the river, _____, there is a rope for swinging out over the water.

7. Write a sentence that contains a parenthetical expression. Remember, there are commas on both sides of a parenthetical expression.

_____

_____

Tips for Teachers

1. Remember that it is not necessary for every young writer to use parenthetical expressions.
2. It is important to teach young writers how to punctuate parenthetical expressions when they begin to use the form in their writing.
3. It is likely that a whole-class lesson will bring several young writers into the parenthetical expression "fold."

It is unlikely that whole-class instruction will ever bring everyone in the class into the parenthetical expression "fold."

4. The essential message for young writers at any age is: **If you have the need for parenthetical expressions in your writing, you also have a responsibility to punctuate them properly.**

LESSON 18: DASHES AND PARENTHESES TO SET OFF PARENTHETICAL EXPRESSIONS

The Conventions

Dashes are used to set off appositives, lists, and explanations. Dashes are longer lines (—) than are hyphens (-), or two keyboard strokes in a row (- -). Parentheses are used to enclose letters or numbers that label items in a list and to enclose examples and other extra information that would interrupt the flow or sequence of ideas in a sentence. The reference above to hyphens is simply to discriminate between hyphen and dash. This lesson is not about writing with hyphens.

Student Writing Samples (not edited for spelling)

1. I was rellay wored (the dog wet on the florr) becuase my day gets mad. [Third Grader]
2. Singing is what I like to do the most in my private place—my room. [Sixth Grader]
3. The only thing I don't like is when I am airbrushing too log, my compressor (the machine that throws air) gets very very hot, and I have to stop while it cools down. [Sixth Grader]
4. My most favorite song of all is from Elvis (It's an oldie). [Sixth Grader]
5. The excitement of the people screeming in the waves—you can just feel it. [Sixth Grader]

Explanation

Dashes and parentheses are used to set off information **within a sentence.** Sometimes the information is extra and may interrupt the flow of the sentence. But in all cases, dashes and parentheses signal the reader that there is an explanation or clarification of some sort.

Dashes are used to signal appositives, lists, and explanations. **There is only one punctuation mark that is formed by making a horizontal line within a sentence—the dash.** In the previous sentence, **the dash is used to signal an appositive—the piece of language that identifies or explains what came before it in the sentence.** The sentence was about a punctuation mark that looks like a horizontal line; the punctuation mark (dash) signaled the reader that the label for the mark (the dash) was to follow. An appositive is an explanation in a sentence about the governor, **Mark Hughes.** Readers will notice that appositives are also set off with commas (see Lesson 13). In less formal writing, the dash will set off appositives, as well.

Dashes also introduce lists. **The book we all read was filled with allusions to wealth—jewels, cars, houses, and the woman's mink boa.** Of course, lists are also introduced by the colon, but writers may use the dash in less formal writing. Do we see a pattern forming here? The dash appears to be a punctuation mark reserved for less formal writing. So far, there is nothing the dash will do that isn't done as well, and more formally, with other punctuation marks.

Then there is using a dash to set off an explanation. **There's always a reason why punctuation is used—to signal meaning.** That's an explanation. The part of the sentence that follows the dash explains the part of the sentence that comes before the dash. In this case, the dash is the appropriate punctuation mark to set off the explanation. In fact, a comma *could* separate the two portions of the sentence, but the dash is clearer, more specific.

Does it appear that these kinds of applications may not be within the range of needs of young writers? Well, that may be true. Most younger writers probably don't write well enough to need the dash and would be better served to learn how to use commas and colons properly, to say nothing of crafting sentences so that dashes aren't necessary to set off explanations that seem to be tacked onto a sentence as an afterthought. **But this book is for all kinds of classrooms—there are all kinds out there—where students may write well enough to need dashes.**

The last sentence in the previous paragraph—the one in bold-faced type—uses dashes on both ends of material that all of a sudden interrupts the flow of thought within a sentence. The interrupting material is explanatory, but it doesn't fit the sentence, so readers need to be told that it's okay to shift gears to the extra material while reading and plug it into the flow of the sentence. The first sentence in this paragraph works the same way. There is a phrase (*the one in bold-faced type*) that doesn't fit the way the sentence is crafted. But you read it anyway and made it fit the flow. You just needed a signal.

There is one other common use of dashes. **Suppose there is a parenthetical expression—a phrase that contains, perhaps, its own commas—and the only punctuation marks the writer has for parenthetical expressions is the comma.** Remember that the reason for punctuation marks is to signal meaning clarification to the reader. If the parenthetical expression in the second sentence of this paragraph were punctuated only with commas, how would the reader know where the parenthetical expression ended? You see, if the parenthetical expression contains its own commas, and, in addition, commas set the parenthetical expression off from the rest of the sentence, there are four commas, and the reader may have to read it at least twice to figure it out. By using dashes to set off the parenthetical expression, we eliminate the confusion.

There are, then, several uses for the dash, two of which are alternatives to using commas—setting off appositives and introducing lists. The other two uses are setting off certain kinds of explanations and setting off parenthetical expressions that contain their own commas.

Young writers, and some writers who are not so young, confuse readers by making their hyphen and the dash in the same way. It may seem a small matter-this dash-making thing-but it can be important if the two marks are mistaken because they look the same. Notice the sentence just before this one. Notice that the dashes are written like hyphens. The hyphen suggests a completely different relationship between words and ideas. With hyphens, it appears that *matter-this, dash-making,* and *thing-but* somehow go together, when, in fact, this is the case only with the second one, *dash-making*. The other two marks should be dashes, not hyphens. Written properly, there is a difference between the two punctuation marks. The difference helps readers avoid confusion.

Young writers often use parentheses (who knows how they get the idea) in their writing. The little arcs set off extra information or commentary that doesn't fit into the flow of the sentence. The opening sentence in this paragraph is such a sentence. Notice that the material within the parentheses is the writer's commentary about the sentence, but it doesn't fit the sequence of the sentence. So the writer puts parentheses around the verbal aside and just goes on. Young writers need to know that there are certain circumstances under which parentheses are used properly. That's one of them.

The other one occurs when the writer wants to make a list and also wants to enumerate the items on the list. **The circumstances under which parentheses are used include (1) enclosing supplementary information, (2) setting off numbers and letters that are used to enumerate items on a list, and (3) enclosing dates that clarify when someone lived or when something happened.** In that sentence, parentheses are used to set off the enumeration of the items on the list.

Examples of Dashes and Parentheses in Sentences

Adventure, comedy, and drama—all are there in *Harris and Me.*

The Giver is a book which takes place in the future—we're not sure when—and describes an unusual way of living.

Gary Paulsen is a distinguished author and—it's obvious from his writing skill, why—*National Geographic* called him and asked where Brian lived.

Teaching Young Writers about Dashes and Parentheses

The uses of dashes and parentheses are among the less frequent punctuation requirements in the elementary and middle school. Given the writing development of students in the six- to fourteen-year range, demand for the two marks will be, at best, small. However, the marks do occur occasionally.

Nine-year-old Damian wrote an autobiographical incident that contained the following sentence.

I was in the kitchen—having supper when the dog barked real loud.

In conference, the teacher asked Damian to read the sentence aloud. "What's this?" the teacher asked while pointing to the dash.

"It's a dash. I saw it in my book."

"Read the sentence without the dash," the teacher directed. Damian read. "The sentence works without the dash. Tell me the reason why you put the dash in there."

"It's because I wanted to say that's why I was in the kitchen. It's like it's a special reason for why I was in the kitchen, so that's why I put in the dash, so it would show the special reason for being there."

The fact is that the dash *does* set off pieces of sentences that are special, or extra. Damian's reason is a good one. It's just that he didn't finish the job. The teacher showed Damian that his reason for using a dash required still another dash. If he wanted to make *having dinner* the special reason for being in the kitchen, he needed to put another dash between *supper* and *when* so the sentence would look as follows.

**I was in the kitchen—having supper—
when the dog barked real loud.**

The teacher also told Damian that dashes are very special punctuation marks that writers can use for very special purposes. She wrote the following example on his paper.

**I was in the kitchen—it was dinner time—
when the dog barked real loud.**

"I want you to see how what I wrote between the dashes doesn't fit the sentence very well, Damian, so I put dashes around it. What you did isn't wrong, but what I did is a better use for dashes." Then the teacher suggested that the next time he felt he needed a dash he should check with her first so she could explain more about dashes. The teacher reported that Damian came by the very next day and asked about using a dash where a comma should be. The teacher reminded him about the comma after a long introductory phrase. That apparently satisfied Damian that commas would do most of what he wanted to do to set off special meanings in sentences.

The teacher didn't teach a lesson to the rest of the class, and dashes never came up again that year. The point of this explanation is not to avoid dashes, and it is certainly not to punish young writers for trying them. The purpose of reporting the teacher's experience is to show that there are all kinds of possibilities under which young writers will experiment with punctuation marks. It is the teacher's job to judge whether direct instruction will help everyone in the class or just the one writer who experiments. If it appears to help only the experimenter, should direct instruction clarify or should it teach for the purpose of generalizing to later writing? This teacher's judgment was for clarification on an individual basis with no intent to generalize past the next experiment. The student's inclination to experiment wasn't compromised at all.

However, there are times when direct instruction with the purpose of generalizing to subsequent independent writing is merited. More frequently used and useful than the dash are parentheses. We've found that the best circumstance in which to emphasize parentheses is in biographical writing, perhaps in the social studies context. It's the fourth grade, and the class is preparing to write biographies on individuals on whom they select to do some reading and research. One of the individuals selected by the class is W. E. B. DuBois. The teacher had written his name and the dates of his birth and death on the board. "Folks, let's begin with his life span, when he was born and when he died. How might a sentence like that read?" Several hands went up. "Dixon?"

"It could say that W. E. B. DuBois was born in 1868 and he died in 1965."

The teacher writes the sentence on the board. "That's one way to write it. Here's another way, and this is the way you see it in history books all the time."

W. E. B. DuBois (1868–1965)

"What else could we put in that sentence?" Someone calls out that he was an early civil rights leader and a founder of the NAACP. Finish the sentence on the board with that information. "Look at how much information we can get in the opening sentence of the biography when we just put the birth and death dates in—what did I do there? Does anyone know?" Ramona will know. She always does.

"It's parentses or something. I know what it is. I just can't say it."

"Parentheses is the word. Parentheses. Let me hear it." She pronounces the word properly. "Everyone say parentheses." Write the word on the board. Put it on a card on The Word Wall.

In the biographical writing thereafter, in fact in all writing that includes dates associated with a subject, use parentheses to enclose the dates. That gets young writers accustomed to using parentheses properly in a predictable and easily understood context.

The other easily understood context for parentheses, the enumeration with letters or numbers of items in sequence, is also predictable in that it works every time. Therefore, just for practice, whenever there is a need for items enumerated within a sentence, direct the use of parentheses to enclose the numbers or letters. This application occurs readily in science writing in which various kinds of simple machines, such as (1) inclined plane, (2) screw, (3) lever, and (4) pulley, help transform energy into more productive work. It also works in science when we write about the men and women, such as (1) Curie, (2) Fermi, (3) Bohr, (4) Einstein, and (5) Oppenheimer, who provided the foundation for the Manhattan Project.

There are, as well, reasons for using parentheses when writing about reasons (1) economic, (2) social, and (3) political for the American Civil War. In each of the three examples above, the enumerated items are an integral part of the sentence. If the reasons for the American Civil War are listed after a colon, they are not enumerated, so there are no parentheses. Such a sentence might read as follows. **There were three reasons for the American Civil War: political, social, and economic.** We recommend not making an issue of the difference between items in a list and items that are an integral part of the sentence, especially with young children.

Writing with Dashes and Parentheses

> ### The dog, barking loudly, kept us up all night.

1. Read the sentence in the box. Rewrite the sentence so that, instead of commas, there are dashes that set *barking loudly* apart from the rest of the sentence.

   _____

   _____

2. Write a sentence of your own that has a construction similar to the one in the box and uses dashes.

   _____

   _____

3. Write a sentence in which the main idea is a cloudy day with a storm approaching. Use the words *dark and angry* to explain something in the sentence, and set those words apart from the rest of the sentence with dashes.

   _____

   _____

4. Write a sentence in which you use a color word to explain something, and construct the sentence so that you set the color word apart from the rest of the sentence with dashes.

   _____

   _____

> ### Isaac Newton was born in 1645 and died in 1727.

5. Read the sentence about Isaac Newton. Rewrite the sentence so that the years of his birth and death are in parentheses and follow his name.

   _____

   _____

6. Write a sentence about Abraham Lincoln in which his birth and death years are in parentheses immediately following his name.

   _____

   _____

7. Write a sentence that includes three things you ate for breakfast. Put numbers in front of each of the things, and enclose the numbers in parentheses.

   _____

   _____

Tips for Teachers

1. One of the most powerful instructional procedures for dashes and parentheses is awareness—reading text that contains dashes and parentheses. Find such material for young writers to read, and call attention to the marks when they occur. In addition, be alert to the marks when they occur in whatever else young writers read during their school day.

2. Direct young writers to notice dashes and parentheses in what they read. Offer a reward (a pencil, for instance) for every five target marks they find and copy for posting in the writing center.

3. The main point of a lesson about dashes and/or parentheses is not to make students use them routinely in their writing. Indeed, most writing does not feature dashes and parentheses routinely. The main point is awareness and proper use when use is necessary.

4. Never include dash and parentheses knowledge in a test.

LESSON 19: COLONS IN SENTENCES

The Convention

The colon is used to introduce and separate. Colons clarify connections between parts of sentences. Colons have several specific introductory roles in sentences: to precede formal lists of items and to precede formal explanations and appositives. A colon may also be used to introduce a long quotation, especially if the quotation contains several sentences. Finally, a colon is used to separate hours from minutes when writing the time of day, to separate titles from subtitles, and to follow salutations (greetings) in formal letters.

Student Writing Samples (not edited for spelling)

1. They have many outside activities: flag football, wiffleball, soccer, and basketball for boys and girls. [Fourth Grader]
2. My brother takes all kind of things at college: math, litichure, sciens, and PE. [Fourth Grader]
3. My best room in the house is the kitchen because it has three things I like best: food, water, and the cat. [Fifth Grader]
4. I was born at 1:45 in the middle of the night. [Fifth Grader]
5. The name of my book is *Social Studies for Living: Fifth Grade*. [Fifth Grader]

Explanation

The two roles, to introduce and to separate, are instructive when thinking about colons. **The colon introduces three kinds of sentence parts: formal lists, formal explanations, and long quotations.** The preceding sentence contains proper use of a colon to introduce a list. There are three items in the list, and the portion of the sentence that comes before the colon can stand alone as a sentence. If the list is an integral part of a sentence, do not use a colon. A colon introduces formal lists, formal explanations, and long quotations.

This business of whether or not a list is part of the sentence (do not use a colon) or added on to the sentence (use a colon) is clarified after lots of exposure. Exposure (practice) leads to sufficiency.

Colons also have several separation roles. A colon separates the hours from the minutes in the time of day (12:30 P.M.). A colon is also used to separate the greeting (salutation) from the body of the formal letter (Dear Ms. Greene:). Finally, a colon separates subtitles from titles (*Punctuation in Writing: Instructional Devices*).

That makes three introductory roles and three separation roles for the colon. We need to pay attention, therefore, to six routine uses for colons. There are a few others, such as separating the numbers in ratios (4:1) and separating chapter from verse in biblical references (20: 1–17), but those applications are far less frequent.

Examples of Colons in Sentences

The Red Pony included several characters: Billy Buck, Jody, Carl Tifflin, and Gabilan (the pony).

There are several poems in *The New Kid on the Block* that name characters: "Clara Cleech," "Drumpp the Grump," and "Granny Grizer."

Maniac did three seemingly impossible things: untangled Cobble's Knot, kicked the football, and braved Finsterwald's backyard.

Teaching Young Writers about Using Colons in Sentences

"My friends, I want you to think of at least three things you study in school that you enjoy, and I want you to think of a sentence that contains the areas of study and the fact that you enjoy them. Think now, and raise your hand when you have a sentence written in your head." (The business of writing sentences in your head is part of every lesson, for the oral part of the writing program is basic to how we teach. We always remind students at all levels that writing is something that goes on in your head; then you either push it out of your mouth or you push it out of your pencil, but it goes on in your head. It doesn't take long for students to realize that when they are directed to think of a sentence, they have a very short time to think, and they can write that sentence in their head in seconds.)

Sam's sentence tells that he likes reading, language, and science the best. Write his sentence on the board.

I like reading, language, and science the best.

"Folks, I want us all to notice another way to write Sam's sentence so it will have the same ideas in it. Watch what I do here."

I like three things best in school

Rebecca's hand is up before you turn around. "You don't have what he likes. It isn't finished." Ask what she suggests. "Put a comma and then reading, language, and science."

"That's not a bad idea, Rebecca. I wonder if there's another idea out there. Is there any other punctuation mark we could use right there before we write the reading, language, and science?"

If there has already been an awareness lesson on dashes, someone will remember. Acknowledge the good memory and tell him that the dash will work even better than the comma, but we learned that the dash is a very informal way to write. "Is there anything else you may have seen in your reading that will introduce the list?" If Gisele is in the class, she'll suggest something about that thing with two dots. If she isn't in your class, put the colon out there for their consideration. Someone will say that he's seen that before.

"It's a colon. It is a punctuation mark that introduces a list." In fact, a colon introduces a list when the text that comes before (*I like three things best in school*) will stand alone, will behave as a sentence behaves, is a sentence sound, and so forth. If the text that comes before does not stand alone, the colon is *not* used. By introducing the colon as shown in the scenario above, the construction of the sentence itself illustrates the circumstance in which the punctuation mark is used. Set up examples with introductory text that stands alone. Then that becomes the circumstance for which youngsters see the colon serving a need, and there is

no need to make an issue of a list that is an integral part of the sentence **(Of the subjects in school I like best, reading, language, and science are the highest.).**

In exactly the same way as in the case of introducing lists, the colon introduces explanations. Given introductory text that will stand alone **(The coach was interested in only one outcome at practice),** there is often an explanation **(making sure her players were ready).** The whole sentence, then, reads as text that will stand alone, colon, and explanation.

The coach was interested in only one outcome at practice: making sure her players were ready.

Then there is the matter of the colon being used to introduce a long quotation, especially if the quotation contains more than one sentence. In the fifth or sixth grade there is some possibility that young writers might get themselves involved with a report of information, for example, about humans' irrational fear of wolves. The student will read Farley Mowat's classic *Never Cry Wolf* and quote from the final chapter.

His pain was shown when he realized what he might have done: "I sat down on a stone and shakily lit a cigarette, becoming aware as I did so that I was no longer frightened. Instead an irrational rage possessed me. If I had had my rifle I believe I might have reacted in brute fury and tried to kill both wolves."

We strongly recommend against teaching the above colon application out of context. When the situation (report of information, biography, and so forth) occurs, the colon is the solution to the problem. Without the situation, the colon has no role.

There are, however, two high-frequency roles for the colon, and those should be taught clearly when the situation comes up. Writing the time of day comes up early in school, perhaps as early as the first or second grade. Here's a scenario: During oral language time first thing in the morning during the second grade, when there are morning greetings, the calendar is upgraded, and three youngsters get to share something that happened recently that made them feel good. The teacher can make note of the time of day and put it in written context. "Yes Mario, it is nine fifteen. Let me show you how that can be written." Write 9:15 A.M. (The abbreviation has been taught several weeks ago.) Call attention to the colon. Call it by name and tell the children that they will use a colon for other reasons as they get older. Do the time of day tomorrow, and the next day. After several times, call on the children to write the time of day on the board. It becomes routine, habitual, and it will be easy to make the transition to their writing the first time the need pops up. "Well Sandie, you remember how we do it in our morning exercises. Do it the same way on your paper."

Then when it comes time to write formal (business) letters, put the colon after the salutation (greeting). They will know what it looks like from the time-of-day activity in the morning. Capitalize on their prior knowledge.

That the colon is used to separate subtitles from titles might be useful when they write bibliographic entries in their term papers, but there they only have to copy from the original source to get it right. If they have to *write*, rather than copy, a title separated from its subtitle with a colon, it will probably be their own title and subtitle. People who write well enough to need a title and subtitle probably know how to use a colon, or they have an editor.

Writing with Colons in Sentences

1. Use numbers and the right abbreviation to write *two fifteen in the afternoon* in the space. _____ Write a sentence that contains the time of day that you wrote in the space.

   _____

   _____

2. Write a sentence that tells what time of day you usually have dinner or supper. When you write the time of day, use numbers and the right abbreviation.

   _____

   _____

3. Think of a way to finish the sentence in the box.

My teacher has a reason for teaching about punctuation

   The text in the box introduces the teacher's reason for teaching punctuation. Think about what that reason might be. In the space below, write the introduction from the box and the reason. Be sure to use a colon in your sentence.

   _____

   _____

4. Write a sentence similar to the one in Exercise 3 above, but make the main idea something about caring for animals. Remember the colon.

   _____

   _____

5. The sentence in the box contains a list of three things Amy likes to eat for breakfast.

I like to eat cereal, toast, and fruit for breakfast.

   Rewrite Amy's sentence so the three breakfast foods are in a list at the end of the sentence. Remember that a colon is used to introduce the list.

   _____

   _____

6. Write a sentence in which the main idea is some things you like about sports. Write the sentence the way you wrote in Exercise 5 above. Make the sentence have a colon that introduces a list at the end.

   _____

   _____

Tips for Teachers

1. Remember, most writers can write most of what they have to write for most of their lives without ever using a colon. Writers can write out the time of day and weave lists into their sentences. Nevertheless, it is a useful mark and should be part of the response to situations young writers meet in their daily writing.

2. Use context for all colon instruction. Bring it up when the children have to write the time of day with numbers, when they have to write formal (business) letters, and when they have to set up long quotations in their term papers. Otherwise, use it to answer young writers' questions about how to solve certain problems when they appear.

LESSON 20: SEMICOLONS IN SENTENCES

The Convention

Semicolons are used to mark major breaks in sentences. They often serve similar functions as commas; but they are more powerful, more pronounced in signaling the pause in sentence flow. Of the several uses of semicolons, four are germane to this book.

- Semicolons are used in compound sentences in which independent clauses are *not* joined by a coordinating conjunction, especially if the clauses themselves have commas in them.
- In addition, if the independent clauses *are* joined by a coordinating conjunction (see Lesson 7 on Commas in Compound Sentences) and the independent clauses contain commas, a semicolon may be used before the coordinating conjunction.
- Two independent clauses may be separated, as well, by connecting words such as *accordingly, however, therefore,* and *then,* in which case the semicolon comes before the connecting word.
- Semicolons are also used to separate items in a series when the items themselves contain commas.

It is apparent that semicolons are used mainly to promote clarity.

Student Writing Samples (not edited for spelling)

1. I'm at Sea World when I see the whales; they make me feel so tiny. [Fifth Grader]
2. I like being there; everybody is nice to me. [Sixth Grader]
3. It snows really hard there; the weather is bad almost all the time. [Sixth Grader]
4. It's really not a beach; it's an island, a really small island with two palm trees, and I'm listening to music and drinking out of a coconut. [Sixth Grader]

5. The baseball stadium is like another world; you can shout or jump or do whatever you want. [Sixth Grader]

Explanation

As indicated in the statement of the convention, there are four routine ways in which semicolons can be used in the sort of writing young writers are likely to read, understand, and write themselves. Each of the uses of semicolons exists for the purpose of ensuring clarity.

The first application of the semicolon occurs when a writer wants to put together two sentences in order to signal a sense of closely related meaning.

It's as though there are two sentences which belong in one; the semicolon joins them.

In the example, the two sentences (independent clauses) have separate but very closely related meanings. A comma could join them if the writer had the right coordinating conjunction, but what conjunction? Not *and* because the two clauses don't have an additive connection. Not *so* because the second clause doesn't follow necessarily from the first. Not *but* because the second clause isn't an alternative to the first. There aren't any coordinating conjunctions that will effectively join the two clauses. Still, they are closely related, and the writer wants them together. The semicolon joins them properly without making the sentence look like a run-on or an awkward comma splice.

There are also sentences in which there are two independent clauses, or simple sentences, and one or the other contains its own commas; and joining them requires a semicolon for clarity. Notice in the immediately preceding sentence that there is an opening independent clause about clauses that contain their own commas. That opening clause does, in fact, contain two commas. If the two independent clauses are not separated with a semicolon, the more definite break between them might not be apparent. The semicolon can signal the break, while at the same time indicating that the independent clauses are related.

There are also independent clauses that are joined by words that show their connection; therefore, a semicolon can be used before the joining word to highlight the connection. In the previous sentence, there are two independent clauses, and the second one follows directly from the first. The connecting word is called a **conjunctive adverb.** Conjunctive adverbs include such words and phrases as *accordingly, furthermore, in addition to, on the contrary, therefore, however, moreover, thus, hence,* and *indeed.* When a writer wants to connect independent clauses with a conjunctive adverb, (s)he can make the connection with a semicolon, then the connecting word. The connecting word between the two independent clauses helps to clarify the nature of the relationship between the two clauses. (A period may also be used after the first independent clause and before the conjunctive adverb. Writers choose the semicolon when they want to highlight the relatedness of the two clauses.)

The fourth common use for a semicolon is also to ensure clarity. If there are items in a series in the sentence and the items contain their own commas, semicolons are used to separate the items in the series. Here's an example:

> **Mrs. Romero, the principal of our school; Mr. Lake, my English teacher; Mr. Rhodes, the art teacher; and Mrs. Jackson, the band teacher, performed a hilarious skit at the spring talent show.**

Notice the commas. They separate the names from the explanations (appositives). Notice also the semicolons that follow the explanations in the first three items in the series. If commas (instead of semicolons) were used between the items, which themselves contain commas, a reader might find the sentence confusing. The semicolon, again, serves the need for clarity.

Examples of Semicolons in Sentences

> Beezus and Ramona are sisters; Henry Huggins has no sisters.
> The Giver helped Jonas and Gabriel to escape their fated lives; but before he did, he cautioned Jonas about the possible risks he was taking.
> Mary was very lonely; the secret garden changed that.

> Mae Tuck said that there was plenty of room; the loft was cluttered, but there were two mattresses on the floor.

Teaching Young Writers about Semicolons

It is almost a cliché to say that when semicolons come up in the fifth-grade language arts book (or the fourth or the sixth), the result is a slew of subsequent papers with semicolons all over them, arranged seemingly at random or even in interesting designs around the page. The fact is that writers use semicolons sparingly because the need is spare. After all, semicolons serve the need to clarify potentially confusing prose. Good writers tend to write so their work isn't potentially confusing. They don't often find it necessary to rescue potentially confusing writing with a punctuation mark; and when they do use a semicolon, it's not to rescue but to clarify mature and, perhaps, complex prose. The reason why broad semicolon instruction doesn't work so well in the fifth grade is because most fifth graders don't compose the mature complexity that semicolons can clarify.

That said, remember that punctuation marks should be taught in the context of need. If a third grader writes prose that demands a semicolon, teach the semicolon to that third grader. It is your authors' experience that for most young writers there is little need for semicolons throughout the elementary school years. However, should the need arise for broad, or whole-class, instruction, it is important to begin, as we have discussed before, with the concept of clarity in writing. Write a sentence on the board.

> **They shouldn't have gone there they should have stayed with the group.**

Solicit someone to read the text aloud. Inquire how the text **could** (note the word) be punctuated. The owner of the first hand will suggest a period at the end of the first sentence (clause) so the piece reads as two sentences. "That will work, Randall. What can we do if we want the whole piece of language to be in one sentence?"

They will probably try to make a compound sentence by inserting conjunctions. But notice what happens with the most common conjunctions. Words such as *and* or *but* and *yet* will tie the two clauses together, but those words don't work properly because they compromise the meaning. Reinforce the student who suggests a complex sentence rewrite: **Because they should have stayed with the group, they shouldn't have gone over there.** "That's a terrific idea, Carlos, but that changes the meaning of the sentence a bit.

"I have another idea, and it's something you've seen before. Look." That's when you put the semicolon between *there* and *they.* Tell them that the semicolon is a more powerful pause than a comma, but it isn't so powerful that it makes a stop as a period does. We use the semicolon when there are two sentences (**clauses,** if the word has clear meaning in your room) that closely and clearly follow one another and are so tied to one another that they just beg to be in the same sentence.

Be prepared to offer a second example; images of language that contain semicolons are important for awareness. Write the second example on the board.

Tell the children about the trip they will be excited to hear about it.

Hands shoot up, for having just seen how the semicolon works, they see immediately where the mark fits in this example. "Justin?" He tells you to put a semicolon between *trip* and *they.* Put it in there, and solicit readers. Then, it's time for them to write. Remember, this is for writing, not editing. Lessons designed for writing rarely work if students don't write with the content of the lessons. Direct everyone to copy the first sentence on their paper. Direct them to copy the second example on their paper. Then direct them to select either the first or the second sentence and write one just like the one they selected except for one or two small changes. Give them an example. "You could write a sentence just like the second sentence on the board except that you could change *children* to *boys; that* would be one small change."

Listen to several sentences. Require that they call the semicolon when it appears in their sentence. Write some of their sentences on the board. Tell them they will be paying lots of attention to semicolons during the next weeks by noticing them in their reading and trying them in their writing. Direct them to notice how hard it is to find semicolons in their reading. **It is important to enter the world of semicolon application slowly, moving through stages of reading, copying, noticing,** and **experimenting.** Over time, some young writers will begin to use semicolons properly. Many young writers will not. That is as it should be; for only a few of the children in the elementary and middle school will write the complex prose that demands semicolons.

Related to the instruction above is the second application of semicolons where there is a joining word. Call the joining words **conjunctive adverbs** if you must, but realize that you are explaining something to fifth graders that many professional writers don't fully understand. We recommend that you call them connecting words and be done with it. If necessary, show them that words such as *however, therefore, accordingly, furthermore,* and so forth don't look like *and, but, so, or, for,* and *yet* (the coordinating conjunctions). The former are preceded by semicolons when they connect independent clauses. On the other hand, the latter, coordinating conjunctions, are used in compound sentences and are usually preceded by commas.

There is a slight complication here, and it represents a third use for semicolons. It is important to note that when compound sentences are joined by coordinating conjunctions and when the independent clauses contain commas, we often use a semicolon, not a comma in front of the joining word. Show youngsters an example such as the following. Begin with a rather straightforward compound sentence.

I like pizza, but my brother doesn't.

Youngsters should be able to talk about what makes this a compound sentence (two independent clauses, or sentences, joined by *but*). Then, give them another example.

I like pizza, the kind with pineapple and Canadian bacon on it, but my brother, who hates pineapple and tomatoes together, always orders a meatball sandwich.

This example is a compound sentence, too. Ask youngsters how they know that it's compound. Someone will likely say it has the word *but* and that there are sentences on both sides of it. This may not be as clear, however, as it was in the first example about pizza. The extra commas, which offset parenthetical expressions, may cloud the issue. To ensure that the sentence reads clearly and that there is a stronger break between the two clauses, show youngsters that it is better to use a semicolon before the word *but.* Then it reads

I like pizza, the kind with pineapple and Canadian bacon on it; but my brother, who hates pineapple and tomatoes together, always orders a meatball sandwich.

Awareness and direct instruction should proceed as above with examples, copying, changing, noticing (in reading), and conversation. It is as clear in the case of compound sentences as it is with other uses of the semicolon, that most fourth, fifth, and sixth graders, to say nothing of many middle and senior high school students, simply don't have a need for semicolons in their writing. It is good for them to know about semicolons and to have studied, found, discussed, and used them; however, it is not critical that they write with them routinely.

In the fourth application of semicolons, your authors have found that there seems to be a greater need for knowledge and use. It's not uncommon for youngsters to write sentences like this:

Erik, my best friend, Bobby, my brother's best friend, and I went to magic mountain.

When that happens, there might be reader confusion about which comma does which separation. In other words, how many people went to Magic Mountain? This is when a semicolon between the items, in this case after both uses of the word *friend,* would clarify who went.

Write an example on the board.

The farmer had three cows, one calf apiece, two pigs, two babies each, and a horse, a black one with a beautiful white blaze on her face.

Then ask, "Quick now, boys and girls, how many items are in the series in the sentence?" With a couple of reads, most of the young writers will have figured out that there are three items in the series. "But it isn't fair to write so that readers have to study the writing in order to figure out what it means. So by using semicolons between the items when there are commas **within** the items, we make it clear that there are only three items in the series."

This application of semicolons seems to have the greatest utility among younger writers because it is more likely that they will write complex items in series than they will write sentences of such complexity that semicolons will solve their syntactic problems.

As you emphasize an awareness of semicolons through the children's reading, focus on two kinds of things. First, make sure young writers notice how hard it is to find semicolons in their reading. There's a message in that. Second, when semicolons do appear, notice how the punctuation mark is used. It may even be useful to have a small panel in the writing center devoted to semicolons. Fifth and sixth graders can build a bar graph to show which of the four semicolon uses is most often represented. In the noticing, they come to "see" the punctuation mark in context and build a sense of what kinds of sentences require it.

Writing with Semicolons

> **Rayford was tired when he got home. He ate dinner anyway.**

1. There are two sentences in the box. Rewrite the two sentences into one sentence that uses a semicolon and the word *however*.

   _____

   _____

2. Rewrite the two sentences in the box into one sentence that uses a comma and the word *but*.

   _____

   _____

3. Rewrite the two sentences in the box into one sentence that begins with the word *although*.

   _____

   _____

> **Rayford was very tired during dinner. He had worked very hard on his project at school.**

4. Rewrite the two sentences in the box by combining them into one sentence that uses a semicolon but not an extra word such as *however*.

   _____

   _____

5. Write a sentence of your own that requires a semicolon to connect two simple sentences or clauses.

   _____

   _____

6. Write a sentence that contains three or more items in a series, and make at least one of the items in the series contain a comma of its own. Use semicolons to separate the items in the series.

   _____

   _____

Tips for Teachers

1. Teach semicolons only because one or more young writers show that they need them. No one becomes a better writer because (s)he knows how to use semicolons.

2. When teaching semicolons, emphasize students' awareness through reading. Help students notice how practicing writers incorporate semicolons into their writing, carefully and sparingly. There's nothing wrong with teaching terms such as **conjunctive adverb,** but it's not the label that's important. It's young writers' ability to apply the connection, appropriately and correctly, that's critical. The only function of the term associated with the concept is as vocabulary to help us talk about the writing.

CHAPTER 4

CAPITALIZATION

This section contains 10 capitalization conventions. As in Chapter 3, the lessons are sequenced to begin with those which have the highest utility for primary grade children. These are the conventions which tend to appear very early in youngsters' writings, and, therefore, should be addressed early in the school curriculum in writing. Actually, nearly all of the capitalization conventions are straightforward and unambiguous. The one most likely to create problems for youngsters is found in Lesson 25 and involves the capitalization (or non-capitalization) of direction words. While not necessarily so complex, the decision to capitalize or not capitalize the first letter in a direction word may require some careful thought. Nevertheless, there is no reason not to expect that most youngsters will master all 10 capitalization conventions by the end of their elementary school years.

As with the lessons in Chapter 3, each lesson in this section involves a high degree of oral and written language participation by youngsters. The activities require that young writers construct meaning by applying what they are learning about language to their writing. In this book, they participate as active members of a learning community where awareness leads to application and, ultimately, to mastery.

TIPS FOR UNDERSTANDING AND USING THE LESSONS

- Remember, as in Chapter 3, the lessons have a general sequence, from higher to lower frequency; however, the overriding criterion for using these lessons is student need.
- Student need is determined through their authentic writing, as well as the teacher's action research.
- These lessons are about capitalization, not grade levels.
- The context for writing is students' construction of meaning in their own sentences. Remember, context is everything.
- Writing is an art and a craft. Part of the art and craft is mastering meaning markers. One of the meaning markers is capital letters.

LESSON 21: CAPITAL LETTERS TO BEGIN SENTENCES

The Convention

Use a capital letter in the first letter of the first word in every sentence. In cases where there is a sentence inside of another sentence (dialogue), the first word of the sentence is capitalized, and the first word of the direct quote is capitalized, as well.

Student Writing Samples (not edited for spelling)

1. I like to go to the cerks and play on the ridtse. [Second Grader]
2. Singing is what I like to do most of all. [Third Grader]
3. After I got there, I said, "It's pretty dark in here." [Fourth Grader]
4. It's like we used to be at home when we were all together. [Fifth Grader]
5. The plane was over the roof at my house, and I thought it might crash, but it didn't. [Fifth Grader]
6. Nobody ever thinks about that. [Sixth Grader]

Explanation

This is one of the two earliest writing conventions that we teach to young writers. One is the capital letter that begins a sentence, and the other is the end mark that finishes one. Together, they allow the youngest writer to make messages that communicate with an audience.

This convention focuses on more than the first word of a sentence, however. It is important to notice that there are sentences **inside** of sentences, and those begin with capital letters, too. Most characteristic of such sentences are those that occur in dialogue. When Susan writes her story about Jean growing up, there is a conversation between Jean and her friend, Ivy. Ivy talks to Jean in the story.

She looked back at Jean and said, "Try to feel the leaves under your feet."

The sentence begins with a capital letter in the first word (*She*), and there is a capital letter in the first word of Ivy's sentence (*Try*). Both are sentences, the larger one that includes Ivy's sentence as well as the sentence that tells what Ivy said.

Then there is another kind of sentence **inside** of a larger sentence. In this case we are not talking about sentences in dialogue, but we are referring to sentences within sentences.

It was Jefferson who was known to have said, "Those who are willing to trade a little freedom for a little security lose both and deserve neither."

Jefferson's epigram, or quotation, is a sentence, and it begins with a capital letter, just as does the sentence that contains Jefferson's quotation. The best way to understand and use this capital letter convention regarding the first word in sentences is to focus on the fact that **every** sentence begins with a capital letter, even those that occur **within** other sentences.

Examples of Capital Letters That Begin Sentences

Jonas lived a life quite different from young boys in the 20th Century.
All the children laughed when they imagined the two ants swirling around in the cup of coffee.
One of my favorite books is *Tuck Everlasting*.

Teaching Young Writers about Capital Letters to Begin Sentences

This lesson first occurs on the day when the teacher first writes a sentence on the board, or reads aloud and discusses what was read. Instruction begins as **awareness.** "Carla, you gave us the sentence that I wrote on the board. What do you notice about that sentence?" If she knows to say that there is a capital letter at the beginning of the sentence, or a period at the end, reinforce her for having noticed and having used the right words. "Yes, Carla. Good for you. The sentence does begin with a capital letter. Those are the big letters, the ones we practice writing in the morning every day. And what is that first capital letter?" Carla peers at the board and has her eyes focused on the proper letter because the teacher is pointing to it. She calls it right by saying that it's a **T.** "So it is. Good for you. It's a capital **T.**

Every time we start a new sentence, we use a capital letter.

"And why do you think we do that? Why do you suppose we always begin a sentence with a capital letter?" The line of conversation here is directed at moving toward the conclusion that we are communicating with an audience. If someone says that the capital letter shows that a new sentence is starting or that's how we know it's a new sentence, applaud the suggestion and enhance it. "Yes, of course. You see, when we write, people far away might read it and you aren't there to explain what you wrote. So we have to give our readers all kinds of signals about how our writing works. Our capital letters help our readers know where the sentences begin."

That's the right moment to ask the other question about how readers will know when our sentences are finished. If you've already taught end marks, someone will say it's a period. If you haven't, someone may refer to the period anyway. But if no one knows, that's the signal for letting children in the kindergarten or first grade in on the two basic mechanical conventions for writing sentences: capital letters that begin the sentence and end marks that end the sentence (see Chapter 3, Lesson 1).

Optimally, these two conventions would be taught at once. It is not possible to make a mechanically accurate sentence in English without these two basic meaning markers. The point here isn't that the first sentences that the very youngest writers write must be mechanically accurate. The point is that when the very youngest writers begin to write, they must begin to think about their mechanical responsibilities as they think about making meaning with strings of words. This is a developmental matter, and the development begins with learners' attention being drawn to the mechanical issue. At the earliest stages of writing, the mechanical issues are the meaning markers that tell readers when a sentence begins and when a sentence ends.

There is merit in working with the capital letters and end marks even during the initial oral language sessions in a writing program. Early on, we are asking young writers to think of sentences and "talk" what they have "written" in their heads. This is the time to direct young writers to "call" the capital letter and end mark when they "read" the sentence they have "written" in their head.

"Marco, read your sentence." Marco recites the sentence he thought of and recorded in his head. (The rain fell yesterday.) "Oh, Marco, that's a sentence. Good for you. Now, I want you to read it to us again, but this time I want you to tell us when you get to the period in the sentence. Remember, the period is the mark that comes at the end of your sentence." Marco reads again.

(The rain fell yesterday period) "Yes Marco, that's what we want.

"Boys and girls, I want you to do the same thing Marco did, except this time I want you to say the capital letter out loud. If you don't know what the letter is, you may just tell us that there is a capital letter. See, if it were me, and I didn't know what the first letter was, I could say it this way."

Capital the rain made it wet outside.

"Carrie, what is your sentence? Remember, say the capital at the beginning of the sentence." Carrie reads. (Capital rain is good for the flowers.)

As time goes on, move the children to the point at which they oralize the capital letter at the beginning of the sentence and the end mark at the end. When they read sentences from the board, call attention to the initial capital letter and the end mark. When they begin writing their own sentences, call attention to the capital letter and the end mark, as well. The key here is specific attention over time. As mechanical issues are given time and attention, they are internalized. That represents development.

And what about the young writer's basic message in the first place? Doesn't what the young writer have to say come first? The answer is that, of course, it does. And, that basic message is sharpened, made clear, because of the conventions used. We do not focus on **either** mechanical control **or** on authentic message. The authenticity of the written message is enhanced **because** it is disciplined, **because** it is mechanically accurate.

Writing with Capital Letters to Begin Sentences

1. Write a sentence that contains your name.

    _____

    _____

    Read your sentence. Does it begin with a capital letter? Look at how you wrote your name. Your name also has to begin with a capital letter.

2. Write a sentence that contains the word *rain.*

    _____

    _____

    Read what you wrote. Make sure the first word in the sentence begins with a capital letter. Make sure your sentence has a mark at the end to show that the sentence is finished.

3. Write a sentence that contains the name of one of your friends. Be sure to think about the capital letter at the beginning of the sentence and as the first letter in the name of your friend.

    _____

    _____

4. Write a sentence by writing one word in each of the blank spaces. Remember to use a capital letter in the first word.

    _____ _____ rain _____ _____

5. Write a sentence that contains the following two words: *pink* and *cloud.*

    _____

    _____

6. On each of the following five days, write one sentence that contains a color word. Make each of your sentences contain a different color word.

Tips for Teachers

1. You must decide when to initiate the sort of independent writing in Exercise 6 above. Clearly, it is not possible to begin independent writing for all first graders on the same day.

2. The youngest writers will become increasingly competent as they write **independently.** Children don't learn to write by being taught to write; they learn to write by practicing writing **under direction and in response to direct instruction.**

3. Do not despair when most of the youngest writers fail to remember the capital letter at the beginning of their sentences. There are nearly two hundred days in the first-grade year. If children write in response to direct instruction every day, and they are held responsible for paying attention to that capital letter every day, everyone will catch on sometime before the end of the school year.

LESSON 22: CAPITAL LETTERS IN NAMES

The Convention

Use a capital letter to show a **proper** name. A **proper** name belongs to someone or something. A child's name is Samuel or Sandra. The dog's name is King or Bunny. When a child is six, and calls her mother, her mother's name is Mother or Mom or Momma. Any word that reflects or takes the place of a name is capitalized.

Student Writing Samples (not edited for spelling)

1. I would sit with Jerry because he is smart, and my homework grage would get hire. [Third Grader]
2. I think Viviana is my very best friend, and she is a berry bood girl. [Third Grader]
3. There is this place in my back yard where there are lots of sticks and stuff, and my friend Pedro and I play there all the time. [Third Grader]
4. I would like Hawaii with Mom and Dad and my brother. [Third Grader]
5. My mom's pretty brown dog is named Teddy, and she also has a lot of chickens. [Fourth Grader]
6. The person that I like best of all is Mrs. Walter. [Sixth Grader]

Explanation

This convention is pretty well ingrained in the psyches of nearly everyone. Very early on everyone learns that his or her name begins with a capital letter, as does the name of everyone else. One of the first rules in school writing is that you use a capital letter when you write a **proper** name. When the rule is taught, however, almost no one knows what **proper** means, and because the rule is one of the very first ones to be taught and ought not have to be taught later, many young writers never come to understand fully what the convention, in fact, entails.

A **name** means precisely that. It means the name used to identify anyone and anything. It may be useful to use that term when teaching the convention. The term is the word *name.* The modifier *proper* doesn't add significantly to the instructive word *name.* After all, what is an improper name? The word is *name,* and by keeping it simple, we clarify enormously.

So we use a capital letter whenever we write a name. Does that mean my own name? Yep. Does it mean all my friends' names? Yep. How about people's names if I don't even know them? Yep, those too. If it's a name, use a capital letter. My dog's name is Hazel. Do I use a capital letter on my dog? Yep. It's a name for your dog, so you use a capital letter. My mom's name is Jeanne, but I don't call her that. I call her Mom. That, too. If that's the name you use for her, write it with a capital letter. Dad, too? Yep.

Examples of Capital Letters in Names

Lenny and George are memorable characters from John Steinbeck's *Of Mice and Men.*
"Hi, Mom," Jennie said as her mother walked into the room.
I named my dog Searchlight, after the dog in *Stone Fox.*

Teaching Young Writers about Capital Letters in Names

On the first day of kindergarten, or at least during the first week, teachers call students' attention to the name on the desk, on the back of the chair, on the carpet square, and at the snack table. The name is always the same. For Ruben, it always says **Ruben.** Each of the signs says **Ruben.** The word always looks the same. The letters are always the same, and the first letter is a big one which, during the first several weeks of school, we learn to call a capital letter. We read our sign each day, and as the weeks wear on, we learn to read other names. Every time we read a name, we see the capital letter, and often the teacher asks about that letter. Everyone has many opportunities to notice and name the capital letter, and everyone has an equal opportunity to notice and name capital letters on many people's names. The whole kindergarten year is an endless opportunity to notice capital letters in names.

During the kindergarten year, of course, everyone is also noticing and calling by name the capital letters that begin sentences. They are also engaged in the penmanship program in which they are writing letters, both capital and lower case, and discrimnating between the two. If nothing else with respect to capital letters goes on during the kindergarten year, the first-grade teacher will receive students fully ready to do far more than mere noticing. But, of course, there is more, for the kindergarten teacher is writing the names of story characters on the board and calling attention to the initial capital letter. As (s)he reads stories aloud and comes to characters' names, (s)he brings students up to see the names. As students read during sustained reading time, they are asked to notice the capital letters in names (and in the beginning of sentences). And for all of the children who approximate writing, there are reminders and practice sessions on capital letters in names (and in the beginning of sentences).

During the first grade, a sort of formal instruction occurs. "My friends, think of a sentence that contains the name of one of your friends." As young writers read what they have written in their heads, write several on the board and make a specific issue out of the capital letter in names. "We always write names with a capital letter, boys and girls. Always. That's what we will be doing this year. We will be practicing writing with names, and each name we write will start with a capital letter. We want to practice so much that those capital letters will become automatic so we don't even have to think about them. That's one of the things that first grade is all about."

In oral sharing, direct students to call the capital letter. "Mavis, when you read your sentence and you come to the name, tell us the capital letter." If Mavis doesn't understand right away, model. "It will sound like this. **My friend's name is capital D Dolly.** Now you do it." The model and Mavis' recitation(s) will set up the recitations for others in the class. The exercise is somewhat tedious, certainly for adults, but for the little ones it is concentration on precisely what we want them to notice and habituate. Remember, habituation or au-

tomaticity comes from practice, and practice is a deliberate, or thoughtful, instance of the target behavior. That's what we're describing here, at least during the initial learning periods.

As young writers get older, they will write thoughtful, planned sentences on paper, and their deliberate attention will be focused on the capital letters that begin sentences and represent names. They should write several every day, under teacher direction at first (guided practice) and independently later (independent practice). There might be a prompt for the first part of the day (Write a sentence that contains a good name for a pet dog.) and another for the second half of the day (Write a sentence that contains a good name for a pet cat.). The first sentence can be put in the Writing Box before morning recess, and the second sentence can be put in the Writing Box before afternoon recess. That's two independent practice sessions every day.

After a week or so, make an assignment to write a sentence for homework. Spot-read the sentences and use some of the characteristically misspelled words as spelling words.

Along the way it is important to stretch the idea of **name** to encompass a larger picture. "Beatrice, what is your mother's name?" You call on Beatrice because you know that she knows her mother's name, and she says it's Helen. "Oh yes, I know it's Helen, but what's the name you call her? What do you call your mother?" Beatrice says that she calls her mother "Mom." "Yes, now I understand. For you, your mother's name is Mom. What might be a sentence that contains the name you have for your mother?"

It's important for young writers to understand that the concept of **name** means anything within the range of names we have for anyone and anything. When Beatrice recites her sentence, almost certainly something like this (My mom is pretty), write it on the board and inquire of Beatrice, "When you talk to your mother, do you say, 'My mom'?" Beatrice may or may not know what you mean. "Well, don't you just call her by name and say Mom?" Beatrice will agree. Ask her to think of a sentence in which she calls her mother by the name she uses. If Beatrice doesn't come through quickly, model what you're looking for. "I think if I were going to try to write that sentence, I might write **The name I call my mother is Mom.** I also might write something I'd say to her. **Mom, may I wear my school shoes to the party?** In both of those sentences you are using Mom instead of your mother's other name."

If that scenario doesn't make sense to the children, it might be too early to try it. Eventually during the year, however, it is important to establish the idea of **personal names** as encompassing a whole range of possibilities.

Writing Sentences that Contain Names

1. Write your first name in the space. _____ Write a sentence that contains your first name.

   _____

   _____

2. Write the first names of two of your friends. _____ _____

   Write a sentence that contains the first name of one of your friends.

   _____

   _____

3. Write a sentence that contains the first names of two of your friends.

   _____

   _____

4. Write a sentence that contains the name of either your teacher or the principal of your school.

   _____

   _____

5. Write a sentence that contains your mother's first name.

   _____

   _____

6. Write a sentence that contains the name you call your mother.

   _____

   _____

7. In one sentence, write the names of two people you know.

   _____

   _____

8. Think of the name of an animal that is a character in a television program. Write the name of the animal in the space. _____ Write a sentence that contains the name of the animal from the television program.

   _____

   _____

9. Read each of the sentences you have written on this page. Make sure every sentence begins with a capital letter. Now, make sure every sentence ends with a period or a question mark. Finally, put a line under every name in every sentence and make sure every name begins with a capital letter.

10. Copy the best sentence you wrote in 1–8 above.

_____

_____

Tips for Teachers

1. Independent practice in the early grades can pose a spelling problem. Establish the "Three before Me" rule in which anyone who has the question (How do you spell. . . ?) must ask three people before asking the teacher. It's surprising how many words other children in the room know.
2. Establish that what young writers write while their paper is on their side of the desk is their business, so they are always encouraged to spell as well as they can (temporary spelling). Establish, as well, that when writing crosses the desk from the writer to the reader, it has to be right. Those two rules formalize the ideas of a real writer's draft and the importance of editing and revising.
3. The capitalization and punctuation lessons are cumulative. It might take a fair amount of time to get very young children to remember several conventions at once, but that sort of memory is precisely what learning to write well means.
4. Regularity is important. Practice under guidance, then independently, is everything. Frequency tells young writers that what they are doing is important. Remember regularity, frequency, and practice, especially for the youngest writers.
5. Finally, remember that mastery of capitalization and punctuation conventions **is not writing.** Writing is meaning-making and sending messages. Mechanical conventions **serve** meaning-making and message-sending. Young writers must be constructing meaning and sending their messages even as they practice writing with the conventions. The goal here is a **balanced** writing program.

LESSON 23: CAPITALIZING *I*

The Convention

Use a capital letter whenever writing the pronoun *I*.

Student Writing Samples (not edited for spelling)

1. I want to see my cousins because I miss them all allot. [Third Grader]
2. Mom and I had a picnic, and I played with the people there. [Third Grader]
3. That's when I moved to Benton. [Fourth Grader]
4. My favorite place is North Dakota because it is green and people are nice there. Also, I like how cold it gets in winter. [Fifth Grader]
5. It's the kind of place where I can just sleep as long as I want to. [Sixth Grader]

Explanation

Whenever the word *I* is written, it is written with a capital letter. The word *I* never appears alone unless it is capitalized.

The pronoun *I* is special. It never appears by itself uncapitalized. The word *a*, on the other hand, may appear capitalized or uncapitalized, depending on context. Those two letters are the only ones that are also words. One, *a*, is capitalized at the beginning of a sentence and uncapitalized within a sentence. The other, *I*, always appears capitalized. There are no exceptions.

There is nothing about this to confuse small children. If it's *I*, it's written with a capital letter.

Examples of the Pronoun *I* in Sentences

I couldn't wait to find out what happens in *The Giver.*

When I read *Woodsong,* I felt that I was right there on the farm with the sled dogs, the chickens, the goats, and the bears.

When Kate told Emily, "I don't like old people," Emily was shocked.

Teaching Young Writers about the Pronoun *I*

This convention is often taught as a spelling word, and that is certainly legitimate because practice tends to habituate the behavior. The more automatic it is, the less the student has to think about it, and the more fluent the student becomes. The pronoun *I* is one of those capitalization conventions that can become automatic quickly and easily through practice, even in isolation.

However, as is the case with every other convention, context is critical because all mechanical conventions exist in context, which is to say, we don't punctuate and capitalize mere words; we punctuate and capitalize on the basis of the context in which words occur. That context, in English, is sentences. Thus, it is critical to focus young writers' attention on sentences that contain the pronoun *I*. If we don't focus on the context, we risk producing youngsters who can "do" the mechanical behaviors on worksheets and tests but not when they write.

As early as the first grade when the children begin writing in sentences, ask for a sentence that tells whether they are a boy or a girl. That cue has always elicited a sentence similar to **I am a girl** or **I am a boy.** Write the sentences on the board and make an issue out of the word *I* and the capital letter. Tell them directly, "Whenever you write the word *I*, always write it with a capital letter." If they are old enough to understand the word *pronoun,* call it the *pronoun I,* but the fact is that no matter how you label the word, it is written with a capital letter.

Play with that a while, but eventually you have to get the word into the middle of a sentence. After all, some children could just assume it is capitalized because it comes at the beginning of the sentence, even though you said directly and explicitly that it is capitalized no matter what. To establish the capitalization clearly and unambiguously, cue the word in the middle of a sentence.

"Think of a sentence in which the word *I* is the third word." If they're confused by the cue, and most first graders are not once they have worked with it, pose the cue in graphic form.

_____ _____ __I__ _____ _____ _____

As they produce sentences in which the word *I* appears in various positions, emphasize the fact that it is capitalized every time. Come back to this thinking and writing task regularly throughout the year in order to **fix** the convention in automatic writing behavior.

If it is clear that the young writers cannot think in and write sentences in which *I* appears in positions other than the first position, perhaps it is too early to worry about the capitalization convention. If they cannot think with the convention in context, it is probably better to focus instruction on the context itself (sentence thinking and writing) and come back to capitalization when it is critical to what they are writing.

Writing with the Pronoun *I*

1. Write a sentence in which the word *I* is the first word.

    _____

    _____

2. Write a sentence in which the word *I* appears but is not the first word.

    _____

    _____

3. In the box is a sentence in which the word *I* appears two times.

I didn't have dinner because I wasn't hungry.

    Write a sentence in which the word *I* appears one time.

    _____

    _____

    Write your own sentence in which the word *I* appears two times.

    _____

    _____

Tips for Teachers

1. Remember that this is an unambiguous capitalization convention. That makes it easier for young writers to master than conventions that have exceptions.
2. If the children have a problem thinking deliberately in sentences, no convention is appropriate for their attention. First come sentences, then come the conventions that serve the sentences. If they don't write the sentences that demand the pronoun *I*, there is no need for the capitalization convention.

3. There are three primary keys to mastery of mechanical conventions:

   - One, establish what the convention is and practice it in the context of sentences;
   - Two, return to the convention for regular reinforcement;
   - Three, hold young writers responsible for adhering to the convention whenever they pass their writing to an audience other than themselves.

LESSON 24: CAPITAL LETTERS IN DAYS OF THE WEEK AND MONTHS OF THE YEAR

The Convention

Begin every word that names a day of the week or a month of the year with a capital letter.

Student Writing Samples (not edited for spelling)

1. My other thing is going to play basketball every Friday. [Third Grader]
2. On Saturday it's my birthday, and I get to go to the park again. [Fourth Grader]
3. Waiting for June is so hard because that's how ong I have to wait to go to my favorite place. [Fifth Grader]
4. I can just imagine it on a Friday afternoon with the curtins closed and me laying down on the bed watching television with a piece of crisp apple pie on my lap and a cold glass of milk on the side. [Sixth Grader]
5. We got home in the night on Thursday after we were in the airplane all day. [Sixth Grader]

Explanation

There are nineteen words in question here, twelve words that name months of the year and seven words that name days of the week.

Examples of Days of the Week and Months of the Year in Sentences

> Maniac Magee loved to run on Sunday mornings.
> Gabilan, the red pony, was born in May.
> My report on *Jacob Have I Loved* is due on Friday.

Teaching Young Writers about Capitalizing Days of the Week and Months of the Year

Remember, there are nineteen words. One of them per spelling list for nineteen weeks will leave nearly half of the year's spelling lists open for doing them again, one word per week. Then there's the calendar during opening exercises each morning. The calendar has a month and seven days named. Every morning, call attention to the name of the month and the fact that it begins with a capital letter. Then call attention to the name of the day and the fact that it, too, begins with a capital letter. All of that is awareness in the kindergarten and first grade.

Each child in the room is certainly able to record his or her own birthday, by day and month, on a 3×5 card and arrange the card on a timeline with the rest of the cards in the room. There are many holidays during the year, many relevant to the diverse cultures in the classroom, and every one falls on one or more days that can be recorded on the calendar by day and month. Those kinds of awareness activities are part of the instruction for capitalization conventions.

However, there must be appreciation of the writing itself. "Manny, think of a sentence that contains the name of the day after Tuesday." Manny recites: "I like Wednesday the most." Write Manny's sentence on the board, and when you get to the instructive word, pause. "Manny, what do I do now?" He says to write **Wednesday.** Tell him that you know that, but how should you begin? He will tell you to begin with a capital. "A capital what?" He says a capital letter. "That's terrific. A capital **H**?" He says no, a capital **W**. "Thank you, Manny. I just wanted to make sure you knew."

Later, "If it's summer, it must be one of the summer months. What month could it be?" The hands go up. "I want you to write a sentence that contains the name of a summer month."

Whenever you write the day when something is due to be turned in, use the name of the day. If there is a party coming up, write its date in full. Take advantage of every opportunity to use the names of the days and months, and every time you write the name of one of the nineteen words, capitalize it and call attention to the capital letter. We also recommend that you write the nineteen words on the Word Wall for young writers' reference, partly as a capitalization reminder and partly to avoid having anyone ask how to spell days of the week and months of the year.

Writing with the Names of the Days of the Week and the Months of the Year

1. Find a calendar for the year and find your birthday. Write the date of your birthday and spell out the name of the day and the month of the year.

   _____

   Write a sentence that contains the name of either the day or the month that you wrote in the space.

   _____

   _____

2. Write the name of a winter month. _____ Write a sentence that contains the name of the month you wrote in the space.

   _____

   _____

3. Write the name of a weekend day. _____ Write a sentence that contains the name of a weekend day.

   _____

   _____

4. Search on a calendar for the date on which Thomas Edison was born. Write a piece of at least two sentences that includes the month in which Thomas Edison was born and one of the inventions for which Thomas Edison is known.

   _____

   _____

5. Write all of the seven days of the week in the seven spaces.

   _____ _____ _____ _____ _____ _____ _____

   Write a sentence that contains two of the words that name the days of the week.

   _____

   _____

6. Write four of the months of the year, and include two that begin with the letter **J.**

   _____ _____ _____ _____

   Write a sentence that names a holiday that falls within one of the months you wrote in the spaces. Be sure to include the name of the month in your sentence.

   _____

   _____

Tips for Teachers

1. This is an excellent sentence thinking and writing convention. Use it to ensure that young writers think and plan. (Write a seven-word sentence in which the name of a day of the week appears in the fourth position.)
2. Notice that this convention offers an opportunity to write short pieces based on social studies and/or science research. Who, for instance, is Neils Bohr and on what day and month was his birthday? How about Thomas Jefferson, John Adams, and Peter the Great? On what day was the Declaration of Independence signed? On what day was the United States Constitution finally ratified? What was the name of the day on which the victory in Europe was secured by German surrender to end that part of World War II? Of course, some of those research foci are advanced beyond the second grade.
3. Remember, the number of times young writers write the names of the days of the week and the months of the year is directly associated with the extent to which they capitalize those nineteen words every time.

LESSON 25: CAPITAL LETTERS IN PLACE NAMES (INCLUDING DIRECTION WORDS)

The Convention

Use capital letters to show the names of places or locations, including direction words when they are used to name a place or location.

Student Writing Samples (not edited for spelling)

1. My faorite place is Mexico. [Second Grader]
2. Although they did not realize it, these first hunters are the first humans ever to set foot on North America. [Third Grader]
3. I would like to go to New Mexico to see lots and lots of robots. [Third Grader]
4. I would like to be in Hawaii and have the rest of my family there too. [Fourth Grader]
5. I would lik to go to San Francisco because my randma and grandpa live there. [Fourth Grader]
6. I like to go to Sivlerwood Lake. [Fifth Grader]
7. The Bahamas is an island where I like to go. [Sixth Grader]

Explanation

To a great extent, this is a "proper name" convention, but it is broken out here in order to clarify the idea of **place** or **location.** For most of what young writers need in their writings, understanding place or location such as country, state, city, and street is sufficient. We can practice those in isolation, in address boxes on worksheets for formal and informal letters and on editing worksheets, and most young writers will get the idea and capitalize location properly most of the time.

However, while this traditional procedure may establish the use of capital letters much of the time, it doesn't establish the basic idea of place or location.

That's the difference between capitalizing on the basis of a rule learned long ago and capitalizing on the basis of understanding. The idea of place and location is not so complex that young writers cannot understand and learn it.

Any word or words that name a place receive capital letters. Boston is a place. It is capitalized. Kansas is a place, and it is capitalized. Leavenworth is a place in Kansas, and it is capitalized. The Olympic Rainforest is a place. Big Bend National Park is a place in Texas, the Delaware Water Gap is a place in Pennsylvania, and the Delaware Canal is a very long place that runs through New Hope in Bucks County, Pennsylvania. All of those capitalized words designate places (Texas) and/or locations (Big Bend National Park). New Hope is a place in Pennsylvania; it is also a location in Pennsylvania. Alabama is a place in the United States.

The states in the United States are all capitalized because they are places. The "states" in Europe, which many people call countries, are all capitalized because they are places. All of the capitals in all of the countries and states all over the world are capitalized as are all of the other cities, towns, communities, hamlets, neighborhoods, and townships. All of the streets in all of those communities are also capitalized because those are places or locations, too.

And then there are some other words that are capitalized when they name a place or location, but they are not capitalized when they do not name places or locations.

The northeastern part of Arizona is the land of the Navajo People. In Arizona, their land is in the Northeast.

The Navajo people's land is in northeastern Arizona (and western New Mexico and southeastern Utah as a matter of fact), but speaking only of Arizona, Navajos live in the **Northeast.** Why is **northeastern** Arizona not capitalized while the **Northeast** is capitalized? The answer is that the first example (northeastern) is a direction word. The place or location is Arizona; the direction is northeastern. Another way to say it is that northeastern merely modifies Arizona; it doesn't name a place.

The **Northeast,** on the other hand, is a place or location. Think about it. What comes to mind when you see the word *Northeast*? Vermont comes to mind, that's what, and New Hampshire, small towns nestled in snow-covered valleys with white church spires, holiday card images, cold, Boston, and so forth. The word brings images of place because the word is a name for place. Of course, when you hear about the northeastern part of the United States, you may get the same images, but the word *northeastern* names a direction, not a place, itself. The place in that context is the United States; the word *northeastern* refers to a directional portion of the place.

This seemingly minor distinction takes a little getting used to. It might be helpful to read several sentences with some direction words used to name places and other direction words used to name directions.

> **In the northern part of Alaska is the Brooks Range. People in the South who have never seen anything like the Brooks Range would find the mountains intimidating, but those from the West who know the Rockies, or even people from eastern Washington, might just look and say, "Well, there's another mountain."**

In the example, there is a word that directs readers in the direction (*northern*) regarding Alaska and another that directs readers in a direction (*eastern*) regarding Washington. Then there is a word that names a place (*South*) where there are no mountains like the Brooks Range and another that names a place (*West*) where there are mountains like those in the Brooks Range. The West and the South are places all by themselves, and Washington is a place all by itself, while the modifier (*eastern*) merely directs readers to a direction in the place.

Examples of Capital Letters in Place Names

In the story *Hatchet*, Brian traveled to the North to find food to eat.

The students at Trinity School were required to sell chocolate in Robert Cormier's book, *The Chocolate War.*

The pioneers traveled to the West to settle the new territory.

Teaching Young Writers about Capital Letters in Place Names

Begin early with this one because it can be used by each child to write his or her address as part of a child safety program. Certainly in the first grade, if not late in kindergarten, the children can be writing their name, address, and telephone number. The writing will help solidify their memory of those critical bits of information. When they practice writing, we can begin introducing the idea of capital letters in words that tell street names, city names, and state names.

Through the early grades, young writers should be writing informal letters to friends and relatives and by third or fourth grade formal letters of inquiry. In all of those letters there are several opportunities to write addresses in which there are place or location words that need to be capitalized. Much of this is routine practice.

Along the way, however, youngsters are engaged in newspaper reading and discussion activities. Nearly every newspaper article contains a reference to place or location. There could be a portion of a bulletin board in which 3×5 cards are pinned, each one naming a place from newspaper discovery with every place name capitalized. The more the children see this capitalization convention in use, the higher the probability it will become automatic. On that bulletin board there should also be place or location names from social studies and science (Where was the book published?) and any other area of content that involves place or location names. Over time, the convention becomes established. (Youngsters can also locate all of the place names on a map and put push pins or stick-on stars on the places they know.)

Of course, children need to be writing with the convention, so it is also useful to direct young writers to write a sentence that contains the name of the town in which they live, the name of the street on which they live, the name of the state closest to where they live, the name of the country (countries) closest to the United States, and the names of parks where they like to have their picnics.

Along about late third grade, maybe during the fourth, it is time to let young writers in on the complexity here. "Boys and girls, I have a new idea I want you to think about. It's a hard one that even many eighth graders may not understand very well, so I want you to pay very careful attention. You remember the other day when we were working on the map and I said that if you drove from Florida to Maine, you would be driving north. Right?" The chorus agrees. "Well, if I started in Florida and drove to California, in which direction would I drive? Alex?" Alex tells us that you'd be driving toward the west. Having written **north** on the board, add **west.** "Someone tell us where to begin and where to drive if we wanted to go east." It will be Tyrone. He's always coming up with clever ideas. He says that you start in Nevada and go to Missouri, and that would be heading east. Write **east** on the board.

"Now here's the hard part. I want you to name a state in the **North.**" The hands all go up. "Wait. I'll get your states in a moment." Write **North** on the board, away from the three direction words. "How do you know where the states from the **North** are?" Tyrone can't control himself and blurts out that you just said where to look, that it's up there. "Up there? Up where?" They point to the **North.** "Oh, so you're saying that I told you a place and you had to name states in that place?" They all agree that that's just what you asked of them. Direct their attention to the board and the capitalized word. "My friends, what do you notice about this word (*North*) and these words (*west, south, north*)?" They'll say that it's capitalized.

"So it is, and do you know why?" Maybe some will, maybe not. If one says because it's a place, offer a great congratulations and explain. If no one speaks up, explain anyway. "You see, the **North** is a place, and we always put a capital letter in when we write the name of a place. Chicago is a place. Wisconsin is a place. Westfield Park is a place. And the **North** is a place. We'll practice that during the next several weeks."

Also during the next several weeks introduce the distinction. "Folks, here in Center Point where we live there are two sides of town." The hands go up. "Curtis?" He tells us that there is the west side of town

and the east side of town. "The side that is western and the side that is eastern. There are two sides. Do they have names?" Someone says that their names are **East Side** and **West Side.** "Do you mean that you can go to a place called **East Side**?" They agree. "Then when we write the name of that place, we use capital letters.

"Suppose we started on Sixth Street and headed toward Central Avenue. What direction is that? Barbara?" She tells us that it's east. "So you're driving east toward **East Side**?" Everyone agrees. Write the sentence on the board.

We're driving east toward East Side.

"What do you notice?" They notice that one word is not capitalized, but the other is. "Which one names a place? Which one names a direction?" That's the distinction. Work with examples of the distinction over time, and it will become clearer and clearer to more and more of the young writers in the room.

Of course they have to write with the distinction, as well. They have to write sentences in which direction words name places and in which they name only direction. They have to write sentences in which direction words are capitalized and in which they are not. They have to write regularly and frequently over protracted time. The more guided, then independent, practice in which they engage, the higher the probability they will begin to understand this capitalization convention.

Writing Place Names with Capital Letters

1. Write a sentence that includes the name of your state.

    _____

    _____

2. Write a sentence that includes the name of your town or city.

    _____

    _____

3. Write a sentence that includes your street address and the name of your town. Remember, there is a comma between your street name and the name of your town or city.

    _____

    _____

4. Write a sentence that contains the name of a country in Europe or Asia or Africa. You select one.

    _____

    _____

5. Write a sentence that contains the name of a river in the United States or a mountain in South America. You select one.

    _____

    _____

6. Write a sentence in which the word *east* must begin with a capital letter because it names a place.

    _____

    _____

7. Write a setence in which the word *south* does not begin with a capital letter because it names a direction, not a place.

    _____

    _____

8. Write a sentence that includes the word *southwest*. Write the sentence so the word *southwest* names a place and is capitalized.

    _____

    _____

    Now write a sentence in which *southwest* names a direction, not a place, and is not capitalized.

    _____

    _____

Tips for Teachers

1. Be sure to allow time. The distinction between place and direction is hard. It takes time.

2. The best way to handle a difficult distinction is to encourage practice, deliver feedback, and practice again. Tests will not establish the idea. Writing over time will.

LESSON 26: CAPITAL LETTERS IN A PERSON'S TITLE

The Convention

Use a capital letter to show a person's title. Titles include designations of gender, relationships, and profession.

Student Writing Samples (not edited for spelling)

1. Th prnsible name is Mrs. Yoder. [Second Grader]
2. When he cam to aur class, Mr. Henning was nise. [Third Grader]
3. We met Mayor Fraiser, and he helped us know about the city. [Fourth Grader]
4. The doctor who did the speech was Dr. Haines, and she helped us learn about how our teeth can be clean and healthy. [Fifth Grader]
5. I want to vote for Congressman Parker if I was old enough to vote. When I am, I will vote for him. [Sixth Grader]

Explanation

This is a relatively early capitalization convention. Most young writers are faced with not only using names that demand capital letters, but using titles, as well. It is not feasible, or useful, to attempt to teach the complete range of titles in the earliest grades, but the alternative is not to avoid the convention.

A title is characteristically a word that comes **before** a name. Thus, the man is a **mister,** and we know him as **Mister Crawford.** We write his name as **Mr. Crawford.** There is the woman who manages the accounts at Mesa Grande Industries. Her name is Elizabeth. We write her name as **Ms. Cooper,** and if she is married and prefers it, we write her name as **Mrs. Cooper.**

Your mother's sister is your aunt. If her name is Edna, you would write her name as **Aunt Edna.** Her husband, who is your uncle, is named Max. You would write his name as **Uncle Max.**

Ms. Whitmore is a senator from a state in the northwestern part of the United States. When we write her name, we write it as **Senator Whitmore.** There's the congressman from the Seventh District, **Congressman Bailey,** and the judge, **Judge Jones.** Over at the university there are all kinds of professors in the 27 departments, but **Professor Asnew** was recently judged by her students the best teacher in the college.

If the word that designates a title names the person (Judge Jones, Professor Asnew, and Congressman Bailey), it is capitalized. If it doesn't, it isn't (Betty Asnew is a professor, Matilda Whitmore is a senator, George Bailey is a congressman, Lena Jones is a judge).

Examples of Capitalized and Uncapitalized Titles in Sentences

Mr. and Mrs. Huggins were very understanding when Henry showed up at the front door with his new dog, Ribsy.

Mary went to live with her Uncle Archibald Craven, who was a very sad man.

In the waiting room of the doctor's office, the nurse announced that Dr. Inman was running a little behind schedule.

Teaching Young Writers about Capitalizing Titles

Write your name on the board (for example, **Mrs. Campion** or **Ms. Campion,** whatever is preferred and known by the children). Inquire as to what the children know about you by reading your name on the board. When Rosemary says she knows you're the teacher, ask what there is about the name on the board that means teacher. In fact, there are all kinds of people who could be named Ms. Campion. Tell the children about them. There is your husband's mother and your brother-in-law's wife and maybe even some other women you don't know, and none of the ones you know are teachers.

Lead the conversation to the point at which it is clear that what they know from the way the name is written on the board is that there is a person named

Campion, and the person is a woman. The name signifies a female person named Campion. "So how do we know the person named Campion is a female person, a woman?" Someone will shoot a hand into the air and announce that it's because of the **Mrs.** "Yes. We know the name is for a woman, a female person, because of the title. The abbreviation *Mrs.* is a title for a married woman. When we write **Ms.,** we are also using a title for a woman, as well, and this title can be used whether or not she is married.

"Who can tell us a title we might use for a man? Right, Calvin, it's **Mr.** There are all kinds of titles for people. What do you notice about the three titles *(Mrs., Ms., and Mr.)* I have written on the board?" Shirlee's hand is up first. She tells us that all of the words have capital letters. "Oh Shirlee, you're so good at noticing things like that. Yes. Every title has a capital letter when it comes in front of the name."

If it seems right for the moment, take another turn in the lesson, but if they've had enough, leave it for the next day. Then there's another point. "You all get a sore toe once in a while, or the flu, and you have to make a little trip to see someone who fixes you up." The hands go up. "Winston?" He tells us that it's a doctor. Write *doctor* on the board. "It's a doctor. You're right. I've written it on the board. It's a word that tells what the person is. She's a doctor. He's a doctor. That's all. No capital letter. Incidentally Winston, what's your doctor's name?" Winston will know. He always knows. You write it on the board. **Dr. Carty.** Shirlee's hand shoots up again. She says that there's a capital letter

again. "Yes, there is, and why do you suppose there is a capital letter in Dr. Carty, but there isn't any capital letter over here where we just said the person who fixes our toe is a doctor?" This may be a hard one. Give it a count or two and announce the answer. "Here we have the title for a person. It's written with the name. Over here we just have the name of something a lot of people do. This one is a person's title, and that's why we use the capital letter. We're going to write with these titles for a while and practice using them."

During the next several weeks, conduct another practice session with a new title, perhaps **Uncle.** Add a new title every couple of days. As each new title is used and practiced, put the title on the Word Wall and several sentences that contain the title in the Writing Center. Titles with which young writers in the first several grades can think and write include the gender words *Mrs., Ms.,* and *Mr.), doctor* (for physician and dentist), *mayor, uncle,* and *aunt* (if the titles are relevant for the children in the room), *reverend, senator, councilman* or *councilperson,* and so forth. Depending on the children, there are other titles. For example, there is no specific title for teacher in the United States, but in Mexico it is *profesora* or *profesor.*

It is not necessary to work through every possible title designation in the early grades. In fact, if the connection between title and capital letter is established with only gender and relationship words, that will suffice. As the children get older and come to know more, the connection between title and capital letter, with minor guidance, will generalize.

Writing with Titles That Are Capitalized

1. Write the abbreviation that we use to show the title of the person who fixes your teeth. _____ Write a sentence that contains the title for a dentist.

   _____

   _____

2. Write a sentence that contains the title for a person who gives you medication when you are sick.

   _____

   _____

3. Think of someone whose name you would use with a title. Write that person's name with the title.

   _____ Write a sentence with the name and title you wrote in the space.

   _____

   _____

4. Suppose that Dr. Elena Medina is married to a doctor named Juan Medina. How would you write Juan Medina's name with the doctor title?

   _____

   How could you write Dr. Medina's last name with a title that doesn't show that he is a doctor?

   _____

   Write a sentence in which it is clear that Juan Medina is a doctor.

   _____

   _____

5. In our town the mayor's name is Miguel Trijillo. Write a sentence in which Mr. Trijillo's last name is used, and the word *mayor* is his title.

   _____

   _____

Tips for Teachers

1. Remember that the children must write with the lesson's focus. The focus here is capitalizing titles. They are writing sentences because that's where the titles are.
2. If you want longer writings, begin with the single sentence to establish the capital letter convention, then direct longer pieces. "Write a paragraph in which the main idea is a trip to the doctor. Use at least three titles that have to be capitalized." When they have written the paragraph, direct them to write the first sentence of the next paragraph.
3. Once the idea of capitalizing titles is established and most young writers can do it properly most of the time, return to the convention with some regularity during the year. Part of learning is establishing the behavior we are seeking. The other part is solidifying the behavior under all kinds of circumstances over time.

LESSON 27: CAPITAL LETTERS IN PUBLISHED TITLES

The Convention

Use capital letters in the main words when writing the titles of published works.

Student Writing Samples (not edited for spelling):

1. I likt it wen you red *Two Bad Ants*. [Second Grader]
2. The book I got from the libery is *Too Many Tamales*. [Third Grader]
3. I liked the poem "Fire and Ice" which is about how the world burns up or freezes. [Fourth Grader]
4. After school, we were all in Grandma's house eating chips and having Cokes and listening to "Mister Rogers" again. It was fun because we didn't listen to him since we were little. [Fifth Grader]
5. The best part of the book is "How It Started." That's in the beginning when there's dinosaurs in the swamps. [Sixth Grader]

Explanation

Lesson 11 in this book is about using punctuation (underlining or italics) in published titles. This is the companion lesson. Not only are certain published titles underlined or italicized, the main words are capitalized, as well. And while the punctuation convention separates published titles into those that are underlined or italicized and those that are quoted, the capitalization convention applies to all published works irrespective of the punctuation.

Thus, we use capital letters to show the main words of a book (*The Best of Everything*), as well as to show the main words of a magazine article ("What Everyone Needs to Know about Being Sixty") and the main words of a chapter title ("Using Capital Letters in the Elementary School"). In that sense, this is an unambiguous capitalization convention. Use it all the time, every time. No exceptions.

Minor ambiguity comes in with respect to what constitutes a main word. There are several attributes of **main words.**

- The first word in a title is a **main** word.
- Almost always, all words that are not articles (*a, the, an*) or prepositions (*to, in, at*) are **main** words.
- A rule of thumb that is not always accurate is that bigger words are **main** words.

In the book noted above, *The Best of Everything*, the first word is a **main** word. The rest of the words, except for the preposition (*of*) are **main** words. In "What Everyone Needs to Know about Being Sixty," there are six **main** words that are capitalized plus two prepositions (*to, about*) that are not. The word *about* confounds that rule of thumb about big and small words, for *about* is a longer word than *know*, yet the latter is capitalized while the former is not. In fact, *know* is a main word because it is crucial to the meaning of the title.

Examples of Capitalized Words in Titles

The book *Two Bad Ants* reminds me of the movie *Honey, I Shrunk the Kids*.

One of my favorite short stories, called "Eleven," is about a young girl who finds out that life is not always fair.

Have you heard the song "I Left My Heart in San Francisco"?

Teaching Young Writers about Capitalizing Words in Titles

This instructional process is very similar to that in Lesson 11 in which young writers punctuated with quotation marks or underlined the words in published titles. Here, they have to become aware of what titles look like when they are capitalized properly. That means the teacher must show lots of titles capitalized properly, on the board, on bulletin boards, and on the overhead projector screen. Whenever there are titles to see and read, attention must be called to the capital letters, the main words, and the general appearance of the title when it is written correctly. Much of this convention is about awareness. The students must see it.   They must also write the convention, and it is probably never too early in their educational careers to begin the writing; however, these procedures are best anchored in the second or third grade and thereafter.

Ask youngsters to think about the book they are reading right now or have read most recently. "Edward, what is your book title?" As Edward reveals his title, write it on the board, then call attention to the capital letters. "Folks, when we write titles of books, and anything else, but we're going to concentrate on books today, we capitalize the important words. Look at how I wrote the title that Edward gave me."

How to Feed Your Cats

"I put a capital letter on every word except *to,* and that's because that word is not one of the most impor-tant words in the title. However, I used a capital letter for all of the other words." Let them know that they will be writing the titles of their books on a special sheet of oaktag that they'll keep at their table, in their cubby, or in their portfolios. That list of titles will reflect the books they have read, are thinking about reading, are reading, or just know about. In fact, if they decide that the key here is to get the longest possible list, and they begin copying the names of books from the library shelf, it is perfectly okay. The reason for the list is to practice writing titles with capital letters. The more, the better.

After a lesson or two and a list or two, it will be useful to conduct a session on sentences that include titles, and then provide some guided practice. Most of those cues or prompts can be taken from Lesson 11. After all, the children need only write a sentence that contains the name of their favorite book, remembering to underline and capitalize properly. When they have collected fifteen or twenty sentences that contain titles, it is time to let them off the hook and merely remind them that from now on, whenever they write a title, they must capitalize and punctuate properly or you will hand their paper back, refusing to read past the error. That's what we do in the fourth or fifth grade. In the second and third, we teach and remind. The point is that eventually we have to pull the string and expect it to be done right.

Writing with Published Titles

1. Write the name of the most exciting book you have read this year.

   _____

   Write a sentence that contains the name of the book.

   _____

   _____

2. Write the name of the book your teacher is reading aloud to the class.

   _____

   Write a sentence that contains the name of the book and something about one of the characters in the book.

   _____

   _____

3. Search through one of the magazines that are in your classroom and find an article that looks interesting for you to read. Write the name of the article in the space.

   _____

   Write a sentence that includes the name of the article and something about why it looks interesting.

   _____

   _____

4. Write the name of a reference book in your classroom.

   _____

   Write a sentence that contains the name of the reference book and something about what the book is a reference for.

   _____

   _____

5. Write a sentence that includes the name of a science book.

   _____

   _____

6. Write a sentence that includes the name of a dictionary in your classroom.

   _____

   _____

Tips for Teachers

1. This is a capitalization convention that can occur at nearly any time in a child's school career.
2. If the young writers in your room aren't writing sentences that include the names of published works, one argument says that there is no reason to bring up the convention.
3. There is another argument to the effect that young writers may begin to include titles of published works if they know how to do it.
4. Wrap Lessons 27 and 11 together whenever possible.

LESSON 28: CAPITAL LETTERS TO SHOW NATIONALITY, ETHNICITY, AND LANGUAGE

The Convention

Use a capital letter to designate the terminology of nationality, ethnicity, and language.

Student Writing Samples (not edited for spelling)

1. American Indians learned how to plant and harvest corn. [Third Grader]
2. The center of Aztec culture was in Tenochtitlan. [Third Grader]
3. Who were the first pepol to discuver Amireca? The Amire Indians discuverd Amireca. [Third Grader]
4. My brother speaks Spanish, but I didn't learn it because my mother speaks English in our house. [Fourth Grader]
5. We all are in the class together and learn at the same time: the Vietnamese, Mexican, and even me who was born here in Arizona. [Sixth Grader]

Explanation

In an increasingly diverse society, there is an increasing need to write words that designate people's nationality, ethnicity, and language(s). Young writers face such terminology more frequently than ever before. The use of capital letters is often encouraged as a matter of respect, but while laudable, that isn't the reason for using capital letters for such words at all. We use capital letters when we write the terminology of nationality, ethnicity, and language because the words themselves fit into the general category of *proper* nouns. They're used to name people and people's origins, so they are capitalized.

There are three categories in this convention, and all three need to be clarified and understood. First, there are **nationality** words. Nationality words include variations on the names of the nation: *French, Italian, Swedish,* and *Polish.* While not precisely terms that designate nationality, variations of state names in the United States are also capitalized. Those include words such as *Kansan, Texan,* and *Arizonan.* Also included in this category are terms unique to the states such as *Hoosier* (Indiana), *Buckeye* (Ohio), and *Ute* (Utah).

It is also important to consider another designation that is capitalized under the umbrella of nationality, even though the words are not precisely nationality terms. Indigenous peoples around the world are referred to as Indians or Indian people or native people, and in the United States, Native Americans. Well, if they're all Native Americans, or Indian people, and those terms designate ethnicity, how do we handle tribal names? The answer is that we write tribal names as though they're nationality. Thus, we capitalize *Muckleshoot* (Washington State), *Standing Rock Sioux* (South Dakota), *Mescalero Apache* (New Mexico), and *Salt River Pima* (Arizona). Any word that names a nationality or Indian tribe is capitalized.

Those folks who live and work around Fort Defiance, Arizona are Navajo people. *Navajo* is the "nationality" or tribal name, but *Indian* or *Native American* is the ethnicity. Those terms are capitalized. **Ethnicity** in the United States is enormously diverse. There are African Americans or Black people. There are folks whose ethnicity is an original Indian/Spanish mix. Their ethnicity is Latino or Latina, although the term *Hispanic* is widely used to specify the European (Spanish) roots. There are various Asian people from any one of many different countries. The terms used to identify the cultural and/or racial backgrounds of our friends and neighbors are ethnicity words because they specify heritage and culture, not just national boundaries.

And there are the **languages people around the world speak.** Usually those language labels are similar to or the same as the nationality term. That is, they are usually derived from the name of the country. Thus, people who speak Italian are Italians and live in Italy. But it doesn't always work that way. People of the

United States speak English plus any one or more of the sixty to seventy other languages spoken in the homes of people who live in our neighborhoods and send their children to school. Those language names are capitalized when they name the language people speak and when they name courses children and youth study in school.

The matter of capitalizing language can produce ambiguity. For instance, both Marco and Julia study **English** and **French** in school. Marco speaks **Spanish** as his native language, and Julia speaks **Italian.** They both study **history** and **government,** as well, but they enjoy **Physical Science 102** most of all. Now, there are four languages represented in the four sentences above and each is capitalized. Then there are two *course labels* not capitalized and *one course title* that is capitalized. When the course is a language, it is always capitalized. When the course is merely labeled (a geography class and another in music), it is not capitalized. When the course is titled (Problems of Democracy, Music 631, and Elementary Geology for Nonmajors), it is capitalized. It needn't be very complicated if we focus on the fact that languages and titles are capitalized.

Examples of Nationality, Ethnicity, and Language in Sentences

> *The Captive* by Scott O'Dell takes place in Mexico, where the primary langauge is Spanish.
> *Encounter* is a story of Columbus, the explorer who sailed under the Spanish flag, though he was actually an Italian.
> *The Rainbow People* is a collection of stories about the Chinese culture.

Teaching Young Writers about Capitalizing Nationality, Ethnicity, and Language

We have still another fine opportunity to expand young writers' range of general knowledge. To write sentences and larger pieces based on the terminology of nationality, ethnicity, and language presupposes that the writer possesses the information on which the terminology rests. Thus, in the second grade, as part of the larger social studies focus on map skills, we pull down a map of North, Central, and South America. "Boys and girls, we are going to spend some time thinking and writing about people who live in the countries on this map. Let's begin with one we know about already." Point to the United States, solicit its name, and ask what we call the people who live there. Someone, maybe several at once, will blurt out that the word is *Americans.* "Yes, so it is. This is the United States, and the people who live here are called Americans." It's second grade,

so it's unlikely that a seven-year-old Juan will raise his hand with a question that you already know. But in later grades, he or she will be in the room and the hand will go up.

"Yes Maria?" Maria says that she lives in the United States, but she's Mexican. "Ah yes, Maria, there are all kinds of folks who live in the United States, and some call themselves Americans, some call themselves by the countries they came from, and some use both names." Maria will nod her head and say that her father says he is Mexican American.

Write all of these words on the board as they come out. Emphasize that each of the words is capitalized. "When we write the words that name our nationality, we use a capital letter." This is a capitalization lesson. It isn't the time to get into a volatile conversation with seven- or even fifteen-year-olds about whether or not people who live in the United States should call themselves Americans first or second. Establish the capital letter.

Point to Canada. "Who lives here?" A second grader will say it's Canada people, but someone else in the second grade, and nearly everyone in the fifth, will say it's Canadians. Write the two words on the board. Point to Guatamala, solicit the word, and write it on the board. They're looking at the map and working on words that name nationality. So far it's not so complicated. But when you point to Peru, be ready for *Peruans.* This is when you get a chance to show that many nationality names are somewhat different from the name of the country, and you show them *Peruvians.*

The words go up on the Word Wall or the social studies bulletin board. After a day or so of the looking and naming, pose the sentence cue: Think of a sentence that names a country and the nationality word we use for the people who live there. There will be lots of sentences that adhere to the format that you virtually dictated.

The people who live in Canada are called Canadians. Bolivians live in Bolivia.

This may feel stilted and nonauthentic, but remember why students are doing this in the first place. This is about practicing capital letters when naming nationality. That's what they are doing, in whole pieces of language in sentences that they construct; and they are doing it several times in order to get the idea. It's not necessary to assign a hundred such sentences. A half-dozen will make the point.

Conduct a similar activity with respect to ethnicity and language. The key is to get the terminology in the open where everyone can see it. To do that means naming countries and generating words that fit. France is inhabited by French people who speak French, but lots of people in France speak English and German, too. There are Mexican American people in the United States who have a Latin or Hispanic cultural heritage or ethnicity and speak Spanish and English. Many Polish people in Chicago speak Polish as well as English. Portuguese is a language spoken in Portugal and Brazil, while German is spoken in Germany and Austria.

This is also an opportunity to mitigate against the monolithic conception of ethnicities and cultures. *Asian* is a word used to name ethnicity, but the more accurate words name countries. Chinese and Vietnamese people are often called Asian, but they are as different from one another culturally and ethnically as are Koreans different from Australians. This study will help youngsters understand the words we use to identify one another, both in the United States and around the world.

Finally, the monolithic notion of Indian people, or Native Americans, will come under important scrutiny, and third and fifth graders will eventually understand that there are four Apache tribes, not one, that the four are dramatically different from one another, and that all four are even more dramatically different from the Quinault people in the Olympic Rainforest. Navajo people are Navajos, Makah people are Makahs, and there are Cherokees, Seminoles, Rosebud Siouxs, and as many as two- to three-hundred more separate and distinct tribal groups in the United States. They're all rather conveniently labeled Native Americans or Indians, but there is enormous educational merit in having elementary school children begin to discriminate among them and call them by their right names, to say nothing of coming to know where many of the tribal groups are located, the language(s) they speak, and the nature of their political systems and economies. This exercise is about capitalization, yet moving in the direction of greater general knowledge can be facilitated by the study of capital letters.

Writing with the Words for Nationality, Ethnicity, and Language

1. Write the word that names a country in Central America. _____

   Write the word that names the ethnicity of the people who live there. _____

   Write the word that names the language that is spoken there. _____

   Write a sentence that contains two of the words you wrote above.

   _____

   _____

   Write a sentence that contains the third word you wrote above.

   _____

   _____

   Write one sentence that combines the two sentences you wrote above.

   _____

   _____

2. Write the name of an Indian tribe in New Mexico. Find out the name of a town where those Indian people live. Write a sentence that includes the name of the tribe, the state, and the nearest nonIndian town. (Example: The people of the Santo Domingo Pueblo live within ten miles of Bernallilo in the community of Santo Domingo.)

   _____

   _____

3. Write a sentence that names the language you might like to study in school.

   _____

   _____

4. If you could speak two languages in addition to what you speak now, what might those two languages be? _____ _____ Write a sentence that contains the name of one of those languages and the name of a country where it is widely spoken.

   _____

   _____

5. Complete the following pairs of words by writing either nationality words or ethnicity words.

   Sweden _____   Denmark _____   Spain _____   Chile _____

   Find all of the four countries on a map. Write a sentence that includes the name of a country that borders on one of the four.

   _____

   _____

Tips for Teachers

1. Use the social studies implications of this capitalization instruction. The more social studies, the more authentic the study of capitalization.
2. This study can lead to writing that is larger than single sentences. There is no reason why young writers should

not be writing reports of information from their map work. If that is the direction, make sure the report of information answers a question that young writers themselves ask in the beginning.

LESSON 29: CAPITAL LETTERS IN TRADE NAMES, COMMERCIAL PRODUCTS, AND COMPANY NAMES

The Convention

Use a capital letter when writing the names of trade names or commercial products and company names.

Student Writing Samples (not edited for spelling)

1. My favorite place is Disnyland, Sea World, and Six Flags Magic Mountens. [Third Grader]
2. My favert ride is Pirets of the Caraben. [Third Grader]
3. On the weekend we always go to Stater Bros. for our food shopping. [Fourth Grader]
4. I have a lot of games for my Sega. [Fifth Grader]
5. My special place to eat in a restrant is Sizzler because you can eat all day there. [Fifth Grader]

Explanation

This is another capitalization convention, just like the one on institutions, associations, and events (Lesson 30), that offers an excellent information-gathering opportunity for young children. They need to know about the companies and corporations in their local area and across the United States, and they should be aware of what those companies do and make. This convention can get youngsters out into their communities and put them in touch with the resources that describe the companies and their products.

There are two kinds of capital letters in this convention: the registered names of products on the market and the names of the companies that make them. Notice that we are talking about **registered** names of products and the companies that make the products. **General Electric Company** makes a refrigerator and a television set. The company (General Electric Company) is capitalized. Neither *refrigerator* nor *television set* is a registered name, so neither is capitalized. However, **Mars Candy Company** (capitalized as the name of the company) makes **M & M's** (capitalized as a registered trade name).

The basic attribute of these capital letters is that they name something specific, again. Most of the capitalization conventions have to do with naming something. In this case the naming is companies and corporations and registered products.

Examples of Capital Letters in Trade Names, Commercial Products, and Company Names

> The soles of Maniac Magee's sneakers, "hanging by their hinges and flopping open like dog tongues," certainly weren't new Nikes.
>
> When Elbert entered the gardener's cottage, he noticed the stove from the Ace Stove Works in West Carrollton, Ohio.
>
> Emily told Kate that if she would come over soon, there would be a tall Black Cow Root Beer waiting for her.

Teaching Young Writers about Capitalizing Trade Names, Commercial Products, and Company Names

We use this convention as another frame of reference for gathering information, for becoming more knowledgeable. "Boys and girls, there is a fast food restaurant near our school. . ." Randall raises his hand. "Yes, Randall." He tells us all, beaming with every word, that it's Richardson's. "Yes, in fact, that's what I had in mind. Someone tell me how to write it on the board." Randall will likely raise his hand again and begin spelling it. He can spell it, of course, because he's seen the word maybe a thousand times, but he won't begin with a capital letter. Write it as he spells it; then ask about the capital letter. They all say that it should be capitalized. Change it on the board. "Boys and girls, whenever you write the name of a company, you use a capital letter.

"But I have another question for you. What is Richardson's best-known meal? What are they known for?" Everyone will participate in the choral response: Richburger. Write it on the board with a capital letter. "Who else makes a Richburger?" They all know that no one else makes it. "You're right, my friends. Richardson's owns the Richburger. They don't own hamburgers, but the Richburger is their own invention. Incidentally, what's good about the Richburger?" Someone will say it's the Swiss cheese and mushrooms. "Does anyone else make that kind of hamburger?" They all agree that Richardson's is the only place you can get that burger. "See, it's their own. They own the burger, and they have named it, so because it's their name, it is capitalized when we write it."

That point is the instructive one. Extend it. General Motors is a car-manufacturing company, but the company doesn't make any car named General Motors. It makes Buick and Chevrolet, among others. General Motors Corporation is the company; Chevrolet and Buick are the trade names or commercial products. General Motors is the only corporation in the world that may call a car a Buick because they own the name; it is registered by them.

"What cars does Ford Motor Company make? How about Chrysler Corporation? What company makes Dr. Pepper? What companies make paper copiers? Who makes personal computers? What companies make refrigerators? Name a German manufacturer. What trade name is the German manufacturer known for?" The children should make a list of the Japanese automobile makers and list the automobiles each company makes. They should make the same lists for auto makers in the United States and Britain. They should make the lists for computers, telephones, and television sets.

There could be a wall in the room devoted to a month-long study of companies and their products, all capitalized, of course. Who makes pencils? Who makes Kleenex? What is Caterpillar? What is International Harvester? What is Allis Chalmers, John Deere, and Massey Ferguson? Who makes ice cream, frozen yogurt, chocolate bars, TV dinners?

Write a sentence that contains the name of a company that makes mechanical pencils. Write a sentence that contains the name of a company that makes electric stoves. Write a sentence that contains one of the candy bars made by H. B. Reese Candy Company. And finally, there is a puzzle. Everyone in the room is faced with a research task: Find out what Swingline Incorporated makes.

Writing with Trade Names, Commercial Products, and Company Names

1. Write the trade name of a product that is made by Motorola. _____

    Write a sentence that includes the name of the product and the name of the company.

    _____

    _____

2. Write a sentence that contains the trade name of your favorite soft drink.

    _____

    _____

3. Include in the sentence the trade name of something made by Proctor and Gamble.

    _____

    _____

4. Find the name of a paper product company. Write a sentence that contains the name of the company and a description of something it makes.

    _____

    _____

5. Find out the name of the company that made one of the chairs in your house. Write a sentence that contains the name of that company.

    _____

    _____

6. Find out the name of the company that manufactured your stove at home. Write a sentence that contains the name of the company and something about your stove.

    _____

    _____

7. Write a piece of at least one paragraph in which you tell about the products made by either an automobile company or a computer company.

Tips for Teachers

1. Use the opportunity to get young writers into the enormous range of information associated with companies and their products.
2. Every one of the companies that young writers find out about exists somewhere. Use that for locational geography.

3. Those companies have histories, as well. Young writers could write short descriptions of the history of major or minor United States' corporations.

LESSON 30: CAPITAL LETTERS IN NAMES OF INSTITUTIONS, ASSOCIATIONS, AND EVENTS

The Convention

Use a capital letter when writing the name of institutions (Shippensburg University), associations (Lions Club), and events (the Penn Relays).

Student Writing Samples (not edited for spelling)

1. Our family would have the Raiders on and my friends would dance to the music. [Third Grader]
2. We looked out the door and saw illegal imergrants next door running from the Border Patrol. [Fourth Grader]
3. This is my school. Its name is Nancy Grayson School. [Fourth Grader]
4. We had a field trip to the college that is Price Laboratory School. [Fifth Grader]
5. When I saw the Super Bowl, I was excited to see my favorite team win. [Sixth Grader]

Explanation

This capitalization convention is about making sure the meaning of various words is clear. There are **lions** and there are **Lions.** The **lions** inhabit the plains of Africa and stalk prey for food. The **Lions** are more likely to inhabit houses and fund eyeglasses for children who can't afford them. One capital letter means everything with respect to discriminating between lions on four feet and those on two feet.

In addition, there are the **relays** out on the asphalt of York Avenue School each spring, but for athletes in Philadelphia, there are the **Relays,** which means those at Franklin Field at the University of Pennsylvania, the **Penn Relays.** The capital letter gives meaning to the word that in one case is a race and in the other is an event.

The capital letter in this convention clarifies formality. There is the university in Arizona, which could mean any of several, but when it is written as Arizona University, it is clearly the one in Tucson. There are congregations of writers, worshipers, and runners, but the Writers Haven, the First Congregational Fellowship, and the Lansdale Track and Field Club are not mere congregations of folks. The capital letters make them formal associations.

And there are bowls of oranges, oranges in a bowl, even orange bowls, but the Orange Bowl is special, and the capital letters take the words out of the world of a painted bowl and what's in it and put the bowl in Miami on New Year's night.

Perhaps a useful attribute for explaining this convention is specialness. There are fellowships, but the Methodist Youth Fellowship is special. There are bowls, but the Rose Bowl is special. There are schools, but James Madison School is unique. There are football games every Sunday, but the Super Bowl is special. The capital letter signifies specialness.

Examples of Capital Letters in Institutions, Associations, and Events

> I wonder if Jonas knew about the Boy Scouts of America.
> Mr. Grayson played baseball in the Texas League.
> Maniac was saved from the Pennsylvania Orphans Association home by his friendship with the Beales.

Teaching Young Writers about Capital Letters in Institutions, Associations, and Events

One of the advantages of teaching several of the capitalization conventions is the cross-curricular context. This convention is an excellent example. Young writers need to know a variety of institutions, associations, and events in order to practice the convention. It is a nearly sure bet that most of the second, third, and fourth graders for whom this direct instruction is intended can benefit from what the almanac, the newspaper, and the local chamber of commerce have available that will require the capitalization convention.

Notice in the final sentence of the previous paragraph the reference to a chamber of commerce. There are all sorts of chambers of commerce around the United States, and virtually every town has one. But it is not capitalized until it is special. The one in Decatur, Alabama is special; it's known as the Decatur Chamber of Commerce. A telephone call by one of the third graders to the director (as opposed to Miriam Cooper, **Director**) will produce a list of every association in the city. Those associations should be printed on large sheets of tagboard and pinned to the wall. Then, during the year, representatives from each of the associations should be invited to spend a few minutes with the class to explain the association and what it does for the community and its members. All of that requires letters of invitation and thank you, and every letter contains the name of the association several times, each time capitalized. Call it a year-long social studies unit on community awareness.

Make it a part of every class presentation by representatives of local associations to include the name of the major annual event that the association sponsors. Those could be included in the local community corner of the classroom. Thus, the Montgomeryville Lions Club sponsors the Annual Clam Bake, the Jamul Toads sponsor the Annual 10K and Fun Run, and so forth. Following each presentation, all of the young writers in the room write a synopsis of the presentation, to include the special event; and the synopses are bound into a book at the end of the year and sent to the chamber of commerce for its display. Of course, every piece of writing contains the name of the relevant event, properly capitalized.

Wouldn't it be interesting for nine- and ten-year-olds to begin inquiring about the nature of higher education institutions, technical schools, and so forth? These are not commitments; they are mere queries. Everyone in the class must write a letter of inquiry to a community college in the area, a four-year college in-state, a four-year college out of state, and a local trade or technical school. In addition, sometime during the year everyone must select a confederation of colleges or universities and list its members (Ivy League: Brown, Pennsylvania, Yale, and so forth). Finally, there are other institutions that students are likely to hear about. There could be in the room a list of the local, state, and federal jails and prisons. Everyone could select one and write a letter of inquiry regarding its capacity, the educational level of its "clients," the average stay, and the per-day cost per "client."

To establish the convention, conduct several writing sessions during which the children write sentences that feature the capitalization convention. Write a sentence that contains the name of our school. Find out the name of the football game played in Pasadena, California on New Year's Day, and write a sentence that contains the name of the game and the most recent winner. Find out the name of the association that owns your favorite professional sports team (San Diego Padres Baseball Club, for instance), and write a sentence that contains the full name of the association.

Writing Institutions, Associations, and Events in Sentences

1. Write the name of the high school that is closest to where you live. _____

   Write a sentence that contains the name of the high school.

   _____

   _____

2. Find out the name of a private school in your community or town. Write its name in the space.

   _____

   Write a sentence that contains the name of the private school.

   _____

   _____

3. Find out the name of a club or association in your community or town that is especially for women. Write the name of the club or association in the space.

   _____

   Write a sentence that contains the name of the club or association you wrote in the space.

   _____

   _____

4. Ask your teacher to name a professional association to which (s)he belongs. Write the name of the association.

   _____

   Write a sentence that contains the name of your teacher and the name of the association to which (s)he belongs.

   _____

   _____

5. What is the name of the special event at which the best movies and performers are given golden statues?

    _____

    Write a sentence that contains the name of the event you wrote in the space.

    _____

    _____

6. Write a sentence that contains the name and date of your favorite sports event.

    _____

    _____

Tips for Teachers

1. This convention has little use out of context. The context is information. Use it for information-gathering and then writing about the information.

2. We strongly encourage a year-long emphasis on this convention because it is an excellent excuse for getting the children into the telephone book, into the reference books, and into the community.

3. Along the way, the matter of *minor words* and *major words* comes up. Wait for it to come up, then deal with it slowly. The difference between a minor word and a major word is more experience than rule. The children will come to understand as they work with institutions, associations, and events that minor words, such as *of, a, an, and,* and *the,* are not capitalized unless they begin the name.

CHAPTER 5

GRAMMATICAL TERMINOLOGY FOR TALKING ABOUT WRITING

This section of the book was written with one purpose in mind, to contribute to writers' ability to manage written language with increasing effectiveness. If you've spent much time reading the first four chapters of this book, you realize that it is clearly not an all-purpose grammar book. It's a book about writing, and everything in it is designed to help children, and anyone else who needs its contents, to become increasingly effective writers by using writing conventions appropriately and accurately. That is the book's primary objective. Its purpose is not to make young, or older, writers more effective memorizers of grammatical terms. This portion of the book exists only to support the primary objective.

To that end, we have defined and discussed six grammatical terms that are directly relevant to the lessons in Chapters 3 and 4. In those lessons you will encounter the following grammatical vocabulary: *nouns, verbs, adjectives, adverbs, prepositions,* and *clauses.* Our intent in the next several pages is to clarify the concepts associated with each term and to provide some instructional processes that can help youngsters understand the functional use of the concepts in their writing. As with the rest of this book, the focus is writing.

TIPS FOR UNDERSTANDING AND USING THE WRITING ACTIVITIES

- The direction to write a six-word sentence with a verb in the fourth position (*Given Word Sentence,* cited earlier) is vastly different from one that requires students simply to write a sentence that contains a verb. The former promotes focused attention to verbs; the latter does not.
- The grammatical terminology and concepts are for communication; there is no assumption, nor evidence for that matter, that knowing the words or terms makes better writers.

NOUNS

Yes, a noun names a person, place, or thing. The **girl** (person) traveled to the **farm** (place) in order to see the new **barn** (thing). But to understand the noun requires more than defining it; understanding means working with how it behaves in sentences.

The word *farm* is a place, thus a noun, except in the sentence about how the man **farms** his land, in which case the word *farms* is a verb. It isn't just that the word got bigger by changing from *farm* to *farms* because when that farmer (noun-person) owns several farms (noun-place), the word becomes a noun again.

A word is a noun when it does the things that nouns do, or it is in a place where nouns tend to be. For example, nouns tend to come after words such as *the, a,* and *an* (articles). They also tend to follow words such as *pretty, bold,* and *defunct* (adjectives).

Nouns often appear as objects after verbs. The **boy** (noun-person) walked **home** (noun-place). In the case of this sentence, the second noun follows the verb. That noun is called an object; it's the *object* of the verb, what the verb acts on.

Nouns also appear as the last word **in a prepositional phrase.** Notice the prepositional phrase in bold type. In that sentence the last word is a noun (a thing). Right before it is an adjective. Remember? Nouns often come after adjectives.

When you teach about nouns, you want youngsters to understand how nouns work, not just how to define and find them. You want youngsters to be able to write with nouns—consciously, on purpose. We can accomplish that by making their noun practice into writing practice.

1. Write a sentence in which *goat* is a noun in the second position in a sentence.
2. Write a sentence in which *goat* is a noun in the third position in a sentence.
3. Write a sentence in which *goat* is a noun in the fourth position in a sentence.
4. Write a sentence in which a noun follows the word *fantastic.*
5. Write a sentence in which a noun is the third word in a prepositional phrase that begins with the preposition *under.*
6. Write a sentence that contains a noun that names a person.

7. Write a sentence in which a noun names a place.
8. Write a sentence in which a noun names a thing and appears in the fifth position.
9. Write a sentence that contains two nouns.
10. Write a sentence that contains three nouns, one of which is plural and one of which must begin with a capital letter.

VERBS

Okay, a verb is defined as a word that shows action or state of being. We all agree on that. The first person who can tell third graders, or 20-year-olds for that matter, what *state of being* means, in words that eight-year-olds will understand, gets an early recess. We ought not suggest to third graders that they have to learn the definitions in their textbooks just because we remember them from when we were in junior high school.

Consider the following sentence. **The man _____ down the street.** The man could *walk, run, saunter, meander, stumble, stagger*, even *crawl* down that street, and all of those words would work in the sense that all of those words paint a picture and *feel* right in that space. They're all verbs, and any word that fits in that space and feels right is a verb.

Any word that doesn't fit because it doesn't feel right isn't a verb. That man won't "elephant" down the street or "luckily" down the street or "under" down the street because none of those words will work as verbs. If a word doesn't do the work of a verb, it isn't a verb, no matter the definition.

Now what's this *state of being* stuff? The *state of being* verbs are the ones in bold type in the box below.

Sarah **is** plain.

All of the girls in Sarah's class **are** from the farm.

They **were** out in the fields.

It **was** late in the day when they **had** dinner.

When it **is** finally dinner time,
they **have** a sumptuous feast.

Those verbs don't describe any action, so they confuse third graders. To third graders, they don't have any states (of being) in them, and they don't have any being, either. In your authors' experience, it works much better to drop the obscure definition and give children something with which to work—in writing.

1. Write a sentence in which the word *walked* is a verb.
2. Write a sentence in which the word *walked* appears as a verb in the fourth position.
3. Write a six-word sentence in which the word *hopping* is the verb in the fourth position.

Think now, as you read: If you were working on these sentences either on paper or in your head, what were you focused on? We think it's a pretty safe guess that your attention was on making the verbs work in sentences. Wouldn't it be useful to get third and fourth graders to focus on how to make verbs work in sentences, too? It's useful because people learn what they focus on.

4. Write the sentence around the verb.
   _____ _____ **is** _____ _____
5. Write another sentence around the verb.
   _____ _____ _____ **were** _____
6. Write a sentence in which the verb *was* appears in the third position.
7. Use the verb *are* in a sentence in which the main idea is mealtime.
8. Write a sentence that contains two verbs.
9. Write a sentence that contains two nouns and one verb.
10. Write a sentence that contains the word *match* used as a verb.

ADJECTIVES

Yes, it is a describing word, but so are lots of other words that aren't adjectives. There are **pretty** trees, **aged** houses, **dilapidated** cars, and **magical** books. All of those trees, houses, cars, and books are nouns that are described by the adjectives that come right in front of them. Adjectives often come right before the nouns they describe. The adjectives change, adjust, give texture to the nouns. In other words, the adjectives *modify* the nouns.

But this can confuse children because the idea of describing words, although it seems to make sense with adjectives, applies to other words as well. You see, or you will see below, that adverbs are describing words, too; it's just that they modify verbs, not nouns. So it's true that adjectives are describing words, but if that's all third graders learn about adjectives, they'll not understand. They have to understand three things about adjectives.

- Adjectives describe only certain kinds of words, and those are nouns and, though not nearly so common, pronouns.
- Adjectives tend to appear in front of the nouns and pronouns they modify.
- Adjectives sometimes follow verbs.

If children come to understand that adjectives describe nouns and pronouns and that they tend to appear in front of the nouns they modify, the following example illustrates an adjective that will throw them off every time. **The boy's wagon is red.** There are two adjectives in that sentence. One of them looks for all the world like a noun (*boy's*), but it isn't, and the other adjective comes after the verb, not before a noun. This is why it's so important to teach what words do, not merely their definitions. See, the first adjective (*boy's*) modifies the noun (*wagon*), and the second one (*red*) also modifies the noun (*wagon*). There are two adjectives in the same sentence, both describing, or modifying, the same noun, each in a different place in the sentence. It isn't fair to teach eight- or eleven-year-olds that adjectives are describing words that come before the noun because both definitions are only partly right.

1. Write a five-word sentence in which *hot* is used as an adjective.
2. Write a six-word sentence in which another temperature word is used as an adjective in the third position.
3. Write a sentence in which a noun appears in the third position and an adjective appears in front of the noun.
4. Write a sentence around the adjective *big*.
   _____ _____ _____ **big**
5. Write a sentence in which an adjective comes after the verb.
6. Write a sentence in which there are two adjectives, one that comes before a noun and one that comes after a verb.
7. Write a sentence in which the word *tiger's* is used as an adjective.
8. Use a plural possessive as an adjective in a sentence.
9. Use a word that ends in *-ed* as an adjective in a sentence.
10. Write a sentence that contains two nouns, only one of which has an adjective in front of it.

ADVERBS

An adverb is also a describing word. When the boy ran **quickly** down the street, we know exactly how he ran because there is a describing word in the sentence, and that word describes how the boy ran. Adverbs are describing words just as adjectives are describing words. The difference is that adverbs describe verbs and adjectives and other adverbs. Adjectives describe nouns and pronouns, so when teachers use *describing word* to define adjectives, there's a host of adverbs lurking in sentences to confuse the children.

It would be far better to talk about describing words, if you must, in terms of the kinds of words they describe, or modify. There are adverbs that describe verbs, adjectives, and other adverbs. No, they're not adverbs just because they describe; they're adverbs because they describe (modify) verbs, adjectives, and other adverbs. And no, it isn't necessary to learn how to diagram sentences in order to understand modification. Modification is a relationship, in this case a relationship between adverbs, on the one hand, and verbs, adjectives, and other adverbs, on the other. Diagramming sentences isn't necessarily bad; it just isn't necessary to understand adverbs and their relationship with verbs, adjectives, and other adverbs.

Look at some examples of the modification relationships between adverbs and the words they modify, or describe.

Linda walked **slowly** back to her house. (modifies a verb)
She was an **extremely** pretty girl. (modifies an adjective)
It was **very** hard for her to understand. (modifies an adjective)
She had been **very** highly recommended. (modifies another adverb)

The focus, again, must be on what adverbs do in sentences. Call youngsters' attention to how adverbs make verbs stronger, clearer, more textured. That man can walk, or he can walk **slowly** or **laboriously.** Of course, he could saunter or stagger, and those verbs are pretty big, clear, and textured. Good writers try to use nouns and verbs that don't need modifiers, but that doesn't mean that modifiers aren't useful. The power in a sentence is in word selection, and the selection of adverbs can bring power to verbs that verbs, themselves, often cannot.

Now, let's try to make adverbs bring some power to sentences.

1. Write a sentence in which *run* or *ran* is the verb, and use an adverb that helps to make the verb clearer.
2. Write a sentence in which the word *packed* is the verb. Use an adverb to describe something about the verb.
3. Write a sentence that contains an adverb that modifies a verb of your choice.
4. Write a sentence in which the word *painfully* is used as an adverb.
5. Write a sentence in which an adverb helps to tell how fast Kristina can run.
6. Write a sentence that contains two verbs, only one of which is modified with an adverb.

7. Write a sentence in which an adjective is modified by an adverb.
8. Write a sentence in which an adverb modifies another adverb.
9. Write a sentence that contains two nouns, one adjective, one verb, and one adverb.
10. Write a sentence in which adverbs are used to modify a verb and an adjective.

PREPOSITIONS

Prepositions are words that draw attention to relationships between ideas in sentences. Let's look at some examples:

Marissa walked **into** the room. All her life, she had been called the pretty girl **with** the red hair. She sat **on** the leather stool and smiled broadly **at** the cameraman as he snapped a series **of** pictures. **After** an hour, it was time **for** a break. Marissa loved those moments **between** sittings. She could wander outside and sit **in** the park **across** the street. Being a professional model **for** a cosmetic company was not her dream **of** a lifetime, but **for** now, she couldn't complain. She made more money **in** a day than her friends did **in** a month.

As you might guess, all the words in bold type are prepositions. They're everywhere, and, in fact, it's rather difficult to write without using them. Prepositions tie ideas together, as you can see as you reread the above paragraph. Prepositions connect their objects (the nouns or pronouns that follow them) with other ideas in a sentence. Prepositions, with their objects, are called **prepositional phrases.** For example, *into the room* is a prepositional phrase, as are *with the red hair, on the leather stool, at the cameraman,* and *between sittings.*

Prepositional phrases always begin with prepositions and end with nouns or pronouns (the object of the preposition). Between the preposition and its object, there may be words that modify the noun or pronoun. In our paragraph, *with* is a preposition, *the* and *red* modify *hair,* and *hair* is the object of the preposition. Here's another example: **After the delicious dinner,** we sat down to a game of Go Fish. *After* is the preposition, and you know the rest.

An aside to teachers: As you know, *after* is not always a preposition. Read the following sentence: *After we played Go Fish, we decided to take a walk. After* is not a preposition in this sentence, and *After we played Go Fish* is not a prepositional phrase. It's a dependent clause, which we'll discuss in the next part of Chapter 5. Here's another sentence: *I like to read. To* is often used as a preposition, as you've noticed in our paragraph above; however, this time it's used with *read,* which is a verb form called an **infinitive phrase.** These are non-examples when it comes to prepositional phrases and are

just something to be aware of when youngsters are learning about prepositional phrases.

Going back to our original idea, prepositions begin prepositional phrases, which end with nouns or pronouns and may contain words that modify them.

You may have heard someone say, as a rather primitive explanation, that prepositions were words that show where you can be in relationship to a cloud: **over** the cloud, **under** it, **through** it—well, you get the picture. This explanation isn't wrong, it's just simplistic and limiting. Prepositions show relationships between their objects (nouns or pronouns) and other words and ideas in sentences. A good language arts text will have a reference list of prepositions, but the objective is not to memorize lists. You have already seen that simply knowing that *to* can be a preposition is insufficient knowledge because *to* can also be part of an infinitive phrase (e.g., I like **to write**).

As with all instances of language use, the key to mastery lies in understanding function and in practicing regularly.

1. Write a sentence using the blanks below.
   _____ _____ *under* _____ _____.
2. Write a sentence that contains the prepositional phrase *outside the window.*
3. Write a sentence that contains the prepositional phrase *after lunch.*
4. Write a sentence that contains the prepositional phrase *to the store.*
5. Write a sentence that contains the prepositional phrase *of the car.*
6. Write a sentence that begins with the prepositional phrase *Between my friend and me.*
7. Write a sentence that begins with the prepositional phrase *across the street.*
8. Write a sentence that ends with the prepositional phrase *across the street.*
9. Use the phrase *with my friend* in a sentence.
10. Use the phrase *into the room* as the last three words in a sentence.

CLAUSES

There are two kinds of clauses, independent and dependent. One is called **independent** because it can stand alone; the other is called **dependent** because it cannot. Here's an example: *Before I go to school, I feed my pet gerbil.* **I feed my pet gerbil** can stand alone. It tells what the writer (or speaker) is doing. It's an independent clause. On the other hand, **Before I go to school** is an unfinished idea. We're left wondering what happened before school. This cluster of words cannot stand alone and, therefore, is called a dependent clause. The dependent and independent clause together make up what is called a **complex sentence** (see Chapter 3, Commas in Complex Sentences).

Let's look at another example: *My best friend and I went shopping, and I bought a new pair of shoes.* This is a **compound sentence** (see Chapter 3, Commas in Compound Sentences). If we look on either side of the *and* that follows the comma, we'll see independent clauses. Each one is independent because the first part of that sentence (before the comma and the *and*) can stand alone. It makes sense. We know what the writer is talking about. The same is true for the words that follow the comma and the *and*. Each part can stand alone and make sense (i.e., **I bought a new pair of shoes**).

The best way to understand dependent and independent clauses is to use them. Each type of clause has a sound to it. Independent clauses sound as though they make sense on their own. Dependent clauses sound unfinished. The following cues ask young writers to write using dependent and independent clauses. When young writers write, ask them to read their sentences aloud so that the entire class can benefit from the sounds of the language.

1. Write a sentence that begins with the dependent clause **Because I like puppies.**
2. Write a sentence that uses *but* between two independent clauses.
3. Write a sentence that begins with the dependent clause **When I go shopping with my friends.**
4. Write a sentence that ends with the dependent clause **after I eat dinner.**
5. Write a sentence that begins with the dependent clause **After I eat dinner.**
6. Write a complex sentence.
7. Write a compound sentence.
8. Write a complex sentence that contains the independent clause **I like to listen to the radio.**
9. Write a compound sentence that joins two independent clauses with *and.*
10. Write a complex sentence in which **because I like to read** is the dependent clause.

CHAPTER 6

THE TEACHER AS RESEARCHER IN THE CLASSROOM

How do teachers know whether their instruction is effective? How do they know whether or not to trust their "gut" feelings or intuitions about the workings of their classrooms? Classrooms are complex, dynamic systems; and although experienced teachers are not wrong to trust their "sense" of how student learning is progressing, intuitions may not always be accurate, nor may they always be easily reportable. They are often difficult to convey to individuals outside the classroom, such as administrators, school boards, and parents.

Part of teachers' professional responsibility is to give substance to their feelings and intuitions, and one way to do that is through **action research.** By becoming **active researchers** in their classrooms, teachers can substantiate for themselves, their students, parents, administrators, and the public in general, the impact of their instruction on the progress, in this case the writing progress, of their students.

There are five steps in this process of conducting clsassroom action research in writing. The first is to decide what question to ask. The question relevant to this book is **"What is the impact of instruction in mechanical control on students' writing?"** The nex four steps are to (1) take a writing sample; (2) implement the instructional strategies students need in order to improve their writing; (3) take subsequent writing samples; and (4) use results to adjust instruction, as well as to communicate performance to students, administrators, parents and other interested individuals.

In the following section, we describe in some detail the procedures for conducting classroom action research. We include prototype forms for reporting results to administrators and parents.

STEP I: COLLECTING DATA

The origin of the data is the writing sample, a piece of writing completed without extensive or systematic preparation and without benefit of revision. Because the point of a writing sample is to find out what young writers can do automatically, it is best conducted as a timed response to a specific prompt or cue. The prompt must be something to which everyone in the room can respond. Our experience is that young writers can always respond to a prompt about where they live because everyone lives somewhere. The characteristic prompt, therefore, is to direct students to describe or write about a room in their house. This is not an especially exciting prompt, and the writing itself tends to be purely descriptive; however, the point here is to collect data regarding mechanical control, not to encourage youngsters to wax poetic.

Our experience is that in a five-minute writing, youngsters produce sufficient text for data collection and analysis. The amount of time given to students is not magical. You may want to set seven minutes or ten or twelve, depending on your own experience and knowledge of your students. Remember, however, the more time, the more writing, and the more writing, the more time you commit to reading and analysis. Remember, as well, that most youngsters, and adults, for that matter, display what they're capable of writing in about 50 to 60 words. The rest requires your time for analysis, yet you learn little more about their writing skill. The most important point is to provide the same amount of time for every writer and with each sample you collect to help legitimize comparisons that are made among them.

Alternative prompts that also work well include writing about a favorite place or about something they do well. As part of the writing prompt, teachers should direct students to write as follows: "Write as much as you can and as well as you can." Say it just that way. Use a stop watch or sweep second hand on the clock. Stop them in five minutes. This isn't about electric prose or finished ideas. It's merely a sample of what they can do automatically.

In scoring writing samples, you must first decide what characteristics you are scoring for. You may be scoring for a variety of traits, such as organization, voice, and fluency. You may decide to include a holistic score, using a particular rubric. This book features a high-utility list of capitalization/punctuation conventions. Therefore, the scoring focus is mechanical control, specifically the extent to which young writers' samples display use of the capitalization and punctuation conventions in this book. Back to the research question we're asking: What is the impact of instruction in mechanical control on students' writing?

We strongly recommend, therefore, that teachers score writing samples for the purpose of analyzing students' use of conventions, specifically those contained in this book. Mechanical control is clearly **only one** criterion among many possible when scoring writing samples, but it is the one that responds to the question about how to know if mechanical control instruction is working. That's the research we're talking about here.

Scoring for capitalization and punctuation means making a tally for each such error, so that having read a student sample, the teacher has **X** tallies that reflect the number of times the student–writer misused or failed to use a capital letter or punctuation mark correctly.

Scoring for Fluency

However, we suggest that if you are going to the trouble of collecting writing samples and scoring them for purposes of reporting to children, colleagues, administrators, and/or parents, you may as well add additional elements to the scoring mix that will offer a more complete picture of writing performance.

Given that everyone in the room wrote for exactly the same number of clock minutes in response to precisely the same cue, it is possible to get a word count on each sample, add the word count, divide the total by the number of students in the class, and come out with an average number of words written by the class. Of what use is that? The individual sample word counts and the average for the room are **fluency** scores. Fluency scores show the extent to which students actually write. If we believe that writing behavior, itself, is a road toward writing skill, then the more they write, the higher the probability they are learning to write. There does appear to be a relationship between fluency (quantity) and quality. In his meta-analysis of 32 studies that looked at the effect of computer use on writing, Bangert–Drowns found that many youngsters using computers tended to write longer compositions and that there was a high corrleation between the longer writings and those that were judged to be of higher quality (Bangert–Drowns, R. L. [1993]. The word processor as an instructional tool: A meta-analysis of word processing in writing instruction. *Review of Educational Research, 63*, 69–93).

Let's say you find that in five minutes the average child in the fourth-grade room is writing 37 words. Given that 37 words in five minutes means between 7 and 8 per minute, it is reasonable to project that with some fluency practice the average score could increase by 20% in the next month. If children's fluency increased by 20% in the first month, 10% in the next, and 5% each month thereafter, a fourth grader who averaged 7 words per minute in September would average about 12 words per minute by May. Fluency, alone, is not a writing program, nor is it the foundation of assessment, but **there is nothing else without it.** (It's a bit like fluency in reading; reading does not occur without it.) All teachers in the Western world would be absolutely delighted if students who arrived in their rooms at the beginning of the year were willing and able to write fluently on cue.

Now, count some more. Count the sentences, or in the case of children who don't use punctuation, count structures that *should* be sentences. Divide the number of words on each child's sample by the number of sentences and you have the average number of words per sentence for each child. There's no evidence to the effect that long sentences are **better** than short ones; but the **capacity** to write longer ones is a worthy objective of instruction, and when young writers are able to write longer sentences, they will tend to do so.

Scoring for Mechanical Control

Next, count the capitalization and punctuation errors. As an aside, we've found that while counting capitalization and punctuation errors, it's just as easy to count sentence errors, such as run-ons and fragments, and spelling errors at the same time. Regardless of whether you analyze students' writings for spelling, run-ons, and fragments, or just for capitalization and punctuation errors, we have found that it is useful to categorize the errors informally as you read and tally. In other words, you'd have a column labeled **Capitalization,** one labeled **Punctuation,** and so forth. Under those headings, you would then place your tallies in the appropriate category.

A very useful score regarding error rate (and error rate, remember, is the key to the question about whether mechanical control instruction is working) is the ratio of errors per sentence (total errors divided by number of sentences). Consider, for example, that if the child writes 50 words in 5 sentences in September and commits 10 errors (2 errors per sentence), then 60 words in 6 sentences in October and commits 10 errors (1.7 errors per sentence), the number of errors has remained the same, but the rate of errors has **decreased.** In fact, if the student continued a reduction of .3 errors per sentence each month, the student would be writing error-free drafts, with greater fluency, in six months. Next year's teachers would be delighted.

STEP II: IMPLEMENTATION OF INSTRUCTION

Based on scores from the first, or baseline, writing sample, teachers can plan to focus instructional attention on the several highest frequency error patterns in the room. Pretend, for example, that in a third grade the most characteristic error patterns are found in students' use (or misuse) of end punctuation, commas in series, apostrophes in contractions, and capitalization of names. In that classroom, the teacher would plan to teach those conventions from the ideas in this book for, perhaps, six weeks. Instruction would occur in some organized manner, maybe three times a week for six to ten minutes each time. This instruction would, of course, accompany students' other daily writing for a variety of purposes across genres and content areas. In other words, even as they are learning to use conventions appropriately, students are practicing the conventions in their ongoing writing projects and activities.

STEP III: COLLECTING SUBSEQUENT WRITING SAMPLES

At the end of six weeks, the teacher takes a writing sample in precisely the same way the baseline sample was collected. The prompt may be, but need not be, the same. The time allowed for writing should be identical to that allotted in the baseline sample. The teacher scores the second sample and compares the data with the first sample.

This is what the research is all about. Data have now been collected to show the degree, if any, of student improvement. Has the instruction worked? Classroom action research helps answer the question. This pattern of research can be repeated throughout a school year, so that teachers and students, as well as their parents and administrators, have evidence of progress and learning.

What if the comparison of data does not show improvement in student writing?

- Is it because the material is too hard?
- Is it because the instructional time was not long enough to allow for student growth?
- Is there actually a better way to teach the material?
- Is it because the six-week timeline was not long enough to be sensitive to growth?
- Is it because the writing sample prompt didn't allow for display of the targeted mechanical control conventions?

There may be more questions. It is important to realize that all good research leads to questions. It is important to remember, as well, that educational research (and any other research, for that matter) does not **prove** anything; it merely narrows the possibility for error.

STEP IV: REPORTING RESULTS

Professional people have a responsibility to inform their peers and the public regarding what they do. There is a sample of a reporting form in this chapter. If in the first six weeks the writing sample data show that the average child in the fourth grade commits far fewer mechanical errors than (s)he did at the beginning of the year, what we know is that there is reason to continue doing what we have been doing, and to continue studying its effect regularly. If the children do not improve, all we know is that it is now necessary to ask some new questions.

Reports to administrators, board members, and parents must be accompanied by a short narrative that details the conditions under which the data emerged. Those conditions include what was taught, when, how often, to whom, and for what purpose. That narrative could be as short as one hand-written page. The authors would be delighted to receive a copy of your report.

DIRECTIONS FOR ANALYTIC SCORING OF WRITING SAMPLES

1. Take a cued five-minute writing sample. Cue: Think about your house, walk around in your house inside your head, notice what is there and who is there; select a room in your house, any room, notice what's in there and who is in there, think about why you selected that room; write about that room in your house, write as much as you can as well as you can; you have exactly five minutes. Go.
2. Call time in exactly five minutes. That's when they put their pencils down.
3. If the children are in the second grade or higher, direct them to count their words. Give them time to count and put the number in a circle at the top of their paper. Then direct them to count again and put the second number at the top of their paper. Teachers count only those on which there are two different numbers. That cuts significant time from the scoring process.
4. Count the sentences. (Count sentences that would be there if the paper were punctuated properly.)
5. Count the capitalization and punctuation errors. (If you like, count the spelling errors and the runons and fragments [the nonsentences] as well, but

the point of the analysis in this book is capitalization and punctuation.)

6. Divide the number of words by the number of sentences. That gives the average number of words per sentence. Calculate for each child; then find the average for the class.

7. Count the number of capitalization and punctuation errors and divide that total by the number of sentences. That gives you the average number of capitalization and punctuation errors per sentence. (You can, of course, find the average number of capitalization errors per sentence and the average number of punctuation errors per sentence if you would like that separation.)

Classroom Data Sheet

Name	# Words	# Sentences	Words/Sentence	Errors/Sentence

SCORED WRITING SAMPLES

The following writing samples have been scored for number of words, number of sentences, words per sentence, and errors per sentence (capitalization and punctuation only).

Sample 1: Fourth Grader

The room has one couch and three chairs in it. It has one big picture in it. My mom teaches violin in the room. There is over one hundred music books in the room. There is one piano in the room. There is a balcony leading into the room. There is some nice clean soft rug on the floor in that room. I like the lights in the room because there are pretty glass-like things on it.

Number of Words:	77
Number of Sentences:	8
Number of Errors:	0
Words Per Sentence:	9.6
Errors Per Sentence:	0

Sample 2: Sixth Grader

It is all yellow, even the bedspread is yellow. It is not that big or that small, it is just right, or at least I think so. Of course it is my room. It is in the middle of a hall, it is between my mom and dads room and my brothers room. In it there is a double bed, a desk, and two dressers. One of my dressers I have a baby hamster, and about six or seven little goldfish and guppies I have quite a lot of stuffed animals on that same dresser. I have a African

Number of Words:	99
Number of Sentences:	11
Number of Errors:	9
Words Per Sentence:	9.0
Errors Per Sentence:	1.2

WHAT HAPPENS AFTER SCORING THE FIRST WRITING SAMPLE?

1. Determine the general capitalization and punctuation needs in the room. Form up to four instructional groups after determining the specific capitalization and punctuation needs of the children and grouping them on that basis.
2. Conduct instruction and practice sessions in either the large group or the smaller groups, focusing on the needs revealed by the writing sample scores. Conduct the instruction and practice at the same time the children are also writing through the genres and across the curriculum. The instruction and practice sessions shouldn't consume more than about six to eight minutes a day.
3. After two to four weeks of instruction and practice, conduct another writing sample, score as above, and compare the results.
4. Discuss the results with the children and remind them that their achievements tell you that they **can** remember, that they **do** know, and that you **will** hold them responsible for writing at least as well as they do in the writing sample.
5. Reconstitute groups to work on the patterns revealed in the second writing sample.

Reporting Form/Letter for Writing Improvement (Class Averages)*

Dear _____:

During the past _____ weeks, the students in my class have worked very hard on basic writing skills. On (date) I collected a writing sample from every student in the class and scored them for fluency, maturity, and mechanical control. The results are listed below:

- Class's average number of words written in a five-minute writing (fluency)   _____
- Class's average number of words per sentence (maturity)   _____
- Class's average number of capitalization and punctuation errors per sentence (mechanical control)   _____

For the next _____ weeks, we worked specifically on increasing both the quantity (fluency) and the quality (maturity and mechanical control) of writing. I then took another writing sample and found the following scores, with differences from the first sample in parentheses.

- Average number of words   _____   (+/–_____)
- Average number of words per sentence   _____   (+/–_____)
- Average number of errors per sentence   _____   (+/–_____)

Understand, these scores reflect only basic writing skills. The children are also writing for content, clarity, and organization. I intend to continue these efforts in writing through the year, and I invite your feedback and recommendations.

Sincerely,

---

*Adjust this letter/form for your audience (i.e., administrators, school board, and so forth).

Reporting Form/Letter for Writing Improvement (Individual Student)

Dear _____:

During the past _____ weeks, the students in my class have worked very hard on basic writing skills. On (date) I collected a writing sample from every student in the class and scored them for fluency, maturity, and mechanical control. The results are listed below:

- Number of words written in a five-minute writing (fluency)   _____
- Number of words per sentence (maturity)   _____
- Number of capitalization and punctuation errors per sentence (mechanical control)   _____

For the next _____ weeks, we worked specifically on increasing both the quantity (fluency) and the quality (maturity and mechanical control) of writing. I then took another writing sample and found the following scores, with differences from the first sample in parentheses.

- Number of words   _____   (+/– _____)
- Number of words per sentence   _____   (+/– _____)
- Number of errors per sentence   _____   (+/– _____)

Understand, these scores reflect only basic writing skills. The children are also writing for content, clarity, and organization. I intend to continue these efforts in writing through the year, and I invite your feedback and recommendations.

Sincerely,

References

The following refer to the literature from which we created sentences in the section of each lesson under "Examples of . . . (the target punctuation or capitalization convention)."

Babbitt, Natalie. (1975). *Tuck Everlasting.* New York: Bantam Skylark Books.

Burnett, Frances Hodgson. (1987). *The Secret Garden.* New York: Random House.

Carle, Eric. (1990). *The Very Quiet Cricket.* New York: Philomel Books.

Cherry, Lynne. (1990). *The Great Kapok Tree: A Tale of the Amazon Rain Forest.* San Diego: Harcourt Brace Jovanovich.

Cisneros, Sandra. (1991). *Women Hollering Creek and Other Stories.* New York: Random House.

Houston, Jeanne W., and Houston, James D. (1973). *Farewell to Manzanar.* Toronto: Bantam Books.

Little, Jean. (1986). *Hey World, Here I Am!* New York: Harper Collins.

Lowry, Lois. (1993). *The Giver.* New York: Houghton Mifflin.

MacLachlan, Patricia. (1991). *Journey.* New York: Delacorte Press.

Milne, A. A. (1928, 1956). *The House at Pooh Corner.* New York: Dell Publishing.

Paulsen, Gary. (1991). *The River.* New York: Delacorte Press.

Paulsen, Gary. (1990). *Woodsong.* New York: Viking Penguin.

Prelutsky, Jack. (1984). *The New Kid on the Block.* New York: Greenwillow Books.

Spinelli, Jerry. (1990). *Maniac Magee.* Boston: Little, Brown.

Soto, Gary. (1990). *Baseball in April and Other Stories.* San Diego: Harcourt Brace Jovanovich.

Soto, Gary. (1993). *Two Many Tamales.* New York: G. P. Putnam's Sons.

Van Allsburg, Chris. (1985). *The Polar Express.* Boston: Houghton Mifflin.

Van Allsburg, Chris. (1992). *The Widow's Broom.* Boston: Houghton Mifflin.

Viorst, Judith. (1980). *Alexander and the Terrible, Horrible, No Good, Very Bad Day.* New York: Atheneum.

Wojciechowska, Maia. (1964). *Shadow of a Bull.* New York: Atheneum.

Wood, Audrey, and Wood, Don. (1988). *Elbert's Bad Word.* San Diego: Harcourt Brace Jovanovich.